A BRIT'S GUIDE

TO

NEW ★ YORK

 2001

KAREN MARCHBANK

In association with NYTAB
The New York Travel Advisory Bureau

foulsham

LONDON • NEW YORK • TORONTO • SYDNEY

foulsham

The Publishing House, Bennetts Close, Cippenham,
Slough, Berkshire, SL1 5AP, England

ISBN 0–572–02651–X

Series title, format, logo, artwork and layout design
© 2001 W. Foulsham & Co. Ltd

Text copyright © 2001 Karen Marchbank

Chapter 4 copyright and reproduction of NYCard
© 2001 New York Travel Advisory Bureau

Other books in this series:
A Brit's Guide to Orlando and Walt Disney World, Simon Veness, 0-572-02649-8
A Brit's Guide to Las Vegas and the West, Karen Marchbank, 0-572-02650-1
Choosing A Cruise, Simon Veness, 0-572-02562-9

Printed in Great Britain by St. Edmundsbury Press, Bury St. Edmunds, Suffolk

CONTENTS

Dedication
For Jennifer, who is just about ready to bite off a chunk of the Big Apple ...

Acknowledgements
With grateful thanks for all their help to Clive Burrows and Audrey Bretillot at the New York Travel Advisory Bureau, plus Sarah Handy and Jo Chamberlain at the New York Convention and Visitor's Bureau. My thanks also to the Lower East Side Tenement Museum, the Metropolitan Museum of Art, Ellis Island Immigration Museum, Museum of Modern Art, Museum of Jewish Heritage, Whitney Museum of American Art, *Intrepid* Sea-Air-Space Museum, the Frick Collection, Skyscraper Museum, National Museum of the American Indian, Children's Museum of Manhattan, *The Beast* Speedboat Tour, Amy Downs Hats, Alik Singer Rubin Singer, NY Waterways, Harlem Spirituals, the Big Apple Greeters, David Watkins and Ponycabs, The Mark, the Queens Jazz Trail, the World Trade Center, American Museum of Natural History, New York Stock Exchange, Souperman, American Park at the Battery, Tapika, Orienta, Serafina Fabulous Pizza, Park View at the Boathouse, Picholine, Sylvia's Restaurant, the River Café, the Water Club, *World Yacht* Dining Cruise and Europa Grill. My thanks also to the following individuals who were a font of great knowledge: Lorraine Heller, Neal Smith, Russell Brightwell, Maria Pieri, Bob Maddams, Leonie Taylor and Neil Wadey.

Introduction

In Las Vegas the New York-New York hotel has a twistin', turnin', rock 'n' rollin' rollercoaster weaving its way around the entire exterior of the building. In New York it is the city itself that is the rollercoaster. Loud, brash, bright, crazy – all the words used to describe the Big Apple speak of its larger-than-life personality that enthrals visitors from the moment they land at JFK or Newark airport. And as more Brits hop on a plane for a long weekend or drop in on their way to other destinations in the US, more are being beguiled by the sheer lunacy of the place and some even wish they could make it their second home.

It may be all those old black and white movies that painted the well-to-do lifestyle of the rich, famous and crooked so vividly or the dark and dangerous movies of the last 30 years, but everyone feels they know the city as soon as they arrive. Hardly surprising – they've seen most of the major sights on celluloid a hundred times over. So, when we Brits arrive in New York, we feel we are stepping into one large, mad, bustling movie set and once we've tasted the excitement, there's no going back. Of all the people I've spoken to who've been to the city in the last five years, not one person

has said they had a bad time or they hated it. Oh no, unbeknown to many New Yorkers, Brits are having their very own love affair with the biggest, brightest, brashest city North America has to offer, and it will be some time before the honeymoon period is over.

I now must admit (and there's no need for sympathy) that I've been forced on several occasions to spend long periods of time in New York – all in the name of research, of course – to bring you this guide to getting the most out of the greatest city on earth. Well, it's a tough job, but someone's gotta do it! Throughout the next twelve chapters I will be bringing you my view of all that is great, all that is unmissable, all that is quirky and all that is fun in this city. After all, when you arrive, you want to know how to eat, drink, shop and be merry in next to no time at all. Hopefully what follows will provide all the insights you need. Having said that, if you come across some wonderfully off-the-wall boutique, nightclub, bar or restaurant that I haven't mentioned, just drop me a line and let me know about it. You never know, it could well be in the next annually updated edition of the book.

One of New York's greatest charms is its cosmopolitan nature, its hugely diverse ethnic mix. In this city you will find any type of cuisine, often available at any time of the day or night. Where music's concerned, everything from jazz and R 'n' B to techno and rap is out there any night of the week and the nightclubs are among the hippest and most happening of any in the world.

Of course, at first it can all seem a bit overwhelming and it doesn't help that everyone gives the impression of being in the biggest hurry ever and far too busy to help. But beneath the ice-cool veneer of most New Yorkers are people who will be willing to answer any question or plea for help you put to them.

One of the biggest drawbacks to New York in previous decades has been the high level of crime, but even that has changed. According to the New York Police Department, murders have gone down by 68 per cent in the last five years, robberies have been cut in half and serious assaults are down by 30 per cent. Indeed, the Convention and Visitors' Bureau now sells New York as the safest large city in America.

★★★★ **INSIDE TRACK** ★★★★
★ ★
★ ★
★ **You must have plenty of** ★
★ **change and singles** ★
★ **($1 bills) to get around** ★
★ **as you'll be tipping** ★
★ **everyone for everything!** ★
★ ★
★★★★★★★★★★★★★★★★★★★★★★

Mayor Rudolph Giuliani, an Italian-American lawyer, has been taking all the credit for these figures, even

though crime has been falling nationally. All the same, the city is also cleaner than it's been in living memory – and that is certainly very much down to Giuliani. Under his Business Improvement Districts programme (BIDs), local businesses and organisations have taken on the responsibility of cleaning their neighbourhoods. It's a policy that has paid off and helped to create New York's pristine new image.

Giuliani did not stop there. He demanded that the police department invoke age-old laws that hadn't been enforced for a long time, banning, for example, drinking in open-air spaces and illegally jumping over subway ticket machines. Instead of turning a blind eye, the police force was instructed to take offenders to police stations, where more often than not it was discovered that they were wanted for other crimes or that they knew about other people's crimes and gave up the information to save themselves.

The Giuliani-enacted, and much contested, adult zoning law forbids a business with adult content to be carried on within 500 feet of a school or church. Under this law, Giuliani's team discovered they could remove all the sex shops from Times Square, which they duly did.

Not all New Yorkers are happy with Giuliani's methods, though, and some hate the sparkling clean and Disney-fied image of Times Square today. Another example of the Giuliani administration's super-tough approach – again, much criticised by some – was the use of property confiscation laws, meant for drug traffickers, to curb drink-driving. Many people thought that having your card taken away before trial smacked of punishment before guilt was proven.

Leaving aside the qualms of some local people, though, Guiliani's methods have helped to create a city that is far more pleasant to visit than at any other time in the last 30 years, so do not allow any worries about crime to put you off the experience of a lifetime – visiting New York City!

A SHORT HISTORY OF NEW YORK

Due to the vast number of movies set in different periods of New York, many of the key people in its history are familiar to us Brits, though I suspect that, like me, you're a little hazy as to what exactly they were famous for.

Understanding a little of the city's history is as good a way as any to familiarise yourself with the different areas of New York and the buildings named after its great movers and shakers. Many of them were men and women of great vision and courage and their contributions to New York's rich and diverse culture, entertainment and business are all part of what makes the city so remarkable today.

The great story that is New York's started in 1524 when Florentine Giovanni da Verrazano arrived on the island now known as Manhattan. It was a mixture of marshes, woodland, rivers and meadows and was home to the Algonquin and Iroquois tribes of Native Americans. No one settled on the island, though, until British explorer Henry Hudson arrived in 1609. Working for the Dutch West India Company, he discovered Indians who were happy to trade in furs, skins, birds and fruit. In 1613, a trading post was set up at Fort Nassau and by 1624 the Dutch West India Company was given the right to govern the area by the Dutch government.

Dutch settlers soon began to arrive; Manhattan was named New Amsterdam and governor Peter Minuit bought the island for $24 dollars' worth of few trinkets and blankets. Peaceful relations between the Europeans and Native Americans were disturbed, however, by the settlers' insistence on taking over the land and a costly and bloody war ensued, lasting two and a half years. Finally Peter Stuyvesant was hired by the Dutch West India Company to restore peace.

Stuyvesant was an experienced colonialist and went about establishing a strong community with a proper infrastructure. One of the first things he did was to order the building of a defensive wall and ditch along what we know today as Wall Street. The new settlement prospered and even doubled in size, but Governor Stuyvesant was not well liked. He introduced new taxes, persecuted Jews and Quakers and even limited the amount of alcohol people could drink. Trouble followed and the locals became less and less inclined to obey him. By the time four British warships sailed into the harbour in late 1664, he had no alternative but to surrender to Colonel Richard Nichols without a shot being fired. The colony was immediately renamed New York in honour of the Duke of York, brother to the English king, and thereafter remained mostly in the hands of the British until the end of the American Revolution.

By 1700, the population had reached 20,000, made up of immigrants from England, Holland, Germany, Ireland and Sweden. It was already the rich melting-pot of cultures and religions that it remains today. Over the next 74 years, the colony gradually began to find its own voice and there was a growing belief among well-educated and powerful Americans – including Thomas Jefferson and Benjamin Franklin – that the government should be fair and democratic.

In 1764, following the Seven Years War between the British and French, the Brits passed a number of laws, including the Stamp Act, allowing them to raise taxes in the colony. In response, Americans from all over the country banded together and rescinded Britain's right to collect taxes from them. The Stamp Act was repealed but it seemed that the Brits hadn't learned their lesson. They introduced the Townshend Act, which imposed taxes on various imports, and led to a bloody

confrontation in 1770. In 1774, the Americans set up the Continental Congress, made up of representatives from each of the colonies. Later that year, those representatives urged all Americans to stop paying their taxes and just two years later the Declaration of Independence was drawn up, largely by Jefferson. During the War of Independence that inevitably followed, New York was considered strategically vital as it stood between the New England colonies and those in the south. In 1776, British commander Lord Howe sailed 500 ships into the harbour and occupied the city. George Washington's army was defeated and forced to leave. The peace process began in 1779 and led to a treaty in 1783. The Brits, who had remained in New York since the end of the war, left just before George Washington arrived.

New York then became the country's first capital and George Washington its first president, taking his oath of office in 1789. The city was capital for just one year, but business boomed. The New York Stock Exchange, established under a tree on Wall Street by Alexander Hamilton in 1792, positively buzzed with activity as new companies were set up, bought and sold. But as the city grew, it became clear that a proper infrastructure and sanitation system was needed, so the governors introduced a grid system throughout the entire island. North of 14th Street, it abandoned all the existing roads except for Broadway, which followed an old Indian trail, and set up wide avenues that ran south to north and streets that ran between the rivers. Everything, it seemed, was pushing the city north, from illness to prosperity: while the grid system was being put on paper, a series of epidemics drove residents from the old Downtown into what is now known as Greenwich Village.

By 1818, reliable shipping services between New York and other American cities and Europe were well established and trade was booming. It was boosted further by the opening of the Erie Canal in 1825, which, together with the new railroads, opened trade routes to the Midwest. With so much spare cash to play with, businessmen started to build large summer estates and mansions along 5th Avenue up to Madison Square. At the same time, many charities and philanthropic institutions were set up and great libraries were built as education was seen as being very important.

But the divide between rich and poor was getting wider. While water supplies, indoor plumbing and central heating were being installed in the 5th Avenue mansions, thousands of immigrant families – particularly from Ireland – were forced to live in the appalling tenement buildings that were being erected on the Lower East Side of Manhattan.

These people were forced to eke out a wretched existence in the old sweatshops by day and contend with the punitive living conditions of the tenements by night. Entire families were crammed into one or two rooms that had no windows, no hot water, no heat and, of course, no bathroom. Toilet facilities had to be shared with neighbours.

The impending Civil War over the issue of slavery became of major issue for the poor of New York, who couldn't afford to buy their way out of conscription. Uppermost in their minds was the concern that freed slaves would be going after their jobs. The fear reached fever pitch and led to America's worst-ever riot, a four-day-long affair in which 100 people died and thousands, mostly blacks, were injured. By 1865, however, the abolitionists won the war, and 4 million black people were finally freed from the plight of slavery.

At the same time, New York and Boston were being hit by great tidal waves of immigrants. In the 1840s and 1850s it was the Irish, fleeing famine, in the 1860s it was the Germans' fleeing persecution, and in the 1870s it was the Chinese, brought into American specifically to build the railroads. In the 1880s it was the turn of the Russians, along with 1.5 million Eastern European Jews. Over 8 million immigrants went through Castle Clinton in Battery Park between 1855 and 1890. Then the Ellis Island centre was built in 1892 and handled double that number. Between 1880 and 1910, 17 million immigrants passed through the city and by 1900 the population of New York was 3.4 million.

Of course, most of the new arrivals who chose to stay in New York ended up in the crowded tenements of the Lower East Side. Finally, in 1879, after the terrible conditions were brought to light, the city passed new housing laws requiring landlords to increase water supplies and toilets, install fire escapes and build air shafts between buildings to let in air and light. The introduction of streetcars and elevated railways also helped to alleviate the transport problem.

Meanwhile, the wealthy were enjoying the Gilded Age, as Mark Twain dubbed it. Central Park opened in 1858 and more and more mansions were built on 5th Avenue for the likes of the Whitneys, Vanderbilts and Astors. Row houses were also being built on the Upper West Side for wealthy European immigrants.

Henry Frick, who made his fortune in steel and the railroads, built a mansion (now a museum) on the east side of the park at 70th Street, just ten blocks from the new Metropolitan Museum of Art. Luxury hotels such as the original Waldorf-Astoria and the Plaza opened, as did the Metropolitan Opera House. The Statue of Liberty, St Patrick's Cathedral, the Brooklyn Bridge and Carnegie Hall were all built at this time.

Those were the days of the people whose names we associate with New York but don't necessarily know why – like Cornelius Vanderbilt, a shipping and railroad magnate; Andrew

Carnegie, a steel and railroad baron; and John D Rockefeller, who made his millions in oil. The names of many of these millionaires live on in the gifts they gave back to the city: they provided concert halls, libraries, and art museums and donated entire collections to put in them. Carnegie built and donated Carnegie Hall to the city. Rockefeller was one of three major backers behind the opening of the Museum of Modern Art, and the Whitneys created a museum containing their own collection of modern American works of art.

At the same time, the structure of the city itself was undergoing a transformation. In 1904, the IRT subway opened 84 miles of track, which meant that people could move away from the polluted downtown areas and by 1918 the New York City Transit System was complete. The turn of the century also saw the birth of another phenomenon, which was to become one of the city's most famous facets – the skyscraper. First to be built, in 1902, was the Flatiron Building, which was completed using the new technology for the mass production of cast iron. Frank Woolworth's Gothic structure followed in 1913. The beautiful Chrysler Building came in 1929 and the Empire State Building in 1931.

In the meantime, the Volstead Act of 1919 banned the sale of alcohol and led to the Roaring Twenties. Fuelled by lively speakeasies, illegal booze, gangsters, the Charleston and jazz, this was the real heyday of famous venues like Harlem's Cotton Club and the Apollo Theater. After several glittering years, the fun and frolics came to an abrupt end with the collapse of the Wall Street Stock Market on 29 October 1929. It destroyed most small investors and led to huge unemployment and poverty right across the whole of America. Things only started to turn for the better after the election of President Franklin Roosevelt who introduced the New Deal, employing people to build new roads, houses and parks.

In New York, Fiorella La Guardia was elected mayor and set up his austerity programme to enable the city to claw its way back to financial security. During his 12 years in office, La Guardia worked hard at fighting corruption and organised crime in the city, and introduced a massive public housing project.

These were also the days of a great literary and artistic scene in the city. Giants of the spoken and written word, including Dorothy Parker and George Kaufman, would meet at the famous Round Table of the Algonquin Hotel, where they were joined by stage and screen legends Tallulah Bankhead, Douglas Fairbanks and the Marx Brothers.

The Second World War was another watershed for New York, as people fled war-ravaged Europe and headed for the metropolis. Both during and after the war, huge new waves of immigrants arrived – fleeing first the Nazis and then the Communists. New York was as affected by

McCarthy's hunt for 'reds' among the cultural and intellectual elite as the rest of the country, but it bounced back when a new building boom followed the election of President Truman, whose policies were aimed specifically at helping the poor.

The Port Authority Bus Terminal was finished in 1950, the mammoth United Nations Building was completed in 1953 and work started on the huge Lincoln Center complex – built on the slums of the San Juan district – in 1959.

By the 1950s, a new period of affluence had started for the middle classes of New York. The descendants of the earlier Irish, Italian and Jewish immigrants moved out to the new towns that were springing up outside Manhattan, leaving space for a whole new wave of immigrants from Puerto Rico and the southern states of America. This was also the decade of the Beat generation, epitomised by Mack Kerovac and Allen Ginsberg, which evolved into the hippie culture of the 1960s, during which Greenwich Village became the centre of a new wave of artists extolling the virtues of equality for all. By the 1970s, however, this laissez-faire attitude, coupled with New York's position as a major gateway for illegal drug importation, and the general demoralisation of the working classes and ethnic groups, led to an escalation in crime. Muggings and murder were rampant, and the city was brought to the brink of bankruptcy.

Complete chaos was only averted by the introduction of severe austerity measures, which unfortunately most affected those who could least afford them – the poor. But good news was just around the corner as new mayor Ed Koch implemented major tax incentives and rejuvenated New York's business community. A boom followed, reflected in the arrival of a series of mammoth new skyscrapers, including the World Trade Center and Trump Tower. The transformation was completed in the 1990s with Mayor Giuliani's clean-up operation. It has to be said that this was unpopular with the more Liberal New Yorkers but there are many who believe that it was his policies that made New York into a city fit for the new millennium.

From the time of the earliest immigrants, New York has represented a gateway to a new life, a place of hope: the American dream offered a future filled with happiness and success. And nowadays New York still draws in people in their thousands. After all, as the song goes, 'If you can make it there, you'll make it anywhere.'

CHAPTER 1

All About New York

We've included diagrammatic maps through the book to help you get to grips with the areas of New York and the locations of the major sights. For accurate bus and subway maps, turn to the inside front cover.

GETTING INTO THE CITY

From John F Kennedy International Airport

JFK is in the borough of Queens and is the best place to enter or leave New York by air. It is 15 miles from Midtown Manhattan, a journey that will take you between 50 and 60 minutes. The cost of a yellow medallion taxi into town is a fixed rate of $30 as set by the New York Taxi and Limousine Commission. Bridge and tunnel tolls are extra (you can pay at the end of the journey). An MTA bus and subway ride will cost you $1.50 each, private bus companies charge between $13 and $16 and the shuttle service costs $16. Private car services vary in price. There are various ways to get into New York.

SuperShuttle: Tel 212-209 7000. A door-to-door shared limo-bus from the airport to your hotel. Operates 24 hours a day, 365 days a year. With your NYCard (see page 33) you'll get a $1 discount off the first person and every other person in your group (friends or family) will only be charged $9 – a great saving.

★★★★ **INSIDE TRACK** ★★★★
★   ★
★   If dialling a 718 area code or   ★
★   anything other than a 212 code   ★
★   while in Manhattan, you must   ★
★   dial 1 first or you won't get   ★
★   through.   ★
★   ★
★★★★★★★★★★★★★★★★★★★★★★★★★

New York Airport Service: Tel 718-875 8200. Runs every 15–30 minutes to Manhattan and also operates a minivan service from drop-off points in Manhattan to many hotels.

From Newark International Airport

Newark is in the borough of New Jersey and is 16 miles from Midtown Manhattan – a journey that will take at least 60 minutes. Set taxi fares start at $34 plus bridge or tunnel toll and tip. Private bus companies charge between $10 and $15 and the shuttle service costs between $13.50 and $18. Again you have a choice of ways to get into the city.

SuperShuttle: See From John F Kennedy International Airport opposite.

The PATH: Tel 800-234 PATH. Rapid transit from Newark Penn Station (but you must take a taxi there from the airport) to Manhattan's World Trade Center and other stops in Lower and Midtown Manhattan. Operates 24 hours, fare $1.

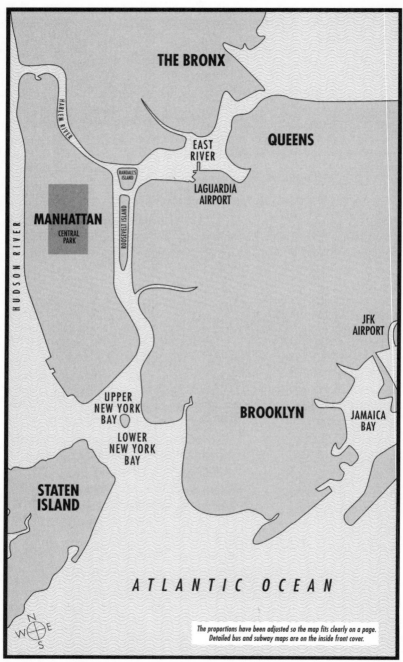

Areas of New York

**Olympia Trails Airport Express
Bus:** Tel 212-964 6233. Operates
between Newark and four
Manhattan locations – Penn Station
(34th Street and 8th Avenue), Port
Authority Bus Terminal (42nd Street
and 8th Avenue), Grand Central (41st
Street between Lexington and Park
Avenues) and World Trade Center
No 1. Also hotel shuttle to all
Midtown points between 30th and
65th Streets. Departs every 20
minutes, fare $10 (hotel shuttle $15).

GETTING AROUND NEW YORK

Orientation

When most people talk about New
York, they actually mean Manhattan,
which is the long, thin sliver of an
island in the middle of the four outer
boroughs of Staten Island, Queens,
the Bronx and Brooklyn. Manhattan
is 13.4 miles long and two miles
wide for the most part and almost all
of it above 14th Street is on the grid
system that was introduced quite
early on in New York's history. The
main exception is Greenwich Village,
which, like Downtown, had already
established its eccentric random
arrangement of streets (like ours in
the UK) and refused to get on the
grid system. The other exception is
Broadway, which follows an old
Indian trail that runs largely north to
south on the west side of the island,
then cuts across to the East Side as it
runs downtown.

Here are a few basic rules about the
geography of Manhattan; it is useful
to aquaint yourself with them as

soon as possible, then you'll be able
to walk around with confidence!

• The city is divided between East
and West by 5th Avenue and all the
street numbers begin there. That
means that 2 West 57th Street is
just a few steps to the west of
5th Avenue while 2 East 57th Street
is just a few steps to the east of
5th Avenue.

• Most streets in Manhattan are
one-way. With a few exceptions,
traffic on even-numbered streets
travels east and traffic on odd-
numbered streets travels west. Traffic
on major 'cross town' streets –
so-called because they are horizontal
on the street maps of Manhattan –
travels in both directions. These
include Canal, Houston (pronounced
Howston), 14th, 23rd, 34th, 42nd,
57th, 72nd, 79th, 86th and 96th
Streets.

• When travelling north to south or
vice versa, it is useful to remember
that York Avenue goes both ways,
1st Avenue goes south to north,
2nd Avenue goes south and 3rd
goes north mostly, though there is a
small two-way section. Lexington
goes south, Park goes in both
directions, Madison goes north and
5th Avenue goes south. Central Park
West goes both ways, Columbus
Avenue goes south, Amsterdam
Avenue north, Broadway goes in
both directions until Columbus Circle,
after which it continues south-
bound only, to the tip of Manhattan.
West End Avenue and Riverside Drive
go in both directions.

• To New Yorkers, 'Downtown' does not mean the city centre, but means south, while 'Uptown' means north. You will need to get used to these terms if you are planning to use the subway – which is simpler to use than it looks at first!

Taking a taxi

This is the preferred means of transport for many visitors to the city but, even though the fares are much cheaper than in London, the cost still mounts up pretty quickly. In any case, you will need to have a good idea of where you are going and how to get there, as most of the cab drivers in New York are the latest immigrants to have arrived and have very little clue about how to get around the city. Fortunately, thanks to the grid system (see page 17), it is relatively easy to educate yourself about where you are going and so you can give good directions.

• First off, never expect the driver to be the kind of chirpy, chatty Cockney character that you're used to in the UK. Most speak very little English and are not interested in making polite conversation, and many can be downright rude.

• Secondly, make sure you get on at the right place. If you are travelling uptown, but you're on a road heading downtown, walk a block east or west so you are heading in the right direction. It saves time and money, and if you don't, the taxi driver will know you're a tourist.

• Always have the full address of the place where you are going.

• Hailing a taxi is not necessarily as easy as it looks – you have to be aware of the lighting system on the top of the yellow medallion taxis. If the central light is on, it means the taxi driver is working and available. If all the lights are out, it means the driver is working but has a fare. If the outer two lights are on, it means the taxi driver is off-duty – look carefully and you'll see the words.

• When you get to a toll, expect the taxi driver to turn around and demand the cash to pay for it, but you are quite within your rights to ask him to add it on at the end.

• Beware of trying to get a cab at around 4pm. This is when most drivers change shifts so getting a taxi is well nigh impossible around this time because they don't want to go anywhere but home!

• Do not expect a taxi driver to change any bill larger than $20.

• In addition to the medallion on the roof, a legitimate taxi will have an automatic receipt machine mounted on the dashboard so that you can get an immediate record.

• If you find yourself below Canal Street after business hours or at the weekend, you may have difficulty finding a yellow cab. Your best bet, rather than jump into any vehicle purporting to be a taxi, is to phone one of the many companies listed under Taxicab Service in the Yellow Pages. Fares are slightly higher than metered cabs, but they are a much safer option than trusting to your luck on the streets.

Subways

The first time you take a look at a subway map of New York, you can be forgiven for thinking you need a degree in the whole system to get anywhere. The confusion is made worse by the fact that the signposts – both outside and inside the stations – are easily missed. Just as you need to get used to how the city is laid out, there are a few rules you'll need to understand to play the subway game. They're worth learning, though, as you'll feel far more confident travelling around Manhattan and will save yourself a fortune in cab fares.

• Don't look for obvious London Underground-type signs; instead look for either the very discreet 'M' signs in blue or the signature red and green glass globes (red means the entrance is not always open).

• Before going down a subway entrance, check it is going in the right direction for you – many entrances take you to downtown or uptown destinations only, not both. It means that if you make the mistake of going in and swiping your ticket before you realise you're going in the wrong direction, you will have to swipe your card again on the other side – so you'll end up paying double. The alternative is to travel in the wrong direction until you get to one of the larger subway stations (such as 42nd Street) and then change.

• Generally, if you're planning to go downtown, use subway entrances on

the west side of the road and if you're going uptown, use subway entrances on the east side of the road. This way you should be heading in the right direction, but do always check before entering.

• If you're in one of the outer boroughs the same rules apply, but look for the sign that says 'Manhattan'.

• To complicate matters further, some trains are express and some are slow. At some stations you have to go down two flights to get to the express trains, while at others you don't, and it is easy to get on an express train by mistake.

• There are conflicting opinions (hotly debated by the locals) as to whether it is worth waiting for an express. On the plus-side, they move damn fast, but on the downside you could end up waiting ten minutes for one, which means you won't have saved any time at all in the end.

• The same subway line (denoted by a specific colour, like red, blue, yellow or green) will have up to three or four different numbers or initials to identify it. For instance, the Red Line has trains with the numbers 1, 2, 3 and 9. Don't worry too much about the colours – they commemorate the different companies that started Manhattan's subway lines. The real trick is to find the station on any colour line that is closest to your destination, avenue and cross-street. In Manhattan, there isn't much difference between the train numbers apart from whether they

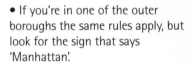

are express or slow, but they will branch off in different directions once they reach the outer boroughs, so beware if you are travelling out of town. A number or letter in a diamond means rush-hour service, in a circle it denotes normal service, and a square indicates a terminus, or the end of a line.

• Take care as some of the numbers don't stop at all stops during off-peak periods, so check what the numbers are against your destination on the subway map. If they are written in a lighter tone, then they are peak-time only.

★★★★ **INSIDE TRACK** ★★★★
★   ★
★   ★
★   **Never lean over the edge of a**   ★
★   **subway platform to look for**   ★
★   **trains. New Yorkers do, but it is** ★
★   **really dangerous and people do** ★
★   **get pushed on to the lines.**   ★
★   ★
★★★★★★★★★★★★★★★★★★★★★★★★

• Just like the London Underground, there are many different lines going to the same destinations, but unlike the London Underground, they are not necessarily apparent. For instance, if you enter the tube at Oxford Circus you will have access to the Bakerloo and Central lines and if you exit it there, you will always be at Oxford Circus itself. But if you arrive at Fulton Street on the New York subway and head for the exit you can come out at four completely different locations. For instance, the Red Line exits at Fulton and William Streets, the Brown Line exits at John and Nassau Streets, the Blue Line

exits at Fulton and Nassau Streets and the Green Line exits at Broadway and John Street – all of which are quite a long way from each other.

• The locals consider that the subway is safe to travel up until around 11pm. After that time opinions vary, but when making up your mind do be aware that the subway service after 11pm is generally incredibly slow. One savvy New Yorker told me that she never uses the subway after 11pm because there is so little traffic on the roads that getting home by taxi is relatively cheap and a darn sight quicker.

• The subway does have one very good point: because the island of Manhattan is largely made up of incredibly strong granite, they did not have to dig as deep as we have to in London to find the really strong foundation level. This means you generally only have to go down one flight of steps to find the line.

• There is a flat fare of $1.50 per subway ride. You can buy tokens for single rides or there are different types of cards. These **MetroCards** can be bought at any subway station and other locations in pre-paid, sometimes, discounted fares from $3 to $80 and also offer free transfers between buses and trains. Seven-day ($17) and 30-day ($63) unlimited-ride MetroCards are also available. Tourists can take advantage of the relatively new **Fun Passes**. They cost $4 a day and entitle you to unlimited rides on trains and buses until 3 the following morning. They are available from newsagents, the Times Square Visitor Center and from vending machines at subway stations. One of the best MetroCards to buy is the $15 card. It gives you 11 rides for the price of 10 and those rides can be taken at any time.

On the buses

Travelling by bus is always a little more nerve-wracking because you can never be sure whether you've arrived at your destination; however, most people are pretty helpful if asked a direct question. I thought that taking to the buses would be more difficult than travelling by subway, but two of my friends put paid to that notion by going everywhere by bus on their first visit to New York. There are a few things that are helpful to know, though, to avoid confusion or embarrassment.

• Often there are no route maps displayed at the bus stops. However, as a general rule they run north to south, south to north, east to west or west to east.

• Generally buses come into their own when you are trying to get 'cross town' as very few subway lines provide that kind of a service (most of the subways run north to south and south to north only).

• Get on the bus at the front and click in your MetroCard or subway token or feed in $1.50. Exact change is essential – and it must be all in coins as no dollar bills are accepted. If you plan to change on to another bus, you must ask for a free transfer ticket when you board.

• Oddly enough, although there are bus exits at the back, you can still also get off at the front!

• Requesting a stop may be a little confusing – there are no clearly marked red buttons to press; instead there are black strips that run the full length of the bus between the windows or at the back along the tops of the handles. Press one of these to request the next bus stop.

• Some bus routes, notably the 1, 5, 6, 10 and 15, run very interesting routes and are a really cheap way of seeing some major sights and getting to know the city. This option works out best on the weekends when the traffic is not too heavy.

Driving

A word of advice: don't even think about it. Most of the streets will be jam-packed, while parking is scarce and astronomically expensive – between $8 and $10 an hour. You can park on the street, but watch out for what is known as alternate-side-of-the-street parking. This means you have to know which day of the week the cleaning truck comes by so you move the car over at the right time. People become obsessed with thinking about where they park their cars and DJs even announce on the radio when alternate-side-of-the-street parking has stopped. Double-parking is common, so it is easy to get boxed in, and frustrated drivers simply get in their cars and honk the horn until the guilty owner moves their car. As one New Yorker told me: 'People do not know how to park here. New Yorkers are not good drivers and are the wildest parkers. Watching a New Yorker trying to park is hilarious!'

If you plan to take a trip upstate, though, and wish to do so by car, then there are some dos and don'ts about car hire. Firstly never, ever, EVER hire a car in Manhattan – unless you want to pay through the nose to the tune of around $90 to $120 a day. Take a ferry to New Jersey and hire a car from there for about $55 to $65 for a medium-sized car with unlimited mileage.

Secondly, don't even think about it in the summer or at weekends, because that's what most New Yorkers will be doing and you'll find hire cars very thin on the ground. Hire cars are also snapped up in the autumn when New Yorkers like to go to the country to see the 'fall foliage'.

THE BEST TIMES TO GO

January to March and July and August are best for accommodation and good for flights. Just bear in mind that July and August are the hottest months, though it is not as bad as you expect because all the shops and cabs have air conditioning and you get blasts of lovely cool air from the shops as you pass.

In the run-up to Christmas it is very difficult to get accommodation in Manhattan, as it is in September and October when there are a lot of conventions. Surprisingly, the times around Thanksgiving and between Christmas and New Year are okay times to go because people want to

be at home with their families. April to June should be pleasantly cool (though it can be warm, actually!) and is a favoured time to go.

★★★★ INSIDE TRACK ★★★★
★   ★
★ In summer watch out for water ★
★ dropping out of air conditioning ★
★ units that have been fitted on to ★
★ the side of apartments. In winter ★
★   take extra care on pavements: ★
★   the grilles over cellars get very, ★
★ very slippery and the worst thing ★
★   is you may not even see them   ★
★   because of the snow.   ★
★★★★★★★★★★★★★★★★★★★★★★★★

In addition to the above advice, check the Festivals, Parades and Dates to Remember section (see page 23) to find out when there are major events happening in the city as it tends to be a bit more crowded at these times.

WHAT TO WEAR

Layers are the key to comfortable clobber in New York, no matter what time of the year you go. In summer the air conditioning in buildings can get pretty cold, while outside it is stiflingly hot. If you take a lightweight, rainproof jacket, you'll be covered for all eventualities, including the odd shower. In winter it is the other way round – warm buildings and cold streets – so it's best to have an overcoat of some sort, but nothing too heavy unless you're planning to be out of doors a lot. At any time of the year, the skyscrapers of the city act as a kind of wind tunnel and unless you're in the sun it can get nippy pretty

CLIMATE

Month	Average Temperature		Rainfall
	Low	High	
January	–3°C/26°F	3°C/38°F	8 cm/3 in
February	–3°C/27°F	5°C/40°F	8 cm/3 in
March	1°C/34°F	9°C/49°F	11 cm/4¼ in
April	7°C/44°F	16°C/61°F	10 cm/4 in
May	12°C/53°F	22°C/72°F	10 cm/4 in
June	17°C/63°F	27°C/80°F	8 cm/3 in
July	20°C/68°F	29°C/85°F	10 cm/4 in
August	19°C/67°F	29°C/84°F	10 cm/4 in
September	16°C/60°F	25°C/77°F	9 cm/3½ in
October	10°C/50°F	19°C/66°F	9 cm/3½ in
November	5°C/41°F	12°C/54°F	11 cm/4¼ in
December	–1°C/31°F	6°C/42°F	10 cm/4 in

quickly – another reason to make sure you have a cardigan or lightweight jacket in the summer. And in the winter, make sure you have a hat, scarf and gloves in your bag for times of emergency.

FESTIVALS, PARADES AND DATES TO REMEMBER

Having decided when to go, you'll want to know what's on while you're there. Happily, New Yorkers like nothing better than a celebration – whether it be for the changing of the seasons, their roots or the arts. They clog up the streets for hours on end but they provide truly spectacular entertainment for the crowds every year. And what's more, apart from the food and drink you choose to imbibe, they're all free!

Events

Winter Antiques Show: Seventh Regiment Armory, Park Avenue (at 67th Street). Tel 718-292 7392. Mid-January. If you're on a cheapie break to New York in the midwinter, then you'll be rewarded with one of the biggest and best antiques fairs in the world. Here you'll find everything from the very old to art nouveau plus vast collections from all over America.

Chinese New Year Parade: Chinatown at Mott Street. Phone 212-481 1222 for information. Held on the first day of the full moon between 21 January and 19 February. Although private fireworks have been banned, there are still plenty of firecrackers and dragons to dazzle onlookers in this stylish Chinese festival. Go to watch, eat, drink and be merry.

Black History Month: See the newspapers and guides for cultural events, concerts and lectures scheduled around the city during the month of February.

American Holidays

(In addition to Christmas and New Year's Days)

Martin Luther King Jnr Day – third Monday in January

Presidents' Day – third Monday in February

Memorial Day – last Monday in May

Independence Day – 4 July

Labor Day – first Monday in September

Columbus Day – second Monday in October

Election Day – first Tuesday in November

Veterans' Day – 11 November

Thanksgiving – fourth Thursday in November

Grammy Awards: The Oscars of the world of TV now take place in Madison Square Gardens. You won't get in but if you'd like a gawk at the stars as they arrive in their limos, why not join the crowd? Late February. Call the MSG on 212-465 6741 for information.

Whitney Biennial: Whitney Museum of American Art (see page

65), 945 Madison Avenue at 75th Street. Tel 212-570 3600. Held every two years (funnily enough!), the Whitney's line-up of what it considers to be the most important art around is as controversial as our British equivalent of a sheep suspended in a glass cabinet. The next show is due to be held in late March to June of 2002.

St Patrick's Day Parade: 5th Avenue (between 44th and 86th Streets). One of the bigger parades the city has to offer, this takes place on 17 March. If you're in town, you won't be able to miss the sea of green that goes with this annual Irish-American day. Kick-off is at 11am for the parade up Fifth Avenue and the festivities go on late into the night at bars all across Manhattan.

Greek Independence Day Parade: Along 5th Avenue from 49th to 59th Streets on 25 March. This one's a Zorba-style parade with Greek food, music and dancing.

Cirque du Soleil: Every other year in spring (more or less) this wonderful Canadian animal-free circus hitches up its tent in Battery Park to the delight of all. Call 800-678 5440 for information, to check the month and see if this is your lucky year.

Easter Parade: 5th Avenue (between 44th and 59th Streets). Annually on Easter Sunday. The steps of St Patrick's Cathedral are generally considered to be the most advantageous viewing spot – so they're very popular. Kick-off is at 11am, so arrive early to bag a space.

New York City Ballet Spring Season: New York State Theater, 20 Lincoln Center Plaza, 65th Street at Columbus Avenue. Tel 212-870 5570. Late April to June. I have to admit I'm a ballet nut, and when away from London and the fabulous Royal Ballet, I can think of nowhere better than the New York City Ballet to see some of the world's top dancers who have made a name for themselves as masters of classics by Balanchine and Robbins.

Ninth Avenue International Food Festival: 9th Avenue between 37th and 57th Streets, mid-May. Feeling a little peckish? Then get on down to 9th where hundreds of stalls line the streets selling every type of food imaginable. Go for lunch and then walk it all off by taking a stroll around down to Chelsea's fabulous art galleries.

Fleet Week: *Intrepid* Sea-Air-Space Museum (see page 58), Pier 86, 46th Street at the Hudson River. Unless you're a boat nut, it's normally not worth visiting the huge armada of US Navy and other ships that visit New York, but if you're here in the last week in May, it'll be hard to miss their presence. Take a wiggle on down to Pier 86 for a closer look.

Washington Square Art Exhibition: An old and revered Greenwich Village event which happens on the last two weekends in May and the first two weekends in September. A huge, outdoor art show with easels and food trolleys set up in the streets all around the park.

Lower East Side Festival of Arts: Theater for the New City, 155 1st Avenue at 10th Street. Tel 212-245 1109. Last weekend in May. Deep in the heart of the neighbourhood that helped create the East Coast Beat movement, method acting and pop art, this is an annual arts festival and outdoor carnival with performances by more than 20 theatrical troupes.

Puerto Rico Day Parade: Fifth Avenue between 44th and 86th Streets. First Sunday in June. You'll get a real flavour of a big New York parade thanks to the bands, floats, colour and noise of this display.

Mermaid Parade: 8th Street between Steeplechase Park and Broadway, Coney Island, Brooklyn. Phone 718-372 5159 for information. Catch the B, D or F trains to Stillwell Avenue on the Saturday following the first official day of summer (late June) to sample a taste of real New York life. It'll be a fishy business, but well worth it!

New York Jazz Festival: Various clubs in early June, phone 212-219 3006 for information. Even those of us who are not true aficionados of jazz can enjoy the festival atmosphere of the 300 acts that take part in this event at ten different venues.

Gay and Lesbian Pride Parade: From Columbus Circle along 5th Avenue to Christopher Street in Greenwich Village. Last Sunday in June. Call 212-807 7433 for information on the week-long events. The Stonewall riots of 1968, when New York's gay community fought for public acceptance, are now celebrated in an annual street parade that gives way to a full week of events including a packed club schedule and an open-air dance party on the West Side piers.

Lincoln Center Festival: For the whole of July and August, a veritable feast of dance, drama, ballet, children's shows and multimedia and performance art involving both repertory companies and special guests is staged at venues inside and outside at the Lincoln Center (see page 130). For information, call 212-845 5400.

Fourth of July: The Americans still insist on celebrating achieving independence from their colonial masters, but at least they do it in style! Throughout New York there are various celebrations going on, but by far the biggest is Macy's Fireworks Display, which is held on the East River between 14th and 51st Streets. A good viewing spot is from the FDR Drive, where you'll see a $1-million firework extravaganza. Another fireworks display is held at South Street Seaport.

Harlem Week: Between West 125th and West 135th Streets. Tel 212-862 8477. Early to mid-August. The largest black and Hispanic festival in the world, its highlight is the street party with R 'n' B, gospel and all that jazz. In addition to the music, there are films, dance, fashion, sports and exhibitions. What a great way to experience Harlem.

West Indian Day Carnival: Eastern Parkway from Utica Avenue to Grand Army Plaza, Brooklyn. Tel 718-625 1515. First weekend in September. Fabulous festival celebrating Caribbean culture. Brightly-costumed marchers put on a special children's parade on the Saturday, with an even bigger event on Labor Day.

Feast of San Gennaro: Mulberry Street to Worth Street in Little Italy. Tel 212-484 1222. Third week in September. Really the best time to see what is left of the once bustling Little Italy that is now reduced to one street – Mulberry. There are lots of fairground booths, plenty of food and even more vino.

Columbus Day Parade: 5th Avenue between 44th and 86th Streets. Second Monday in October. The traditional celebration of the first recorded sighting of America by Europeans is now somewhat controversial in some quarters but, despite its lack of political correctness, Columbus Day still gets the big 5th Avenue parade treatment, which is well worth a view.

Halloween Parade: 6th Avenue between Union Square and Spring Street, Greenwich Village. Tel 212-475 3333, ext 7787. 31 October, 7pm. Although a recent addition to the plethora of parades in the city, New York's latest is also one of the best, thanks to the outlandishly over-the-top costumes of many of its participants. The organisers decree a different theme each year and a lot of work goes into the amazing outfits that range from the exotic to the nearly non-existent. It attracts between 60,000 and 100,000 ghouls, ghosts and onlookers.

New York City Marathon: Starts at the Staten Island side of the Verrazano Narrows Bridge as a mad pack of 35,000 men and women run 26.2 miles around all five boroughs, to finish at the Tavern on the Green in Central Park at West 67th Street. Last Sunday in October/first Sunday in November. If you want to enter the marathon you need to fill out an application form, pay a small fee, and then wait to see if you get picked. Contact the New York Road Runners Club by e-mail at **www.nycmarathon.msn.com** or **www.nyrrcc.org** or write to New York City Marathon, International Lottery, 9 East 89th Street, New York, NY 10128, or call 212-860 4455.

Macy's Thanksgiving Day Parade: From Central Park West at 79th Street to Macy's (see page 115) on Broadway at 34th Street. Tel 212-494 4495. Thanksgiving Day at 9am. Definitely one for the family, this is the Big Mama of all New York's parades, with enormous inflated cartoon characters, fabulous floats and the gift-giving Santa Claus himself. It is even televised for the rest of America. If you miss the parade, you can go to see Santa at Santaland in Macy's until Christmas.

Christmas Tree Lighting Ceremony: 5th Avenue between 49th and 50th Streets. Tel 212-484 1222. Early December. The Rockefeller Center (see page 38) in

front of the towering RCA building provides the magical setting for the switching-on of nearly five miles of lights on the huge tree.

New Year's Eve Fireworks: 5th Avenue and 90th Street or Bethsheda Fountain (Central Park at 72nd Street) are the best viewing spots. The hot apple cider and spirit of camaraderie begin at 11.30pm.

Spare a thought. . .

There is a downside to the parades. As one local told me: 'I first thought parades were a blessing because they are so beautiful and some people live for them, but they all go to the Upper East Side where I live to start and finish. Now I feel battered by parades and am surrounded by strangers who are drunk. St Patrick's Day Parade is the biggest in New York and you just can't get past these drunk kids to get anything done or even just have a cup of coffee. The New York marathon is another force to be reckoned with. A lot of streets are blocked off and it is hard to get to the subway. It means you have to be patient and one thing we New Yorkers are not is patient!'

New Year's Eve Ball Drop: Times Square (see page 40). This event is a real New York classic, though you may prefer to watch safely on TV rather than be packed in with the freezing masses. Remember, Times Square is a misnomer – it's a junction, so there isn't really that much room and all the side streets

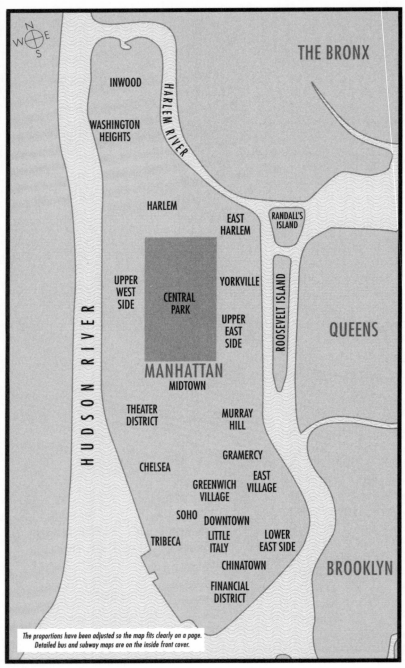

Areas of Manhattan

THE BRONX

INWOOD

WASHINGTON
HEIGHTS

HARLEM RIVER

HARLEM

EAST
HARLEM

RANDALL'S
ISLAND

UPPER
WEST
SIDE

CENTRAL
PARK

YORKVILLE

UPPER
EAST
SIDE

ROOSEVELT ISLAND

QUEENS

MANHATTAN
MIDTOWN

HUDSON RIVER

THEATER
DISTRICT

MURRAY
HILL

GRAMERCY

CHELSEA

GREENWICH
VILLAGE

EAST
VILLAGE

SOHO

DOWNTOWN

TRIBECA

LITTLE
ITALY

LOWER
EAST SIDE

CHINATOWN

BROOKLYN

FINANCIAL
DISTRICT

*The proportions have been adjusted so the map fits clearly on a page.
Detailed bus and subway maps are on the inside front cover.*

get packed too. If you do manage to get a good spot, though, you'll see the giant glitterball of 180 bulbs and 12,000 rhinestones being dropped to bring in the New Year.

Free events

Great news for visitors – particularly those on a budget: a lot of life in New York is free, especially in the summer. Here is a list of some of those regular events, but it is also a good idea to pick up a copy of the Free Time newspaper for information about free concerts, cinema showings and street fairs. Play your cards right and you could end up spending very little on entertainment!

Thursday Night Concert Series: Main Stage, South Street Seaport, South Street at Fulton Street. Tel 212-732 7678. From the last Monday in May (Memorial Day) to the first Monday in September (Labor Day). Enjoy all types of music in a series of free concerts.

Museum Mile Festival: 5th Avenue between 82nd and 104th Streets. Phone 212-606 2296 for information. Museum Mile is neither a museum nor a mile, but a series of museums stretching out along 5th Avenue and Central Park on the Upper East Side. All are worth a visit and on the second Tuesday in June you can get into nine museums including the fabulous Metropolitan for free, as part of the open-house festival. An added perk is the fascinating street entertainment.

Central Park SummerStage: Rumsey Playfield, Central Park (at 72nd Street), June to August. Tel 212-360 2777. You can experience many kinds of entertainment for free in New York and one of the best is the free weekend afternoon concerts put on by the SummerStage, featuring top international performers. On weekday nights there are also dance and spoken-word events.

Metropolitan Opera Parks Concerts: Various sites in June, phone 212-362 6000 for information. If you can't afford to see the Metropolitan Opera at The Met, take advantage of their free open-air concerts in Central Park and other locations. But, be warned, they're popular events so you'll have to arrive very early to bag a seat.

New York Shakespeare Festival: Delacorte Theater, Central Park (at 81st Street). Tel 212-539 8750. Late June to late August. See how top American actors do the Bard – for free. There are two plays each year – one Shakespeare and one American.

Bryant Park Free Summer Season: 6th Avenue at 42nd Street. Tel 212-922 9393. Bryant Park is one of the few green spaces available in the Midtown area, and between June and August things get even better when there is a series of free classical music, jazz, dance and film showings during the day and evening.

Summergarden: Museum of Modern Art (see page 57), 11 West 53rd Street between 5th and 6th

Avenues. Tel 212-708 9400. An added bonus to visiting the little gem that is MoMA is the series of free classical concerts that are presented in the museum's garden between July and August each year.

Celebrate Brooklyn! Performing Arts Festival: Prospect Park Bandshell, 9th Street (at Prospect Park West), Park Slope, Brooklyn. Tel 718-855 7882. Here's a very good reason to break out of Manhattan and visit one of the outer boroughs – a series of free music, dance, theatre and film events that lasts a full nine weeks.

Useful websites

www.citysearchnyc.com Calendar of events happening in New York.

www.cityguideny.com The on-line site of the weekly *City Guide* which is provided to hotels.

www.clubnyc.com Complete list of what's cool, where and why.

www.halloween-nyc.com The official Halloween Parade site with history, how to get involved and information about the forthcoming event.

www.nytab.com The New York Travel Advisory Bureau's site helps in trip planning and gives information on major savings.

www.nycvisit.com The New York Convention and Visitors' Bureau's comprehensive listing includes suggested itineraries for where to stay and shop and what to do.

www.villagevoice.com The on-line site of the *Village Voice*.

VOCABULARY

It has often been said that the Brits and Americans are two races divided by a common language and when you make an unexpected faux pas you'll certainly learn how true this is. For instance, never, ever ask for a packet of fags as this is the American slang word for gays and a sense of humour is not their strong point! Also, when you need to pee, never ask for the toilet – always use the favoured euphemisms of bathroom or restroom. There are plenty of other differences, too, which may not necessarily cause offence, but which will cause confusion, so to help you on your way, here is a guide to American-speak.

Travelling around

Aerial	Antenna
Articulated truck	Semi
Bonnet	Hood
Boot	Trunk
Caravan	House trailer
Car park	Parking lot
Car silencer	Muffler
Crossroads/junction	Intersection
Demister	Defogger
Dipswitch	Dimmer
Dual carriageway	Four-lane (or divided) highway
Flyover	Overpass
Give way	Yield
Jump leads	Jumper cables
Kerb/kerbside	Curb/curbside
Lorry	Truck
Manual transmission	Stickshift
Motorway	Highway, freeway, expressway
Pavement	Sidewalk

Petrol	Gas
Petrol station	Gas/service station
Request stop	Flag stop
Ring road	Beltway
Run in (engine)	Break in
Slip-road	Ramp
Subway	Pedestrian underpass
Turning	Turnoff
Tyre	Tire
Underground	Subway
Walk	Hike
Wheel clamp	Denver boot
Windscreen	Windshield
Wing	Fender

Eating and stuff

One of the biggest disappointments I had on my first trip to America was to use what I thought was the correct lingo when ordering my breakfast eggs 'sunny side up' one morning, only to end up with what seemed like a half-cooked egg! The Americans don't flick fat over the top of the egg when frying it, but turn it over to cook on both sides. So for eggs the way I like them, cooked on both sides but soft, I have to order eggs 'over easy' and if you like yours well done, then ask for eggs 'over hard'.

There are plenty of other anomalies. Many standard American dishes come with a biscuit – which is a corn scone to us and all the more strange for breakfast! Breakfast may also include something called grits, which is a porridge-like dish made out of ground, boiled corn, and hash browns, which are grated, fried potatoes. Here are some other differences in food-speak.

Aubergine	Eggplant
Bill	Check or tab
Biscuit (savoury)	Cracker
Biscuit (sweet)	Cookie
Chick pea	Garbanzo bean
Chips	(French) fries
Choux bun	Cream puff
Clingfilm	Plastic wrap
Coriander	Cilantro
Cornflour	Cornstarch
Courgette	Zucchini
Crayfish	Crawfish
Crisps	Chips
Crystallised	Candied
Cutlery	Silverware or place-setting
Demerara sugar	Light-brown sugar
Desiccated coconut	Shredded coconut
Digestive biscuit	Graham cracker
Double cream	Heavy cream
Essence (eg vanilla)	Extract or flavoring
Filled baguette	Sub or hero
Fillet (of meat/fish)	Filet
Fizzy drink	Soda
Golden syrup	Corn syrup
Grated, fried potatoes	Hash browns
Grilled	Broiled
Icing sugar	Powdered/ confectioners' sugar
Jam	Jelly/conserve
Ketchup	Catsup
King prawn	Shrimp
Main course	Entrée
Malt liquor	Strong beer
Measure	Shot
Mince	Ground meat
Off-licence	Liquor store
Pastry case	Pie shell
Pips	Seeds (in fruit)
Plain/dark chocolate	Semi-sweet or unsweetened chocolate
Pumpkin	Squash

Scone	Biscuit
Shortcrust pastry	Pie dough
Single cream	Light cream
Soda water	Seltzer
Sorbet	Sherbet
Soya	Soy
Spirits	Liquor
Sponge finger biscuits	Lady fingers
Spreading of cream cheese on a bagel	Schmear
Spring onion	Scallion
Starter	Appetiser
Stoned (cherries etc)	Pitted
Sultana	Golden raisins
Sweet shop	Candy store
Take-away	To go
Toilet	Restroom (public) bathroom (private)
Tomato purée	Tomato paste
Water biscuit	Cracker

Shopping

Braces	Suspenders
Bumbag	Fanny pack
Chemist	Drug store
Ground floor	First floor
Handbag	Purse
High Street	Main street
Jumper	Sweater
Knickers	Panties
Muslin	Cheesecloth
Pants	Underpants
Pyjamas	Pajamas
Queue	Line, line up
Suspenders	Garters
Till	Check-out
Tights	Pantyhose
Trainers	Sneakers
Trousers	Pants
Underpants	Shorts, underwear
Vest	Undershirt
Waistcoat	Vest
Zip	Zipper

Money

Bill	Check
Banknote	Bill
Cheque	Check
25 cents	Quarter
10 cents	Dime
5 cents	Nickel
1 cent	Penny

General

Air hostess	Flight attendant
Anti-clockwise	Counterclockwise
At weekends	On weekends
Autumn	Fall
Behind	In back of
Camp bed	Cot
Cinema	Movie theater
City/town centre	Downtown (not lower Manhattan!)
Coach	Bus
Cot	Crib
Diary (appointments)	Calendar
Diary (records)	Journal
From... to...	Through
Lift	Elevator
Nappy	Diaper
Ordinary	Regular, normal
Paddling pool	Wading pool
Post, postbox	Mail, mailbox
Pram, pushchair	Stroller
Tap	Faucet
Trunk call	Long-distance call

New York talk

Of course, in addition to the differences between American- and Brit-speak, the locals have a dialect and phraseology all of their own. There are two overriding influences that affect much of the local dialect: Brooklynese, ie the Brooklyn accent, and Mafia-speak, which has made its way into everyday use, thanks largely to the huge number of movies made about the New York Mafia. A lot of these words and phrases are fun to know about, rather than being essential to finding your way around the city – though they may help you better understand all those movies!

All right already   Stop it, that's enough!

Alphabet City   A nickname for the part of Manhattan's East Village, located between Avenues A and D

Atomic wedgie   From the Seinfeld show. To have an atomic wedgie means to have one's underwear gathered in an extremely uncomfortable position between the buttocks

Barrio   A Spanish-speaking neighbourhood or district

Big one   A $1,000 bill

Bloomies   A popular nickname for Bloomingdales

Bonebreaker   Enforcer for the Mafia

Borscht belt   A resort area in the Catskill Mountains of upstate New York

Bridge and tunnel   A term used by Manhattanites to describe (usually negatively) commuters to the city, who arrive via the bridges and tunnels

Brotherhood   A synonym for the Mafia

Button man   Soldier or low-ranking Mafia member

Capeesh   Pronunciation of *capisce*, Italian for 'understand'

Capo di tutti capi Italian for 'the boss of all bosses'

Cattle call   A large casting call at a Broadway theatre

Communion   A killing by a Mafia enforcer in which the body is made to disappear by burying it in the concrete of a building foundation

Cosa Nostra   Italian for 'our thing' and another name for the Mafia

Dead soldier   Empty beer can or bottle

Do me a solid   Do me a favour

Don't jerk my chain   Don't fool with me

Do the number on To kill, assassinate

DP   Dom Perignon champagne

DPh   Damned fool, based on transposing PhD

Eighth Wonder of the World   The Brooklyn Bridge

Family   An original Mafia unit headed by a don or godfather

Family hammer   Hit man or assassin for a family

Finger Another name for mechanics, dips, cannons, goniffs, moll buzzers or pickpockets

Flip someone   Mob talk for making someone a turncoat

Friend of ours   Someone who is a made man in the Mob

Hitter   Assassin or hit man

Life   Either the term for mob life in the Mafia or the life of a prostitute

Make one's bones   To kill one's first victim to become a qualified man in the Mafia

Mazel tov   Literally means 'good luck' in Hebrew, but is widely used to say congratulations or best wishes

Mazuma   Slang for money

Meet me between the lions   A favourite meeting place – the lion statues in front of the New York Public Library

Met   The Metropolitan Opera House, although many people now use it as an abbreviation for the Metropolitan Museum, too

Moll buzzer   Highly skilled pickpocket, who specialises in opening women's handbags and stealing their purses

Mutt   Stupid criminal (used by police)

No problem   You're welcome

Nudnik or nudge   A persistently dull and boring person

On line   Stand in a queue

Outfit   The Mafia

Out in left field   Weird or unorthodox

Ozone   Very fresh, pure air

Patza   Amateurish chess player who often plays in parks

Pig in a blanket   A small frankfurter encased in a dough and baked

Send up the river   Send to prison – refers to Sing Sing Penitentiary, which is up the Hudson River

Shoot the works   Gamble or risk everything

Silk-stocking District   Manhattan's Upper East Side

Slice   Shorthand for a piece of pizza

Stick   Marijuana cigarette

Straphanger   Subway commuter

Sugar Hill   Prosperous area in Harlem

Suit   Slang for businessman

The city   Manhattan

The Street   47th Street, as referred to by people in the diamond trade. It handles more than half of the finished diamonds in the world. Wall Street is also called The Street

Unshushables   Incessant talkers at cinemas (came from Seinfeld)

Yard   Back garden

Views of the World Trade Center and the financial district, overlooked by the Statue of Liberty

Above: Statue of Liberty

Above right: Empire State Building and the Chrysler Building

Right: Rockefeller Center

CHAPTER 2

Sightseeing

When you fly into New York, seeing all the skyscrapers from your lofty perch makes Manhattan look pretty small; but do not be fooled by this. Because it is a narrow island that is quite long – 13.4 miles in fact – you can easily be duped into believing that it is easy to walk from downtown Manhattan to the Upper East Side. Nothing could be further from the truth. For this reason, when planning your activities for the day, it is best to stick to one particular area so that walking everywhere, which really is the best way to see the city, won't be so tiring.

To try to make your life a little easier I have indicated the location of each of the following sights. Furthermore, in Chapter 4, I have tried to give a comprehensive overview of many of the neighbourhoods so that you can really get a feel for the extremely different areas and cultures of New York – and have plenty of fun in the process.

I have not included in this chapter the many museums and galleries or shopping 'Meccas' that are also worth visiting. It is best to read the other chapters dealing with these, too, before deciding what you want to do for a day, in order to make the most of your time. Finally, make sure you read the section entitled Orientation (see page 17), which should help you make sense of those New York streets!

NYTAB DISCOUNTS

The New York Travel Advisory Bureau produce a wonderful little blue book full of information about New York, and they also have their great discount card – the NYCard, which gives you valuable money-off savings to many sights and museums. Discounts include money off cruises and museum entry and even cheap phone calls.

You'll find your personal NYCard on the inside back cover of this book, plus the Bureau's contact details and information on discounts on pages 193–4. Check their website **www.nytab.com** for the latest information.

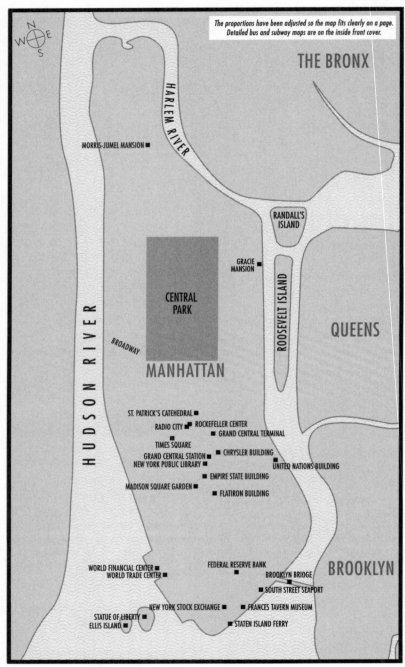

Major Sights in Manhattan

THE BIG ONES

Empire State Building

350 5th Avenue at 34th Street. Tel 212-736 3100. Subway B, D, F, Q, N, R to 34th Street. Open from 9.30am to midnight, last tickets sold at 11.25pm. Entrance $6 adults, $3 under 12s. No credit cards. Area: Murray Hill.

It is hard to believe that the Empire State, which was for almost 40 years the world's tallest building, was nearly not built at all. Just weeks after its building contract was signed in 1929, the Wall Street Crash brought the financial world to its knees. Fortunately, the project went ahead and was even completed 45 days ahead of schedule, rising to 1,454 feet tall in 1931. The lobby interior features art deco design incorporating rare marble imported from Italy, France, Belgium and Germany. A six-year-long renovation was recently completed at a cost of $67 million – $26 million more than the whole original building cost!

★★★★ **INSIDE TRACK** ★★★★

If you want some light refreshments at the Empire State, there is a snack bar on the 86th floor.

There are two observation decks, one on the 86th floor and another on the 102nd floor, but be warned, there is usually a queue on the 86th to go all the way to the top. You buy your tickets on the concourse level below the main lobby, but don't have to use

them on the same day. The building now also has two virtual reality rides that simulate a flight around the skyscrapers and bridges of New York. The New York SkyRide is found on the second floor and is open seven days a week from 10am to 10pm. Entrance $11.50 adults, $8.50 four to 12-year-olds.

World Trade Center

West Street between Liberty and Vesey Streets. Tel 212-323 2340. Subway 1, 9, N, R to Cortlandt Street. Open 9.30am to 9.30pm September to May and 9.30am to 11.30pm June to August. Entrance $13 adults, $9.50 senior citizens, $6.50 six to 12-year-olds, under sixes free. $2 discount with your NYCard. Area: Financial District.

If you have even the slightest fear of heights, then this building will get to you. The indoor observation deck of Tower 2 is on the 107th floor and has floor-to-ceiling glass walls – enough to bring on a spinning head. Even worse, though, you can take the escalator ride to the outdoor observation level. I'm still not certain how I managed to walk around it, especially as my companion gaily told me that someone had walked a tightrope between the two towers (it was mad Frenchman Philippe Petit in 1974). Just thinking about it now is enough to turn my stomach!

Try a virtual reality ride on a helicopter in the amusement arcade on the 107th floor. The Trade Center also houses the **Greatest Bar on Earth** and **Windows on the World** restaurant.

★★★★ **INSIDE TRACK** ★★★★
★   ★
★   ★
★ To avoid the long queues at the ★
★ World Trade Center, get there   ★
★ first thing in the morning.   ★
★   ★
★★★★★★★★★★★★★★★★★★★★★★★

The Empire State v the Trade Center

Many people are torn between whether to go up the Empire State Building or the World Trade Center. Some people swear by the Trade Center, which provides clear views across all of Manhattan and other boroughs of New York, while romantics just love the feel of the Empire even though it is a little overshadowed by neighbouring skyscrapers. Probably the best solution is to make the Trade Center your first port of call. That way you can get a pretty clear picture of the lie of the land, which will make orientating yourself easier once you're back at ground level. Then visit the Empire just before sunset and see it when it is at its electrifying best – when it is all lit up.

Rockefeller Center

West 48th to West 50th Streets between 5th and 6th Avenues. Tel 212-632 3975. Subway B, D, F, Q to 47th–50th Streets/Rockefeller Center. Area: Midtown at 5th Avenue.

Built in the art deco style in the 1930s, the Center was named after the New York benefactor whose fortune paid for its construction. As well as Radio City Music Hall (see page 39), it houses opulent office space, restaurants, bars, shopping on several levels and even gardens. To help you find your way round the 19 buildings that make up the Center, you can collect a map at the lobby of the main building (30 Rockefeller Center). At Christmas time, the sunken plaza in the middle is turned into an ice-rink and a massive Christmas tree with five miles of fairy lights draws huge crowds.

★★★★ **INSIDE TRACK** ★★★★
★   ★
★ If you're holidaying in New York ★
★ in winter, make it a priority to ★
★ visit the beautiful ice-rink at the ★
★ Rockefeller Center.   ★
★   ★
★★★★★★★★★★★★★★★★★★★★★★★

Ticket to ride

The CityPass is an excellent way to avoid long queues and save money. It includes half-price admission to the American Museum of Natural History, the Empire State Building, the *Intrepid* Sea-Air-Space Museum, the Guggenheim Museum, the Museum of Modern Art and top of the World Trade Center. You can pick up a CityPass from any of the participating attractions for $26.75 adults (normal combined price $53.50) and $21 ages 13 to 18 (normal combined price $42).

Radio City Music Hall: 50th Street and 6th Avenue. Tel 212-632 4041. Tours Mon to Sat 10am to 5pm, Sun 11am to 5pm. Entrance $12 adults, $6 children. Subway B, D, F, Q to 47–50th Streets/Rockefeller Center. Area: Midtown at 5th Avenue.

The whole building has been fully restored to its original art deco movie palace greatness and is utterly beautiful. This is where the great films such as *Gone With The Wind* were given their premieres and it has the largest screen in America. Make a point of visiting the loos – they have a different theme on each floor, from palm trees to Chinese and floral. There are even cigar-theme loos for the boys. On the tour you are shown around the whole building and then introduced to a Rockette.

★★★★ INSIDE TRACK ★★★★
★   ★
★   **To see the Radio City Music Hall,**   ★
★   **you have to buy your ticket in**   ★
★   **the morning to see what time**   ★
★   **your tour is, but it is well worth**   ★
★   **planning your day in Midtown**   ★
★   **around this attraction.**   ★
★★★★★★★★★★★★★★★★★★★★★★

NBC Tours: Lobby level of 30 Rockefeller Plaza. Tel 212-664 7174. Mon to Sat 9.30am to 4.30pm. Entrance $8.25. Subway B, D, F, Q to 47–50th Streets/Rockefeller Center. Area: Midtown at 5th Avenue.

A brief, not very detailed and disappointing look behind the scenes at NBC.

Statue of Liberty and Ellis Island Immigration Museum

Reached via the Circle Line/Statue of Liberty Ferry (tel 212-269 5755), which leaves every 30 minutes from Gangway 5 in Battery Park. Subway 1, 9 to South Ferry; 4, 5 to Bowling Green. Open 9.30am to 5.30pm. Tickets $7 adults, $3 under 18s, under threes free. No credit cards. Area: Bowling Green.

The ferry stops off at the Statue of Liberty before moving on to Ellis Island. It is great to get a good close-up view and picture of the French lady, but forget about walking up to the top. There are 154 steps to the observation level where all you can do is squint through a narrow hole and the whole ordeal takes about three hours. Once you've got your exterior photos of Madame, get going to the Ellis Island Immigration Museum. This is the most visited museum in New York, particularly beloved of crowds of Americans who come to take a look at where their immigrant ancestors arrived. In use from 1892 to 1954, it 'processed' up to 10,000 immigrants a day. Each person was examined and then interviewed to find out if they could speak English. Some were rechristened, and a luckless two per cent were turned away.

Visitors follow the immigrants' route as they entered the main baggage room and went up to the Registry and then the Staircase of Separation. Poignant exhibits include photos, video clips, jewellery, clothing, baggage and the stark dormitories.

The Immigrant Wall of Fame lists half a million names, including the grandfathers of Presidents Washington and Kennedy, whose descendants contributed to the $150-million restoration of the main building with its copper roof and railway station-like glass and wrought-iron entrance.

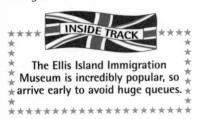

★★★★ **INSIDE TRACK** ★★★★
★ ★
★ ★
★ The Ellis Island Immigration ★
★ Museum is incredibly popular, so ★
★ arrive early to avoid huge queues. ★
★ ★
★★★★★★★★★★★★★★★★★★★★★★★

South Street Seaport

Water Street to the East River between John Street and Peck Slip. Tel 212-732 7678. Subway A, C to Broadway/Nassau Street; J, M, Z, 2, 3, 4, 5 to Fulton Street. Area: Financial District.

You don't have to pay to enter the museum to get a feeling of the maritime history of the city – the ships are all around you. The Seaport is a rare New York approximation of a typical American shopping mall and is full of dining options. You can even eat outside overlooking the Brooklyn Bridge.

Times Square and the Theater District

Broadway at West 42nd Street. Subway 1, 2, 3, 7, 9 to Times Square/42nd Street.

A real tourist Mecca, visit Times Square at night to see crowds of people weaving their way between hotels, restaurants and Broadway shows. The world-famous neon signs are still here, but the sleaze and the pimps have largely gone, thanks to a clean-up campaign launched by Mayor Giuliani. Nowadays more respectable firms of publishers and investment bankers have taken the place of less salubrious businesses. Even Disney has an outlet here and Madame Tussaud's are opening a branch of the great London institution on the south side of 42nd Street, between 7th and 8th Avenues. Close to Times Square is the intersection with Broadway. The Theater District contains about 30 stages, with many others in Manhattan and elsewhere make up Off Broadway and Off Off Broadway. The Times Square Visitor Center is situated in the Embassy Theater, whose glorious dark wood entrance, decorated in glass and brass, is on the east side of Broadway, between West 46th and West 47th Streets.

★★★★ **INSIDE TRACK** ★★★★
★ ★
★ ★
★ Visit Times Square at night to see ★
★ the neon signs at their brightest! ★
★ ★
★★★★★★★★★★★★★★★★★★★★★★★

Brooklyn Bridge

Considered one of the modern engineering feats of the world when it was completed in 1883 after 16 long years of construction, this was the world's largest suspension bridge and the first to be built of steel. The walkway is a great way to see some incredible views of the downtown skyscrapers. Take the A, C or F train to Jay Street–Borot Hall station and stroll back on the walkway.

★★★★ **INSIDE TRACK** ★★★★
★   ★
★ On your Brooklyn Bridge walk, ★
★ take a cassette guide that has   ★
★ been put together by TALK-A-   ★
★ WALK (see page 51).   ★
★   ★
★★★★★★★★★★★★★★★★★★★★★★

Bronx Zoo

Bronx River Parkway and Fordham Road. Tel 718-367 1010, website at **www.wcs.org** Subway 2, 5 to Bronx Park East. Open Mon to Fri 10am to 5pm, weekends and holidays until 5.30pm, Nov to March 10am to 4.30pm daily. Entrance $7.75 adults, $4 under 12s, under twos free. Wednesdays free. Children under the age of 17 must be accompanied by an adult. Cheaper rates Jan to March. Area: The Bronx.

The Bronx Zoo is respected worldwide for its tradition of conservation and ecological awareness, and the naturalistic habitats if provides, such as its African Plains where antelope roam. The latest exhibit to open is the Congo Gorilla Forest, a $43-million six-acre rainforest, inhabited by two troops of gorillas. Disney-style rides include a guided monorail tour through Wild Asia, an aerial safari, camel rides and a zoo shuttle. There is also a children's zoo. Some of the exhibits and rides are only open between April and October.

For a tour by Friends of Wildlife Conservation, call 718-220 5141.

★★★★ **INSIDE TRACK** ★★★★
★   ★
★ Make the most of a day out to ★
★ the Bronx Zoo by having lunch in ★
★ the nearby Little Italy of Arthur ★
★ Avenue. People travel from miles ★
★ around to tuck into the delights ★
★   of this little-known Italian   ★
★   quarter.   ★
★★★★★★★★★★★★★★★★★★★★★★

New York Botanical Garden

200th Street and Southern Boulevard. Tel 718-817 8700. Subway 2, 5 to Bronx Park East. Tues to Sun and Mon holidays 10am to 6pm April to Oct, 10am to 4pm Nov to March. Entrance $3 adults, $1 under 12s, under threes free. Area: The Bronx.

These world-class gardens are set in 250 acres of land, featuring a vast conseratory, housing over 3,000 plants, and the Bronx River Gorge, where the river follows a natural rocky chasm formed millions of years ago by the retreat of the Wisconsin ice sheet.

The botanical gardens are situated just across the road from the Bronx Zoo. Unfortunately, the road between them is an eight-lane highway and the entrances are situated a mile apart. If you decide to do the gardens and the zoo in one day (and they are worth separate visits), the best way to cross the highway between them – and to get to Little Italy for lunch – is by taxi. The ride will only take a few minutes. Call Miles Taxi Co., 718-884 8888.

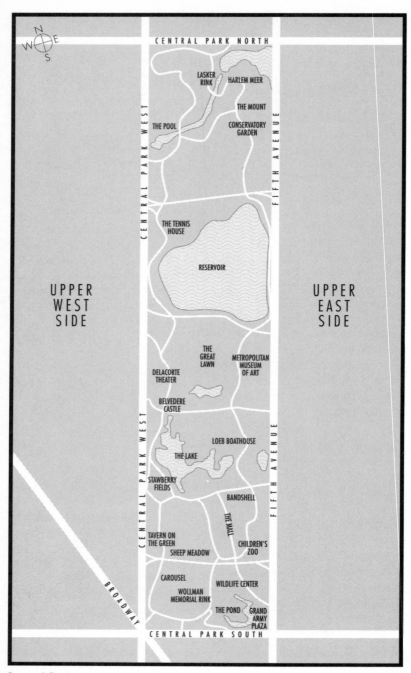

Central Park

Central Park

This is the New Yorkers' playground and meeting place and attracts
15 million visitors every year. Its 843 acres stretch from Central Park South
at 59th Street to Central Park North at 110th Street, with 5th Avenue and
Central Park West forming its eastern and western boundaries. It was
created over a 20-year period by architect Calvert Vaux and landscaper
Frederick Law Olmsted and was completed in the 1860s.

To enter from the south, cross the street from Grand Army Plaza at 59th
Street. Immediately in front of you is the **Pond,** and then the **Wollman
Memorial Rink**, which is open for rollerskating in the summer and ice
skating in the winter. Close by is the **Visitor Information Center**, where
you can pick up free maps and schedules of events, including the series of
free concerts and dramas performed at the **SummerStage** – in the summer,
of course (see page 29 for details). Here also are the **Gotham Miniature
Golf Course**, a gift from Donald Trump, the **dairy** and the antique
carousel. The **Children's Zoo and Central Park Wildlife Center**, just to
the right, costs $3.50 for adults and 50 cents for over threes.

The Sheep Meadow to the north of the carousel is much used by New
Yorkers for picnics and sunbathing. To its left is the **Tavern on the Green**
restaurant (see page 146) and to the right is **The Mall**, a tree-lined
walkway. Follow The Mall to the top and you will find the **Central Park
Bandshell**, another concert venue in the park. Furthern north is the **Loeb
Boathouse** (see Chapter 10 for details of sporting activities in the park),
which is also home to the **Park View at the Boathouse** restaurant.

Continuing north, you will find **The Ramble**, a heavily wooded area which
leads (if you can find the way through) to the Gothic revival **Belvedere
Castle**, housing another information centre. Also here are the **Delacorte
Theater**, home to summer productions by the New York Shakespeare
Festival (tel 212-861 7277 for tickets) and the **Great Lawn**, where the
Metropolitan and City Opera (tel 212-362 6000) stage open-air productions
during the summer months. See page 29 for details of both of these.

Further north again is the huge **reservoir**, which is ten blocks long.
The path here is well-trodden by joggers but few people venture beyond
this point as the nearby neighbourhoods are considered unsafe. However,
in other parts of the Park, there is more to see, including the **Conservatory
Garden**, bequeathed by the Vanderbilt family, where there are free
tours and concerts in the summer, the **Tennis House**, the pool and the
Lasker Rink.

Staten Island Ferry

Ferry Terminal, Battery Park. Tel 718-815 2628. Subway 1, 9 to South Ferry; 4, 5 to Bowling Green; N, R to Whitehall Street. No charge. Area: Battery Park.

Probably the best sightseeing bargain in the world, it passes close to the Statue of Liberty and gives dramatic views of Downtown. Runs 24 hours a day.

St George Historic District

St Mark's Place: St George, Staten Island. Area: Staten Island.

If you take the Staten Island Ferry and decide to get off, then you have two places of interest to visit – St Mark's Place and Historic Richmond Town. The former is on the hill above the St George Ferry terminal and is the only landmarked historical district on Staten Island. Here New York's fabulous skyline forms a dramatic backdrop to a wonderful collection of residential buildings in Queen Ann, Greek revival and Italianate styles. Look on the web for a self-guided walking tour at **www.preserve.org/stgeorge**

Historic Richmond Town: 441 Clarke Ave, Richmondtown, Staten Island. Tel 718-351 1611. Take the S74 bus from the ferry to Richmond Road and St Patrick's Place. Area: Staten Island.

A magnificent 100-acre village that features buildings from 300 years of life on the island including the oldest schoolhouse still standing, which was built in 1695 (that's really old by American standards!). In the summer season, costumed interpreters and craftspeople demonstrate the chores, gardening, crafts and trade of daily life in this rural hamlet.

Federal Reserve Bank

33 Liberty Street between William and Nassau Streets. Tel 212-720 6130. Subway 4, 5 to Wall Street. Area: Financial District.

For a free one-hour tour, you must phone at least seven days in advance. Your name will be placed on a computer list, but the minimum age is 16. Passport or picture identification is essential.

BUILDINGS OF NOTE

Chrysler Building: 405 Lexington Avenue at 42nd Street. Subway S, 4, 5, 6, 7 to Grand Central/42nd Street. Area: Midtown.

Opened in 1930, this was William van Alen's homage to the motor car. At the foot of the art deco skyscraper are brickwork cars with enlarged chrome hubcaps and radiator caps. Inside, see its marble and chrome lobby and inlaid-wood elevators. Its needle-like spire is illuminated at night and the building vies with the Empire State for the prettiest-of-them-all crown.

Flatiron Building: 175 5th Avenue between 22nd and 23rd Streets. Subway F, N, R, 6 to 23rd Street. Area: Flatiron District.

The Renaissance palazzo building was the first-ever skyscraper when it was completed in 1902 and is held up by a steel skeleton.

Fantastic fun for free

You don't have to pay for everything in New York and while summer is generally the best time for free concerts and plays – particularly in Central Park – there are good freebies to be bagged at other venues all year round. Here are a few:

The Museum of American Folk Art: Enjoy folk paintings, furniture, pottery, quilts and other decorative arts from the 18th century to the present. Entrance free Tues to Sun until 7.30pm. Tel 212-595 9533, or see their website at **www.folkartmuse.org**

The Cooper–Hewitt National Museum of Design: (See page 62.) Historical and contemporary designs can be viewed for free on Tuesday evenings from 5pm to 9pm. Tel 212-849 8400, or see their website at **www.si.edu/ndm**

Take a guided tour with a Big Apple Greeter: Get a feel for New York as a real New Yorker sees it (see page 45).

World Financial Center's Winter Garden: (See page 74.) Enjoy concerts and dance performances under huge palm trees at this stunning, glass-enclosed shopping and business complex on Lower Manhattan's waterfront. Special summer events are held out of doors. Tel 212-945 0505, or see their website at **www.worldfinancialcenter.com**

New York Mercantile Exchange: (See page 41.) Watch millions of dollars worth of commodities change hands. Monday to Friday trading at the Comex Division is from 8.30am to 2.30pm, trading at the Nynex Division is from 9.30am to 9.30pm. Tel 212-299 2499.

See a taping of a TV show: By calling in advance, you can attend free tapings of popular TV shows like *Late Night with David Letterman* (tel 212-975 5853) and *The Montel Williams Show* (tel 212-830 0364).

Rockefeller Center: (See page 38.) Explore a famous art deco masterpiece on a free, self-guided tour of this majestic building. Pick up maps in the main lobby at 30 Rockefeller Center where you can also enjoy the summer gardens or view the spectacular Christmas tree during the holiday season. Tel 212-698 2950.

Union Square Green Market: Taste farm-fresh produce, homemade breads, cheeses, cider and more; some vendors offer free samples. Tel 212-477 9220.

6th Avenue Antiques Market: Browse for bargains at the famous market between 24th and 27th Streets (free admission weekends only). Other outdoor markets include the famous fleas at Columbus Avenue and West 76th Street (Sundays only) and the weekend market on Houston Street between Sullivan and Thompson.

New York Philharmonic, City Opera, Shakespeare in the Park: Revel in the best classical music, jazz, drama, opera and dance that New York has to offer at free warm-weather performances in the city parks by these and many more. Tel 212-360 3444.

Cathedral of St John the Divine: See the world's largest Gothic cathedral, near Columbia University in Harlem and explore its Biblical garden and children's sculpture garden. Tel 212-316 7540, or see their website at **www.stjohndivine.org**

New York Public Library: (See page 47.) Explore thought-provoking exhibitions at this breathtaking *beaux arts* library. Tel 212-592 7000. Time your visit well and you could then enjoy free concerts, outdoor movies and other special events in the adjacent Bryant Park, tel 212-983 4142.

Battery Park Esplanade: Catch the breeze and enjoy stunning views of New York Harbour and the Statue of Liberty. In nearby Hudson River Park, the Battery Park City Authority presents a Sounds at Sunset summer series of poetry readings, cabaret and classical music. Tel 212-416 5394.

Gracie Mansion: Carl Schurz Park, 88th Street at East End Avenue. Tel 212-570 4751. Subway 4, 5, 6 to 86th Street. Area: Yorkville.

Now the official residence of the mayor, you must phone ahead to make an appointment to see it and it's only open on Wednesdays. The tour takes you through the mayor's living room, a guest suite and smaller bedrooms. The best part, though, is the view down the river.

Grand Central Station: East 42nd Street between Lexington and Vanderbilt Avenues. Subway S, 4, 5, 6, 7 to Grand Central/42nd Street. Area: Midtown.

Even if you're not going anywhere by train, this huge, vaulted station, which was opened in 1913, is well worth a visit. A $196-million, two-year renovation programme was recently completed and the ceiling once again twinkles with the stars

and astrological symbols of the night skies, and to the chandeliers, marble balusters and clerestory windows of

★★★★ **INSIDE TRACK** ★★★★

If you go to Grand Central Station on a Wednesday at 12.30pm, you can go on a free tour sponsored by the Municipal Arts Society. Tel 212-340 2345.

the main concourse. It now also houses a Mediterranean restaurant, Michael Jordan's Steakhouse and a cocktail lounge modelled on a Florentine palazzo. The lower level dining concourse will offer meals to take away, while shopping outlets include Banana Republik, Godiva chocolates and Kenneth Cole. Complete your trip to this elegant edifice by tucking in at the gorgeous Oyster Bar.

Merchant's House Museum: 29 East 4th Street. Tel 212-777 1089. Subway 6 to Astor Place. Area: East Village.

Built in 1832 as a row house, this was home to prosperous merchant Seabury Tredwell and his family for nearly 100 years.

Morris–Jumel Mansion: Roger Morris Park, 65 Jumel Terrace at 160th Street. Tel 212-923 8008. Subway B, C to 163rd Street. Open Wed to Sun 10am to 4pm. Entrance $3 adults, $2 children. Two-for-one admittance with your NYCard. Area: Harlem.

Built by British colonel Roger Morris in 1765, this is the oldest house in Manhattan. It was confiscated by George Washington in 1776 and briefly used as his war headquarters until the Brits kicked him out of New York. Dickens visited it, and if you want to see a really historical sight so should you!

New York Public Library: 5th Avenue between 40th and 42nd Streets. Tel 212-592 7000. Subway B, D, F, Q, 4, 5, 6, 7 to 42nd Street. Area: Midtown.

Opened in 1911, this is one of the best examples of the city's *beaux arts* architecture. If you go inside you'll find more than 8.5 million volumes guarded by the twin marble lions of Patience and Fortitude.

New York Stock Exchange: 20 Broad Street at Wall Street. Tel 212-656 3000. Subway 4, 5 to Wall Street; J, M, Z to Broad Street. Area: Financial District. Entrance free, but you need tickets, which are handed out from 9am, so go early.

Amazing fact: the Stock Exchange was founded by 24 brokers meeting beneath a tree; now more than 1,300 members crowd on to the building's trading floor.

Riverside Church: Riverside Drive between 120th and 122nd Streets. Subway 1, 2, 3 to 116th Street. Area: Harlem.

Famous for having the world's largest tuned bell and has Carillon concerts on Sundays at 12.30pm and 3pm. You can also go for the great views of Upper Manhattan and the Hudson River.

St Patrick's Cathedral: Fifth Avenue and 50th Street. Subway 6 to 51st Street and B, D, F, Q to 47th–50th Streets/Rockefeller Center. Area: Midtown.

The seat of New York's Catholic Archdiocese, it took 21 years to build, but the impressive design and gorgeous stained glass windows were worth the wait.

Trump Tower: 5th Avenue between 56th and 57th Streets. Subway B, Q to 57th Street. Area: Midtown.

Donald Trump's monument to opulence includes an extravagant pink marbled atrium with waterfalls and plenty of upmarket shops.

United Nations Building: First Avenue and 46th Street. Call 212-963 4440 for tour reservations. Subway 6 to 51st Street. Area: Midtown. Subway: Grand Central/42nd Street.

Tours of the General Assembly, the Economic and Social Council and other areas every half-hour. Be warned – despite its fame, this is not the most exciting tour in the world!

Woolworth Building: 233 Broadway at Park Place. Subway 2, 3 to Park Place; N, R to City Hall. Area: Financial District.

There is no official tour of this the city's second skyscraper, which was built in 1913 at a cost of $13.5 million, but it's worth taking a sneak look inside the lobby. Incidentally, one-time shop assistant FW Woolworth's building was derided as a 'cathedral of commerce' when it opened, but the millionaire took this as a compliment. Just to prove a point, he can be seen counting his money in the carved ceilings.

TOURS

Boat tours

The Beast: Pier 16, South Street Seaport. Tel 212-630 8885. Subway J, M, Z, 2, 3, 4, 5 to Fulton St. Area: Financial District. Also Pier 83 West 42nd Street. Subway A, C, E to 42nd Street. Area: West of Theater District. Open May to Oct, daily, 10am to 7pm. Tickets $15 for adults, children $10. $3 discount with your NYCard.

Take a spin on a thrilling speedboat ride for a quick and memorable tour of Lower Manhattan and see the sights fly by as you reach an incredible speed of 40mph. *The Beast* stops by the Statue of Liberty for photos. Boats leave on the hour.

Bateaux New York: Pier 61 at Chelsea Piers. Tel 212-352 2022. Subway A, C, E to 23rd Street. Area: Chelsea. Tickets from $45.75 to $91.50.

Indulge in a dinner (7pm to 10pm daily) or brunch (noon to 2pm weekends) cruise around Lower Manhattan.

Circle Line: Pier 83, West 42nd Street. Tel 212-748 8782. Subway A, C, E to 42nd Street. Area: West Midtown. Tickets available for full island, semi-circle or sunset/harbour lights cruise. Prices start from $14 adults, $7 for 12 and under. In addition, you can take a three-hour **Latin DJ** dance cruise, a full-day cruise to **Bear Mountain** ($33 adults, $30 12 and under), a **Seaport Liberty** cruise and a **Seaport live music** cruise. $3 off all cruises with your NYCard.

NY Waterway: Pier 17 at South Street Seaport. Tel 212-512 0550. Subway J, M, Z, 2, 3, 4, 5 to Fulton Street. Area: Financial District. Harbour cruise prices start at $10 adults, $5 children and go up to $17 adults, $8 children. Discount of 15 per cent off all cruises with your NYCard.

Offers a wide variety of special sightseeing options all the year round, including New York Harbor cruises and evening cruises with on-board entertainment. Also available in the summer are day-trip cruises to Sandy Hook Beach and, for baseball fans, cruise packages that include a round-trip sail on the *Yankee Clipper*

Greetings from the Big Apple

It's certainly a novel idea and it's also a winner – the Big Apple Greeters are ready to take you on a personalised and entirely customised tour of any part of New York any day of the week and it costs exactly zip, zilch, absolutely nothing. Amazing, huh? The idea is simple: New Yorkers who are proud of their local neighbourhoods and have a little spare time on their hands are available to spend between two and four hours with you. They will take you round any area you like and help you do just what you want to do, be it shopping, sightseeing or eating and drinking. They'll also do it come rain or shine. This is an excellent way to orientate yourself in Manhattan or any part of the city that takes your fancy and is particularly good for the lone traveller in need of a little confidence boost. All you need do is make your request at least ten working days in advance (the more the better) and confirmation will be awaiting you upon your arrival at your hotel. The service is entirely free and no Big Apple Greeters worth their salt will take a tip, but I found that it was no problem to get them to agree to letting me pay for a spot of brunch or lunch. And why not? They're well worth it.

To get in touch with the BAGs, call 212-669 8159, fax 212-669 3685, e-mail **big apple@tiac.net** or look them up on the web at **www.bigapplegreeter.org**

or *Mets Express*, tickets, souvenirs and the ubiquitous hot dog.

Bus tours

Cemetery Tours: PO Box 750841, New York, NY 11375. Tel 718-760 4000. Prices vary according to size of group.

Okay, so technically this is not a bus tour as your mode of transportation will be a hearse, but it still has wheels and travels on roads ... As the title indicates, you'll get a fully detailed tour of New York's cemeteries, visiting gravesites of well-known VIPs, celebrities, politicians and sports stars. Er, enjoy!

Gray Line Port Authority Bus Terminal: 8th Avenue at 42nd Street. Tel 212-397 2600. Subway A, C, E to 42nd Street. Area: West Midtown. From $20 to $50.

Offers a huge selection of tours covering every aspect of Manhattan.

Harlem Spirituals: 690 8th Avenue between West 43rd and West 44th. Tel 212-391 0900. Subway A, C, E to 42nd Street. Area: Midtown. Tickets $33–$85 adults, $23–$50 children.

Gospel tours include walking and riding tours of Harlem on Sunday when you attend a church service and hear a gospel choir; having brunch at a soul food restaurant; and weekday gospel tours with lunch. Heritage and jazz tours include a combined walking and riding tour through Harlem's historical sites, soul food and jazz lunches and a night at the Apollo.

There is also a selection of combined Bronx and Brooklyn tours starting at $35 adults, $23 children.

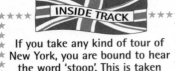

★★★★ INSIDE TRACK ★★★★
★   ★
★ If you take any kind of tour of   ★
★ New York, you are bound to hear   ★
★   the word 'stoop'. This is taken ★
★   from a Dutch word by original   ★
★ settlers and refers to the steps up ★
★   to a townhouse.   ★
★   ★
★★★★★★★★★★★★★★★★★★★★★★★★

Air tours

Liberty Helicopter Tours: VIP Heliport, West 30th Street and 12th Avenue. Tel 212-967 6464. Subway A, C, E to 34th Street Penn Station. Area: Theater District.

Simple bird's-eye-view tours of Manhattan cost $48 Mon to Thurs and $52 Fri to Sun. The most expensive tour, which includes views of all five boroughs and Ellis Island, costs $155 Mon to Thurs and $180 Fri to Sun.

Bike tours

Bite of the Apple Tours: Tel 212-541 8759. A two-hour Spring Celebration bike tour of Central Park from April to June that includes stops at Shakespeare Garden, Strawberry Fields, Belevedere Castle and other sights.

Ponycabs: Tel 212-254 8844. Technically not bicycles, but three-man tricycles (one 'driver' to pedal and two passengers!). So amazing-looking that even seen-it-all-before New Yorkers stop to stare. That may

be a little off-putting for some, but I found it an excellent way to see SoHo without breaking into a sweat or breaking the bank! My Ponycab was powered by actor and teacher David Watkins, who was a mine of information about New York. $15 for half an hour, $30 for an hour and don't forget to tip – 'drivers' earn their money! In good weather only.

A taste of paradise

For a truly unique insight into the fine foods and culinary skills of some of New York's finest restaurants, look no further than **Savory Sojourns**. They promise to give you an insider's guide to New York's best culinary and cultural destinations followed by a great slap-up meal. Areas covered include Upper East Side, Chinatown, Little Italy, Greenwich Village, Flatiron, Meat Market and Chelsea Market. Prices range from $85 to $250. For more information, contact Savory Sojourns at 155 West 13th Street, or call 212-691 7314 or go to the website at **www.savorysojourns.com**

Walking tours

Alliance for Downtown New York: Tel 212-566 6700 or see their website at **www.downtownny.com** Tour starts every Thursday at noon on the steps of the Smithsonian Institution Museum of the American Indian, 1 Bowling Green. Subway 4, 5 to Bowling Green. Area: Financial District.

Free walking tour for individuals and groups exploring the 'birthplace' of New York, including the Customs House, Trinity Church, Wall Street and the Stock Exchange (see page 47), amongst many others.

Big Onion Walking Tours: PO Box, 20561, Cherokee Station, New York, NY 10021-0070. Tel 212-439 1090. Always call after 10.30am on the morning of your tour to verify schedule. $10 adults, $8 students.

Amazingly informative ethnic, architectural and historic walking tours led by Columbia University historians, mostly at the weekends. See their website at **www.bigonion.com** for more information.

Joyce Gold History Tours of New York: 141 West 17th Street. Tel 212-242 5762 or see their website at **www.nyctours.com** Tours begin at 1pm, last two to three hours and cost $12.

Specialists in unusual, in-depth weekend forays into many of the city's distinctive neighbourhoods. Fascinating tours include East Village, culture and counter-culture, downtown graveyards and Greenwich Village Highlights.

Kramer's Reality Tour Pulse Theater: 432 West 42nd Street between 9th and 10th Avenues. Tel 212-268 5525. Subway A, C, E to 42nd Street/Penn Station. Area: West Midtown. Sat and Sun at noon. Tickets $37.50.

The real Kramer behind the Seinfeld character, Kramer has come out of the woodwork and invented his own three-hour tour based on all the Seinfeld spots in the city. Kenny Kramer will answer questions, share backstage gossip and reveal the real-life incidents behind many of the show's storylines.

Municipal Art Society: 457 Madison Avenue between East 50th and East 51st Streets. Tel 212-935 3960. For details of walks, call 212-439 1049 or visit their website at **www.mas.org** Subway: 6 to 51st Street or E, F to 5th Avenue. Area: Midtown.

Walking tours taking in both historical and architectural sights. Well-run, informative – and very enjoyable.

Savor the Apple: PO Box 914, Ansonia Station, New York, NY 10023. Tel 212-877 2903. Prices vary.

Marlayna gives her personal tours of different parts of the city, but is particularly knowledgeable about Greenwich Village, the East Village and Harlem, where she has many personal contacts.

TALK-A-WALK: 30 Waterside Plaza, New York, NY 10010. Tel 212 686 0356, fax 212-689 3538.

Walking tour guides on cassettes – they're excellent. It's best to order them before you leave home and they'll post them to you. There is a choice of four, each looking at the history and the architecture of historic Downtown, which cost $9.95 each.

FINDING A WC

I think it's worth raising this subject early as you'll probably be spending quite a lot of time walking around and you could easily get caught out. It is wise to know that public lavatories are thin on the ground in New York. In addition, subway loos – if they are actually open – are dangerous and unhygienic. I should also point out is that it is considered impolite to use the word 'toilet' (*très* common, I'm afraid) – in America it is always referred to as the 'restroom'!

Okay, so you're in the middle of Greenwich Village, you're desperate, you don't want to pay through the nose for a beer so you can use the bar's facilities, so what do you do? I have it on good authority from those New Yorkers in the know that you should use the following:

Hotels: The restrooms are usually on the ground floor or you can ask and will be told (amazing, huh?!).

Public libraries: They all have public loos.

Department stores: They are hidden away, however, and you have to ask where they are (this is to deter street people from using them).

Restaurants: Some have signs saying 'For customers only', but if you ask authoritatively enough and look okay, they'll probably let you use them. The alternative is to stop for a cup of coffee and then you can use the restroom.

Government buildings: Try places like the United Nations, though you'll have to go through a security check.

Barnes & Noble: This is a newish chain of bookstores that offers restrooms because the company wants people to treat the stores as public meeting places. They tend to be hidden away at the back, so you'll have to ask the way and be prepared for a bit of a wait – sometimes the queues are quite long. The good thing is that Barnes & Noble are just about everywhere in New York now, though they have put a lot of independent booksellers out of business (see the Meg Ryan/Tom Hanks movie, *You've Got Mail*).

McDonald's and Burger Kings: Unisex toilets that are usually clean and modern because they have been built to the McDonald spec rather than the typical New York building spec.

Statue of Liberty: In the gift shop.

World Trade Center: At the top, so go while you're up there!

Lincoln Center: There are ten 'stalls' open to the public, close to the entrance. No tips needed.

CHAPTER 3

Museums

The museums and other cultural institutions of New York are a major reason why people visit the city, and I for one couldn't wait to check out the Metropolitan or discover the delights of the Museum of Modern Art. There's a huge range to see, though, and on your first visit you want to be sure that you won't feel that you've wasted your time. For this reason, I've given you my Top Ten and I'd be pretty darn surprised if anyone hated any of them. You never know, though, so if you've a different opinion, please don't hesitate to let me know ...

TOP TEN MUSEUMS

It is generally the case that when visiting New York we Brits do run out of time more quickly than we expect, so it's useful to make a list of the museums you most particularly want to see. As you get to know New York, you'll form your own opinions, but, in the meantime, here are my favourites. They cover a broad spectrum, from the history of New York to world art and the world's amazing natural history, and should keep you out of mischief!

Metropolitan Museum of Art

American Museum of Natural History

Ellis Island Immigration Museum (see page 39)

Lower East Side Tenement Museum

Museum of Modern Art (MoMA)

Museum of Jewish Heritage

Intrepid Sea-Air-Space Museum

Frick Collection

Solomon R Guggenheim Museum

Skyscraper Musuem

Metropolitan Museum of Art

5th Avenue at 82nd Street. Tel 212-535 7710, website at **www.metmuseum.org** Subway 4, 5, 6 to 86th Street. Open Sun and Tues to Thurs 9.30am to 5.15pm, Fri and Sat 9.30am to 8.45pm. Suggested price: $10 adults, $5 students, under 12s free with an adult. Area: Upper East Side.

With 5,000 years of art spread over 1.5 million square feet, it's impossible to see everything and you won't absorb much if you attempt it. On my first visit, I thought it would be good to see something American as I was in that country, and was delighted by the **Tiffanys** in the American Wing. It also has American arts and crafts and neoclassical sculptures in the garden court. Perhaps the two real 'musts' for the first visit are the **Temple of Dendur,** which was built by Egypt to thank the American people after America helped rescue monuments threatened by the Aswan Dam, and the **Egyptian art exhibits** next door.

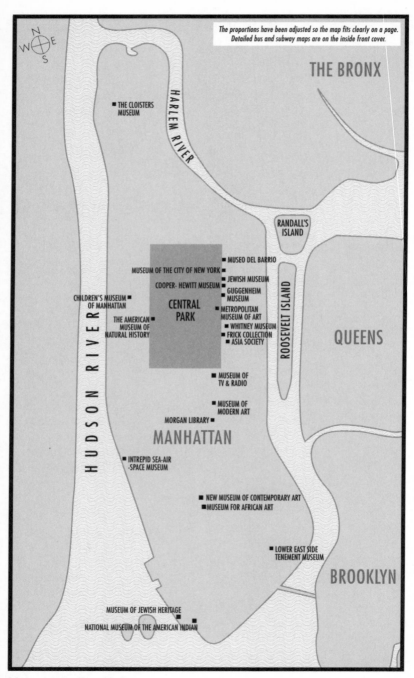

The proportions have been adjusted so the map fits clearly on a page.
Detailed bus and subway maps are on the inside front cover.

THE BRONX

HARLEM RIVER

THE CLOISTERS MUSEUM

RANDALL'S ISLAND

MUSEO DEL BARRIO

MUSEUM OF THE CITY OF NEW YORK

JEWISH MUSEUM

COOPER- HEWITT MUSEUM

GUGGENHEIM MUSEUM

CHILDREN'S MUSEUM OF MANHATTAN

CENTRAL PARK

METROPOLITAN MUSEUM OF ART

THE AMERICAN MUSEUM OF NATURAL HISTORY

WHITNEY MUSEUM

FRICK COLLECTION

ASIA SOCIETY

ROOSEVELT ISLAND

QUEENS

HUDSON RIVER

MUSEUM OF TV & RADIO

MUSEUM OF MODERN ART

MORGAN LIBRARY

MANHATTAN

INTREPID SEA-AIR -SPACE MUSEUM

NEW MUSEUM OF CONTEMPORARY ART

MUSEUM FOR AFRICAN ART

LOWER EAST SIDE TENEMENT MUSEUM

BROOKLYN

MUSEUM OF JEWISH HERITAGE

NATIONAL MUSEUM OF THE AMERICAN INDIAN

Museums in New York

Other 'greats' include the recently updated **Greek and Roman displays,** the **Japanese and Chinese exhibits** and the **medieval art.** To make life a little easier, free hour-long tours leave from the front hall at 10.15am and 11.15am and 1.15pm, 2.15pm and 3.15pm. Also included in the admission price is admission on the same day to **The Cloisters** (see page 62).

★★★★ INSIDE TRACK ★★★★
★ Take a break in the fabulous ★
★ rooftop garden, which has ★
★ magnificent views of Central Park ★
★ and is something of a meeting ★
★ place for single New Yorkers. ★
★ Generally it is open May to ★
★ October depending on the ★
★ weather. ★

American Museum of Natural History

Central Park West at 79th Street. Tel 212-769 5000, website at **www.amnh.org** Subway B, C to 81st Street. Open Sun to Thurs 10am to 5.45pm, Fri and Sat 10am to 8.45pm. Suggested admission: $9.50 adults, $6 under 13s. Combined entrance and ticket to the Space Show (call 212-769 5200 for recorded information) $19 adults, $11.50 for under 13s. Area: Upper West Side.

Like the Metropolitan (see page 53), this is another epic of a museum, which is best seen in parts rather than attempting the whole. The new **Rose Center for Earth and Space** is like a spectacular museum within a museum and incorporates the newly revamped **Hayden Planetarium** as its centrepiece. This is the place to come to learn about both the inner workings of Earth and the outer reaches of the universe. Top of the pile of must-see exhibits include the **Space Theater,** which is billed as the most technologically advanced in the world and shows incredibly realistic views of outer space. The **Big Bang Theater** gives a dramatic recreation of the first minutes of the origins of the universe and is found inside an 87-foot-wide sphere that appears to float in a glass-walled ceiling. The Rose Center also has a dining area and its own museum shop. If you can, try to leave a little time for other magnificent exhibits such as the amazing **dinosaur collection,** the **Native American section** and the **seven continents.** It is worth noting that there is much fun to be had, too – as you trace the roots of evolution you can travel back in time by using the many interactive computer exhibits. Other highlights include the **Imax** theatre, which shows exciting nature programmes, and the amazing **collection of gems** – worth a staggering $50 million – including the famous Star of India blue sapphire. Remember, if you can't

★★★★ INSIDE TRACK ★★★★
★ Make the most of your time at ★
★ the American Museum of Natural ★
★ History and go on a free guided ★
★ tour, starting every hour from ★
★ 10.15am to 3.15pm. Meet at the ★
★ Hall of African Mammals on the ★
★ first floor. ★

fit it all in it gives you an excuse to return to the wonderful Romanesque Revival building.

Lower East Side Tenement Museum

90 Orchard Street at Broome Street. Tel 212-431 0233, website at **www.tenement.org** Subway F to Delancey Street; B, D, Q to Grand Street; J, M, Z to Essex Street. There are three tours available, costing $8 adults, $6 students for one tour; $14 adults, $10 students for two tours; $20 adults, $14 students for three tours. A discount of 25 per cent with your NYCard. Area: Lower East Side.

After they had gone through Ellis Island, what happened to many of those millions of immigrants? They ended up in tenements on the Lower East Side of New York and now there is a museum that tells their poignant stories. One such was Nathalia Gumpertz, a German Jew with a husband called Julius and four children. One morning she gave Julius his bread and coffee for breakfast as usual and sent him off to his job as a shoemaker at the Levy workshop on the nearby Dey Street – and he never came home. This was not an unusual occurrence in those tough days – many men disappeared leaving their wives and children to cope alone. And Nathalia had a lot to cope with. Her family lived in three tiny, dark rooms built on a 100ft-by-25ft lot intended for a single-family home. Conditions were smelly, noisy, unsafe and insanitary. Shortly after Julius disappeared, Nathalie's son

Isaac fell ill and died. Nathalie had no choice but to try to make a living as a seamstress and she taught her daughters how to sew, too. For nine years she had no idea where Julius was and eventually wrote to his father to seek some news. She was told that her father-in-law had died, leaving the huge sum of $600 to his missing son – enough to transform the lives of the Gumpertz family. Nathalie petitioned the courts to declare Julius legally dead and then claimed the inheritance for her family. Finally, in 1884, they moved uptown, closer to middle-class respectability and the fulfilment of the American dream. Glimpses of these lives and others are preserved today at the same address where the Gumpertz and at least 7,000 other immigrant families lived between 1864 and 1935: 97 Orchard Street.

★★★★ **INSIDE TRACK** ★★★★

Before you take one of the walking tours at the Lower East Side Tenement Museum, it is worth watching the slide show and film which gives a tear-jerking insight into the lives of impoverished immigrant families.

The museum consists of several tenement houses – essentially America's first public housing, predating almost every housing law in the US. These houses contain several apartments, faithfully restored down to the last detail, complete with furniture and clothes. It's a must-see for an understanding not only of this neighbourhood, which continues to function as a launching pad for fresh generations of artists and retailers, but also of the American success story. It's also very popular with children as they're allowed to try on the clothes.

Museum of Modern Art

11 West 53rd Street between 5th and 6th Avenues. Tel 212-708 9400, website at **www.moma.org** Subway E, F to 5th Avenue. Open Sat to Tues and Thurs 10.30am to 6pm, Fri 10.30am to 8.30pm. Entrance $10 adults, students $6.50, under 16s free if with an adult. Also open Fridays 4.30pm to 8.15pm, pay what you wish. Area: Midtown.

Founded in 1929 by three private citizens, including Abby Rockefeller, this was the first museum to devote its entire collection to the modern movement. Since then it has retained its pioneering sense of the new, and was the first museum to see architecture, design, photography and film as art forms. The museum's collection, which started with a gift of eight prints and one drawing, dates from the 1880s to the present day and now encompasses more than 100,000 works. Many of the icons of modern and contemporary art are here including Van Gogh's *The Starry Night*, Monet's *Water Lilies*, Picasso's *Les Demoiselles* and Andy Warhol's *Gold Marilyn Monroe*. The collection includes paintings, sculptures, drawings, photographs, films, film stills and videos. Films are screened daily in the two cinemas

(cost included in the museum entrance price, though you need to get a special ticket to reserve your place). Free gallery talks are given at 1pm and 3pm every day except Wednesday and on Fridays at 6pm and 7pm for $4 you can take a personalised audio self-guided tour.

NB: MoMA is building an extension and work may disrupt some programmes. Call ahead for details.

★★★★ INSIDE TRACK ★★★★
★ ★
★ **Break for lunch in the Sette** ★
★ **MoMA Italian restaurant** ★
★ **overlooking the Abby Aldrich** ★
★ **Rockefeller Sculpture Garden** ★
★ **before checking out the MoMA** ★
★ **book and print store. Also, every** ★
★ **Friday (except during the** ★
★ **summer) is Jazz Night in the** ★
★ **Garden Café.** ★
★★★★★★★★★★★★★★★★★★★★★★

Museum of Jewish Heritage: A Living Memorial to the Holocaust

18 First Place at Battery Place, Battery Park City. Tel 212-509 6130. Subway 1, 9 to South Ferry or N, R to Whitehall or 4, 5 to Bowling Green. Open Sun to Wed 9am to 5pm, Thurs 9am to 8pm, Fri and eve of Jewish holidays 9am to 3pm in winter, 5pm in summer. Saturdays and Jewish holidays closed. Entrance $7 adults, $5 students, under sixes free. Area: Battery Park City.

Joy, tradition, tragedy and unspeakable horror are the powerful themes of this museum, which tells the moving story of 20th-century Jewish life from the perspective of those who lived it. Created as a living memorial to the Holocaust, it puts the tragedy into the larger context of modern Jewish history and is organised into three sections – Jewish Life a Century Ago, The War Against the Jews and Jewish Renewal.

The exhibition includes 24 original films that feature testimonies from Steven Spielberg's Survivors of the Shoah Visual History Foundation as well as the museum's own video archive.

Before entering the museum, take a look at the six-sided shape of the tiered roof, a symbolic reminder of the six million who died in the Holocaust and of the Star of David.

Anyone who has ever been to one of the former concentration camps in Europe will be aware of the stark reality of the Holocaust, but this museum does offer some relief in the form of the story of survival and what the Jewish people have achieved since those grim days.

★★★★ INSIDE TRACK ★★★★
★ Make the most of your visit to ★
★ the Museum of Jewish Heritage ★
★ by renting an audio guide, ★
★ narrated by Meryl Streep and ★
★ Itzhak Perlman, cost $5. ★
★★★★★★★★★★★★★★★★★★★★★★

Intrepid Sea-Air-Space Museum

USS *Intrepid*, Pier 86, 46th Street at the Hudson River. Tel 212-245 2533. Subway A, C, E to 42nd Street. Open from the last Monday in May to the first Monday in September Mon to

Sat 10am to 5pm, Sun 10am to 6pm. The rest of the year, Sun to Wed 10am to 5pm. Entrance $10 adults, $5 under 12s. $2 off with your NYCard. Area: Midtown West.

★★★★ INSIDE TRACK ★★★★
★ ★
★ The only way to see the ★
★ submarine at *Intrepid* is on a tour ★
★ and long queues build up very ★
★ quickly, so get there early and see ★
★ it before anything else. ★
★ ★
★★★★★★★★★★★★★★★★★★★★★★

A thoroughly enjoyable museum, which appeals to all ages and sexes. All the staff are very friendly and there are former members of the crew around the ship who are happy to give an insight into its history and life on board. *Intrepid* was one of 24 Second World War US aircraft carriers and despite incidents of serious damage to these ships, none of them were ever sunk during the war. *Intrepid's* worst moment came on 25 November 1944 when two Kamikaze pilots hit the ship five minutes apart, killing 69 men and seriously injuring 85 others. The second plane exploded on the hangar deck and the ship burned for about six hours, but *Intrepid* made it back to America for repairs and returned to the war. Stories of life on board the ship are told by veterans at film screenings throughout the ship and there are also plenty of hands-on exhibits to keep children happy. One of the best exhibits is the F-18 navy jet flight simulator, which costs an extra $5, but is great fun.

Frick Collection

1 East 70th Street at 5th Avenue. Tel
212-288 0700, website at
www.frick.org Subway 6 to 68th
Street. Open Sun 1pm to 6pm, Tues
to Sat 10am to 6pm. Entrance $7;
children under 10 not admitted and
under 16s must be with an adult.
Area: Upper East Side.

★★★★ **INSIDE TRACK** ★★★★
Don't miss out on the free
ArtPhone self-guided tour of the
mansion, which gives historical
information about Frick and his
home and about some of the
works of art on show.

When it opened to the public in
1935, the limestone mansion that
was built for coal and steel
industrialist Henry Frick quickly
became a popular attraction in New
York. The Frick now offers an
intimate look into what was once a
grand home in the last days of
America's Gilded Age. Its artwork and
objects from the 14th to the 19th
centuries, such as fine French
furniture, bronzes, Chinese porcelains
and Limoges enamels, are arranged
as if the Fricks still lived here. The
walls are lined with Holbeins,
Vermeers, Rembrandts, Turners,
Gainsboroughs and Van Dycks. This is
the closest that the Americans will
come to creating the atmosphere of
an English stately home, and the
serenity of this bijou museum is
particularly lovely. You can get a
preview of the whole thing before

you even set off for New York –
there is also a fabulous new virtual
reality tour of the Frick on its
website.

Solomon R Guggenheim Museum

1071 5th Avenue at 88th Street. Tel
212-423 3500, website at
www.guggenheim.org Subway 4, 5,
6 to 86th Street. Open Sun to Wed
9am to 6pm, Fri to Sat 9.30am to
8.30pm. Entrance $12 adults, under
12s free. Area: Upper East Side.

The main Guggenheim Museum in
New York is probably best known for
its beautiful building, which was
designed by Frank Lloyd Wright and
is now one of the youngest buildings
in the city to be designated a New
York City landmark. It houses one of
the world's largest collections of
Kandinksy, as well as works by
Chagall, Klee, Picasso, Cézanne,
Degas, Gauguin and Manet. It also
has Peggy Guggenheim's entire
collection of cubist, surrealist and
abstract expressionist works of art.

★★★★ **INSIDE TRACK** ★★★★
Check out the Guggenheim's
sculpture gallery for some of the
best views of Central Park.

Skyscraper Museum

110 Maiden Lane, New York, NY
10005. Tel 212-968 1961, website at
www.skyscraper.org

Located in New York City, the world's
first and greatest vertical metropolis,
the museum celebrates the city's rich

architectural heritage and looks at what historical forces and which individuals shaped the different skylines of its history. Through exhibitions, programmes and publications, the museum offers a fascinating insight into how individual buildings were born, complete with detailed information about how the contractors bid for the work, what was involved and how the building work was executed, all with comprehensive photographic illustrations.

Since 1997, the museum has presented exhibitions in temporary spaces – two vacant banking halls on Wall Street in the heart of New York's historic financial district – including Downtown New York, Building The Empire State and Big Buildings. There is currently no show, but you can call the number given for information on upcoming lectures, exhibitions and walking tours.

Entrance to the museum when it has an exhibition is generally free, though it is suggested that you give a donation of $2. In the autumn of 2001 the museum will open its permanent home in Battery Park City.

A–Z OF MUSEUMS

The Alternative Museum

594 Broadway between Prince and Houston Streets. Tel 212-966 4444. Area: SoHo.

A small series of galleries focusing on contemporary art and culture that has shown groundbreaking work by

Andres Serrano and David Hammonds, among many others. Check out their website for full details at **www.alternativemuseum.org**

American Craft Museum

40 West 53rd Street between 5th and 6th Avenues. Tel 212-956 3535. Subway E, F to 5th Avenue. Open Tues 10am to 8pm, Wed to Sun 10am to 5pm. Entrance $5 adults, $2.50 students, under 12s free. Area: Midtown.

Just across the way from the MoMA (see page 57), this is an easy museum to fit in – especially as the MoMA doesn't open until mid-morning. And it's worth the effort if you're at all interested in American crafts as it has everything from wood and metal to clay, glass and fibre. In addition to the permanent collections, there are temporary shows too.

American Museum of the Moving Image

35th Avenue at 36th Street, Astoria. Tel 718-784 0077. Subway R to Steinway Street or N to 36th Avenue. Open Tues to Fri noon to 5pm, Sat and Sun 11am to 6pm. Entrance $8 adults, $5 students. Area: Queens.

★★★★ **INSIDE TRACK** ★★★★
★ Astoria is the heart of New York's ★
★ Greek community and filled with ★
★ delis and restaurants. After ★
★ you've been to the museum, head ★
★ to 31st Street and Broadway for ★
★ a spot of lunch. ★
★★★★★★★★★★★★★★★★★★★★★★★

The inside story

A fairly new phenomenon in New York is the introduction of super-sleek, one-hour tours of many of the major institutions in the city to give people the chance to make the most of their valuable time. From January to March and July to September, the **Insider's Hour** gives you a quick peek around the most diverse art collections, wondrous gardens, fascinating animals, backstage magic, historical exhibitions and interactive exhibits. Participating institutions include the Metropolitan Museum of Art (see page 53), Lower East Side Tenement Museum (see page 56), *Intrepid Sea-Air-Space Museum* (see page 58), American Museum of Natural History (see page 55), Bronx Zoo (see page 41), Museum of Modern Art (see page 57), Museum of Jewish Heritage (see page 57) and National Museum of the American Indian (see page 64).

For a complete list of participating institutions and to learn more about the Insider's Hour programmes at each of them, send a stamped, self-addressed envelope to Insider's Hour, NYC & Co, 810 7th Avenue, 3rd Floor, New York, NY 10019. Detailed information about days and times of the programmes are available at the NYC & Co website at **www.nycvisit.com** or CitySearch at **www.newyork.citysearch.com** Have fun!

If you're into everything to do with the making of films, then you will want to make the 15-minute train ride out to Queens to see this museum. Set in the historic Astoria Studios, which are still used today, it is home to screening rooms, rebuilt sets, costumes, props, posters and other memorabilia. Probably the best thing to see is the interactive Behind the Scenes exhibit, where you can see how everything is done and even make your own short film.

Asia Society

502 Park Avenue at 59th Street. Tel 212-288 6400, website at **www.asiasociety.com** Subway 4, 5, 6 to 59th Street. Open Mon to Sat 10am to 6pm. Entrance $4 adults, $2 students, under 12s free if with an adult. Area: Midtown.

Founded in 1956 by John D Rockefeller III, with his collection of Asian art, the society aims to build an awareness of the 30 Pan-Asian countries, which include Japan, New Zealand, Australia and the Pacific Islands. To this end it runs films, lectures and seminars in conjunction with its exhibitions and even has a regular schedule of Asian musicians who play at the museum. Currently it is housed in a temporary building while the headquarters undergo an expansion, but it will return to 725 Park Avenue in autumn 2001.

Brooklyn Museum of Art

200 Eastern Parkway at Washington Avenue. Tel 718-638 5000. Subway 2, 3 to Eastern Parkway. Open Sun 11am to 6pm, Wed to Fri 10am to

5pm, Sat 11am to 9pm. Suggested donation $5, children $2. Area: Brooklyn.

The saddest thing about this huge museum, which is housed in a beautiful 19th-century *beaux arts* building, is that not many people bother to come out to Brooklyn to see it. However, the good thing is that it means all the more space for you to admire one of the best collections of Egyptian art in the world. It also has African art, Middle Eastern art, a collection of pre-Columbian textiles and an impressive Native American section.

The Cloisters

Fort Tryon Park, Fort Washington Avenue at Margaret Corbin Plaza, Washington Heights. Tel 212-923 3700. Subway A to 190th Street. Open March to Oct Tues to Sun 9.30am to 5.15pm, Nov to Feb Tues to Sun 9.30am to 4.45pm. Suggested donation $10 adults (includes free admission to the Metropolitan Museum of Art – see page 53 – on the same day), $5 students, under 12s free if with an adult. Area: Washington Heights/Inwood.

Rockefeller cash allowed the Metropolitan Museum to buy this beautifully red-tiled Romanesque building 70 years ago. Now it is used purely to display examples of medieval art and architecture, including five cloisters – hence the name – from ruined French monasteries dating from the 12th to the 15th centuries. It is stunning to look at and houses some really exciting exhibits.

Cooper-Hewitt National Design Museum

2 East 91st Street at 5th Avenue. Tel 212-849 8400. Subway 4, 5, 6 to 86th Street. Open Sun noon to 5pm, Tues 10am to 9pm, Wed to Sat 10am to 5pm. Entrance $8 adults, under 12s free. Free on Tues from 5pm to 9pm. Area: Upper East Side.

The only American museum devoted entirely to historical and contemporary design, the Cooper-Hewitt covers everything from applied arts and industrial design to drawings, prints, textiles and wall-coverings. Before entering, take time to look at the exterior of the building itself, which was designed in a Georgian style for tycoon Andrew Carnegie.

El Museo del Barrio

1230 5th Avenue between 104th and 105th Streets. Tel 212-831 7272, website at **www.elmuseo.org** Subway 6 to 103rd Street. Open Wed to Sun 11am to 5pm. Suggested donation $4 adults, $2 students, under 12s free with an adult. Area: Spanish Harlem.

Opened in 1969 by a group of Puerto Rican parents, teachers and artists, it houses 8,000 objects of Caribbean and Latin American art from pre-Colombian times to date. Exhibits include musical instruments, miniature houses, dolls and masks.

Fraunces Tavern Museum

54 Pearl Street at Broad Street, first and second floors. Tel 212-425 1778. Subway 1, 9 to South Ferry. Open Mon to Fri 10am to 4.45pm and Sat

MUSEUMS

noon to 4pm. Entrance $2.50 adults, $1 children. Area: Financial District.

When New York was (briefly) capital of America, the Fraunces Tavern housed the Departments of Foreign Affairs, Treasury and War and was where George Washington delivered his famous farewell speech to his officers. Now, nestled among the skyscrapers of the Financial District, this well-preserved 18th-century building, along with four adjacent 19th-century buildings, houses a fine museum dedicated to the study of early American history and culture.

Gagosian

136 Wooster Street between Houston and Prince Streets. Tel 212-741 1111. Area: SoHo.

Given that Guggenheim's SoHo branch is rumoured to have leased space to Prada, which is a reflection of what's going on in this neighbourhood, this gallery is now considered part of SoHo's old guard, yet it represents heavyweight controversials such as Richard Serra and Damien Hirst. Check out their website at **www.gagosian.com**

Guggenheim Museum SoHo

575 Broadway at Prince Street. Tel 212-423 3500. Subway N, R to Prince Street. Open Sun and Wed to Fri 11am to 6pm, Sat 11am to 8pm. Entrance $8 adults or free with ticket to the Solomon R Guggenheim Museum (see page 65). Area: SoHo.

Opened in 1992, the downtown Guggenheim is known for its up-to-date and cutting-edge art shows.

Julia de Burgos Latino Cultural Center and Taller Boricua Gallery

61680 Lexington Avenue at 106th Street. Tel 212-831 4333. Open Tues to Sat, noon to 6pm. Area: Harlem.

Another excellent location to see works by Latino artists. Around the museum, watch out for sidewalk artwork by James de la Vega, a young local artist.

Jewish Museum

1109 5th Avenue at 92nd Street. Tel 212-423 3200, website at **www.thejewishmuseum.org** Subway 4, 5, 6 to 96th Street. Open daily 11am to 5.45pm except Tues (11am to 8pm). Closed on Fridays. Free admission on Tuesdays from 5pm to 9pm. Area: Upper East Side.

In addition to impressive annual exhibitions, the core exhibit is called The Jewish Journey and sets out how the Jewish people have survived through the centuries and what is the essence of Jewish identity. Many of the objects were actually rescued from European synagogues before the Second World War.

Morgan Library

29 East 36th Street between Madison and Park Avenues. Tel 212-685 0008, website at **www.morganlibrary.org** Subway 6 to 33rd Street. Open Tues to Thurs 10.30am to 5pm, Fri 10.30am to 8pm, Sat 10.30am to 6pm, Sun noon to 6pm. Entrance $7 adults, $5 students, under 12s free with an adult. Area: Midtown East.

A gem of a museum, housed in an Italianate building that was once Pierpoint Morgan's library. The collection contains medieval and Renaissance manuscripts; drawings and prints from the 14th century onwards, including works by Degas, Blake, Pollock and Rubens; ancient Middle Eastern seals and tablets; and music manuscripts including original handwritten works by Beethoven, Bach, Brahms and Schubert.

Museum for African Art

593 Broadway between Houston and Prince Streets. Tel 212-966 1313, website at **www.africanart.org** Subway B, D, F, Q to Broadway/Lafayette Street; N, R to Prince Street; 6 to Bleecker Street. Open Tues to Fri 10.30am to 5.30pm, Sat and Sun noon to 6pm. Entrance $5 adults, $2.50 students and children, Sundays free. Area: SoHo.

When the museum moved to its new headquarters in Soho, acclaimed designer Maya Lin, creator of the National Vietnam Veterans' Memorial in Washington, completely redesigned the interior to create a wonderfully serene setting. Exhibitions change approximately every six months.

Museum of Television and Radio

25 West 52nd Street between 5th and 6th Avenues. Tel 212-621 6600, website at **www.mtr.org** Subway E, F to Fifth Avenue; B, D, F, Q to 47th–50th Streets/Rockefeller Center. Open Tues, Wed, Sat, Sun noon to 6pm, Thurs noon to 8pm, Fri noon to 9pm. Entrance $6 adults, $4

students, $3 under 13s. Area: Midtown West.

In addition to the exhibits, the museum also has a daily programme of screenings in two cinemas and two presentation rooms. Pick up a copy of the daily schedule in the lobby on your way in. You can also make an appointment with the library to check out the museum's collection of over 100,000 radio and TV programmes before accessing them on the custom-designed database.

Museum of the City of New York

1220 5th Avenue at 103rd Street. Tel 212-534 1672, website at **www.mcny.org** Subway 6 to 103rd Street. Open Sun noon to 5pm, Wed to Sat 10am to 5pm. Suggested donation $12 families, $7 adults, $5 children. Area: Spanish Harlem.

★★★★ **INSIDE TRACK** ★★★★
The Museum of the City of New York is very relaxed about you defining what – or who – your family is. So if you're travelling with a group of friends, feel free to buy a family ticket.

The entire breadth of New York's history and the people who played parts in its development are celebrated at this museum. Prints, photographs, paintings and sculptures and even clothing and decorative household objects are used to tell the story of New York. It is particularly noted for its Broadway memorabilia.

National Museum of the American Indian

George Gustave Heye Center, US Custom House, 1 Bowling Green between State and Whitehall Streets. Tel 212-668 6624. Subway 1, 9 to South Ferry; N, R to Whitehall Street. Open daily 10am to 5pm. Entrance free. Area: Financial District.

The first museum dedicated entirely to Native American history, art, performing art and culture. The collection includes fabulous leather clothing, intricately beaded head-dresses, sashes, hats and shoes, explaining the white man's influence on Indian culture as well as their own centuries-old traditions. Despite the size and grandness of the beautiful building, it only has 500 pieces on display and thus seems quite small. However, it is very well laid out and the explanations of each piece have usually been given by Native Americans.

New Museum of Contemporary Art

583 Broadway between Houston and Prince Streets. Tel 212-219 1222, website at **www.newmuseum.org** Subway B, D, F, Q to Broadway/ Lafayette Street; N, R to Prince Street; 6 to Bleecker Street. Open Wed to Sun noon to 6pm, Thurs to Sat noon to 8pm. Entrance $6 adults, $3 students, under 18s free. Free on Thursdays 6pm to 8pm. Area: SoHo.

When they say 'contemporary', they really mean it. All the works exhibited are by living artists, often looking at social issues through

modern media and machinery. The area downstairs at the museum is open free to the public and contains the bookstore, a spacious reading room and an exhibition space for interactive projects, installations and performances.

Studio Museum in Harlem

144 West 125th Street between 7th and Lenox Avenues. Tel 212-864 4500. Open Wed to Thurs noon to 6pm, Fri noon to 8pm, Sat to Sun 10am to 6pm. Entrance $5 adults, $3 students and seniors, $1 children. Area: Harlem.

Works of art by African/American, African and Caribbean artists.

Whitney Museum of American Art

945 Madison Avenue at 75th Street. Tel 212-570 3676. Subway 6 to 77th Street. Open Wed and Fri to Sun 11am to 6pm, Thurs 1pm to 8pm. Entrance $12.50 adults, $10.50 students, under 12s free. First Thursday of every month, 6pm to 8pm, pay what you wish.

The Whitney may be housed in one of the most ghastly-looking buildings in the world – a grey, granite series of cubes designed by Marcel Breuer – but it has a world-class collection of 20th-century art. And yet it all came about almost by accident. Gertrude Vanderbilt Whitney offered her entire collection to the Metropolitan but was turned down, so she decided to set up her own museum. As a result, in 1931 the Whitney was founded with a core group of 700 art objects.

Subsequently the museum's holdings have been greatly enriched by other purchases and the gifts of other major collectors. It now has a permanent collection of 12,000 works including paintings, sculptures, drawings, prints, photographs and multimedia installations and is still growing. As well as the wide range of artists in its collection, the Whitney has huge bodies of works by artists including Alexander Calder, Edward Hopper, Georgia O'Keefe, Gaston Lachaise and Agnes Martin.

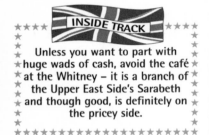

★★★★ **INSIDE TRACK** ★★★★
★ ★
★ **Unless you want to part with** ★
★**huge wads of cash, avoid the café** ★
★ **at the Whitney – it is a branch of** ★
★ **the Upper East Side's Sarabeth** ★
★ **and though good, is definitely on** ★
★ **the pricey side.** ★
★ ★
★★★★★★★★★★★★★★★★★★★★★★★

The Whitney has another branch, called the **Whitney Museum of American Art** at Philip Morris, 120 Park Avenue at 42nd Street. Tel 212-878 2550. Subway S, 4, 5, 6, 7 to 42nd Street/Grand Central. Open Mon to Fri 11am to 6pm, Thurs 11am to 7.30pm. The Sculpture Court is open Mon to Sat 7.30am to 9.30pm, Sun 11am to 7pm. Entrance is free.

The midtown branch of the Whitney is devoted to exhibitions of individual contemporary artists.

MUSEUMS FOR CHILDREN

Children's Museum of Manhattan

212 West 83rd Street between Broadway and Amsterdam Avenue.

Tel 212-721 1234. Subway 1, 9 to 86th Street. Open Wed to Sun (and public school holidays) 10am to 5pm. Entrance $6 adults and children, infants under one year free. Area: Upper West Side.

A museum entirely dedicated to children under the age of ten – and their families. This is a fabulous place and almost worth a visit even if you don't have kids! Its mission statement is to inspire children and their families to learn about themselves and our culturally diverse world through a unique environment of interactive exhibits and programmes. And they certainly achieve it with their inspiring exhibits. Most recent of all is the zany and fun-filled **Body Odyssey,** which shows children just what they're made of. Youngsters aged five and over can rush through the blood tunnel, hold their noses and slime around in the digestive tract, or take deep breaths and wind their way down the windpipe. On the way, they will learn about where burps come from, what makes a cut stop bleeding, where shed skin goes and what life is like inside an asthmatic lung. Other exhibits include **WordPlay** for tots aged six months to four years, where they enter a tiny word-drenched town, plan a meal in apartment ABC and climb up the Chatterbug tree. The **Time Warner Media Center** helps children aged six and above to get behind the scenes of a professionally equipped TV studio and produce their own show, and the **CMOM Theater** takes

Top: Skyline from
Brooklyn Bridge

Above: Times Square

Right: Broadway

Above: Brooklyn Bridge

Below: New York Botanical Garden

Above: Staten Island Ferry
Right: Grand Central Station
Below right: New York Stock Exchange
Below: UN Building

Left: Chinatown

Below: New York street scene

Bottom: Winter Garden

Bottom left: Little Italy

children into a magical world of dance, music, theatre and puppetry.

More museums for children

There are many museums – and not necessarily children's ones – that provide entertaining programmes for young people.

American Museum of Natural History: (See page 55.) Excellent exhibits for children. The **Hall of Planet Earth**, a spectacular, state-of-the-art addition to the museum, explains how the earth evolved, why there are oceans, continents and mountains, and all about earthquakes and storms.

The New York Hall of Science:

4701 111th Street, Flushing Meadows/Corona Park at 47th Street, Queens. Tel 212-699 0005.

The bubble-shaped building features memorable daily science demonstrations and 175 interactive exhibits explaining the mysteries of digital technology, quantum theory, microbes and light and also offers seesaws, slides, whirligigs, space nets and a giant teeter-totter.

Bronx Zoo: (See page 39.) The Children's Zoo gives kids the chance to learn about wildlife by crawling through a prairie dog tunnel, climbing a spider's web or getting close to domestic animals. They'll also really love the new Congo Gorilla Forest.

New York Botanical Garden: (See page 41.) Has a new Everett Children's Adventure Garden with 40 hands-on plant discovery activities throughout 12 acres of gardens and wetlands.

Museum of Modern Art: (See page 57.) Pick up a guidebook from the gift shop for children aged between five to 12, and go on an Art Safari which helps them to explore eight artworks featuring animals and encourages them to look, question and talk about what they see. The museum also has special family tours on Saturdays from 10am to 10.45am (before the museum opens to the public) after which a film series is screened at noon.

Metropolitan Museum of Art: (See page 53.) Self-guided children's tours called Art Hunts with special themes. In addition, it has special tours for groups of children aged from six to 12 and their families in which they are taken to a specific part of the museum and encouraged to hunt for items to do with the theme of the day and then draw those items. Beyond that, two must-see exhibits that always wow children are the awesome **Egyptian Temple of Dendur** and the **medieval armour** collection.

Whitney Museum: (See page 65.) Free Look Out! tours for children at 1pm on Saturdays with a teenage guide who will tell the youngsters about the artists and their work. From October to May, they also run workshops in which children get to discover the inside world of an artist, but you must book the $6 tickets in advance.

Solomon R Guggenheim Museum:
Occasional tours on Sundays
between 2pm and 4pm when
children from five to 10 can see
special exhibitions and afterwards
take part in an art workshop. See
also page 59. Its sister museum in
SoHo, the **Guggenheim Museum
Soho** (see page 63) has a programme
for very young children from the
ages of three to five. They are shown
some works of art before
participating in an art odyssey with
game playing and story telling.

Children's Museum of the Arts:
182 Lafayette Street between
Broome and Grand Streets. Tel 212-
274 0986. Under sevens can have an
artistic ball here, with art computers,
an art playground and a giant
chalkboard.

Brooklyn Museum of Art: (See
page 61.) Offers a drop-in
programme called Arty Facts for
four to seven-year-olds, in which
they learn about different works of
art between 11am and 2pm on
Saturdays.

**Staten Island's Children's
Museum:** 1000 Richmond Terrace,
Staten Island. Tel 718-735 4400.

Science and nature are the order of
the day here – children will love
exhibits like Bugs and Other Insects,
where they get to crawl through a
human-sized anthill, and Pigtails and
Hardhats, where they'll learn the
basics of home construction through
the classic story of The Three Little
Pigs.

The Jewish Museum: (See page 63.)
Offers a new children's exhibit called
Pickles and Pomegranates: Jewish
Homes Near and Far, in which
youngsters can play house in a
replica of a Lower East Side
tenement and a home in Persia
during the same period.

**Lower East Side Tenement
Museum:** (See page 56.) Similar
themes of struggle and triumph
among America's first urban pioneers
spring to life, with a hands-on tour
of the 1916 Confino Family
Apartment that lets children try on
period clothing and operate an
authentic Victrola, a hand-cranked
gramophone.

CHAPTER 4

Getting to the Core of the Big Apple

Whatever your reason for coming to New York, it certainly isn't to rest. Shopping, culture, dining, sightseeing – probably a mixture of all the above. The trick in this, the world's fastest-moving city, is to move just as fast. Hit the ground running as soon as you land. This doesn't mean you have to kill yourself; it means planning what you want to see and do. As a *Brit's Guide* reader, you don't want to join those aimlessly milling around midtown.

NYTAB, the New York Travel Advisory Bureau, is expert at preparing itineraries for top journalists who have not a minute to waste. The following tours were specially constructed by them for *Brit's Guide* readers, with some extra inside track tips from *Brit's Guide* research.. They cover different areas and interests, from hip shopping on the Lower East Side to off-the-beaten-track sightseeing. They include the really important must-sees and some true insider secrets. Each itinerary takes a manageable chunk of the city and should take a reasonable 3–4 hours to complete. Even if you only pick a few, you will be more at home in the areas you cover than most visitors: you'll have more knowledge, more shopping accomplished, more sights seen, and more tales to tell.

The maps that accompany these itineraries don't necessarily include every street. You can, however, rely on them to take you from one point to another and to re-orient yourself should you become lost.

DOWNTOWN AND THE FINANCIAL DISTRICT

Nearly 400 years ago a small group of families came on the ships of the Dutch West India Company and set up camp on Nut (now Governors) Island, just off the tip of Downtown Manhattan. The New World represented a way out, a fresh start, the same new hope it has offered to many millions since then.

★★★★ **INSIDE TRACK** ★★★★

Travelling up and down Manhattan is very easy by subway. Almost every line was designed north to south. Travelling across town is best done by bus on the major (two-way) streets.

New York has always been America's principal gateway for new arrivals, and for many years Downtown was New York. This is where Washington was sworn in as the first president, where Congress first sat, where new states were carved out to add to the 13 born of the 13 colonies.

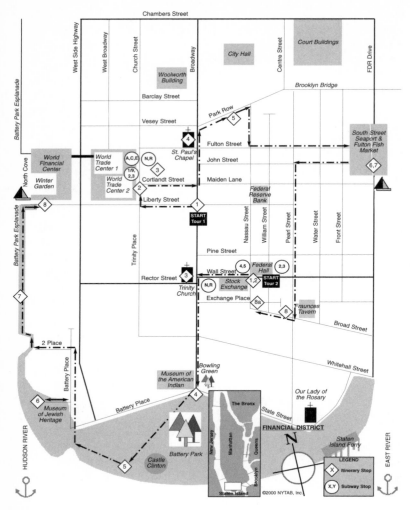

Peter Stuyvesant, New York's first Governor, erected a small wooden barrier at the northern edge of what was then New Amsterdam against possible attack by the Indians or the British. The wall was never tested but the name lived on in Wall Street. The great banks and financial institutions now sited here or nearby affect commerce around the world. The contrasts, of cobblestone and skyscraper, land and water, history and the future, all make for a unique atmosphere.

There's a lot more to Downtown nowadays. To build high you must dig deep, which in turn means you have a lot of excavated debris to dispose of. The original shoreline has, over hundreds of years, literally been extended on all sides by landfill. Once upon a time, the houses on State Street immediately overlooked Upper New York Bay and St. Paul's Chapel faced west on the Hudson shoreline. Water Street and Pearl Street were named because they were at or near the water's edge. In the 1960s, the construction of the World Trade Center yielded enough material to create 23 acres of new land, which became home to Battery Park City and the World Financial Center.

★★★★ INSIDE TRACK ★★★★
★   ★
★ **Make your trips to Downtown on** ★
★ **a weekday. The world's most** ★
★ **powerful financial centre has an** ★
★ **extra hum about it during the** ★
★ **working week.** ★
★   ★
★★★★★★★★★★★★★★★★★★★★★★★★

The following itinerary makes up a very full day, but it breaks quite naturally at lunch. The earlier part emphasises shopping and sightseeing and the second half history and 'culture'. If you decide to attack the second half only, we still suggest you begin or end with a trip up to the observation deck at the World Trade Center. If you wish to go inside the Stock Exchange, you must go there first at 9am for your tickets – they go fast. However, a lot of the action on the floor actually takes place on computers, and so this may be the one to miss if you feel pressed for time. And if you have just arrived, remember, the best way to deal with

jet lag is to hit the ground running and to keep the adrenaline level just above normal until dinner time.

1 Breakfast along Broadway: Take the N or R subway train to Cortlandt Street station; the 4 or 5 subway train to Fulton Street station.

A good way to get native quickly is to have breakfast where the locals go. If the weather is nice, get a coffee and a bagel from one of the vendors on Broadway and watch the morning hustle in the World Trade Center's plaza.

2 Top of the World Observatories: World Trade Center, 107th and 110th floors. Entrance on mezzanine level. Tel 212-323 2340. See page 37 for further details. Discount with your NYCard.

Quite simply the best views on the planet, and it helps you get to grips with the city's geography. If you arrive in New York in the afternoon on a clear day, make this your first stop even if you don't have time for the rest of the itinerary – you can always come again. Also on the mezzanine is a TKTS booth (the other one is in Times Square, closer to the theatres but with much longer queues) where you can get same-day half-price tickets for Broadway shows, as well as next-day tickets for matinees.

3 Century 21: 22 Cortlandt Street between. Broadway and Church Street. Tel 212-227 9092.

There's a shopping concourse on the lower level of the World Trade

Center, but resist and head straight for this: it's one of New York's most famous discount department stores.

★★★★ INSIDE TRACK ★★★★
★ For an exhaustive list of sales all ★
★ over the city, classified by ★
★ designer/brand or merchandise ★
★ type, check out the website: ★
★ www.inshop.com ★

4 St Paul's Chapel: Broadway and Fulton Streets. Tel 212-602 0874.

Seem familiar? Maybe you've seen St Martin in the Fields in London. This is the only building in the city to have survived the Revolutionary War intact. George Washington and all of Congress prayed here after the first presidential inauguration. Washington continued to attend services for the two years New York was the country's first capital. His pew is still here under the first depiction of the presidential seal. Note the rendering of a crown on the pulpit – very rare in a country that rejected monarchs.

5 J & R Computer, Music and Electronics: 31 Park Row between Ann and Beekman Streets. Tel 212-238 9100

The source for software, manuals, electronic gizmos and what-nots. A pretty good music selection too. Ask the store to keep your purchases while you complete your tour.

6 Circle Line – *The Beast* **Speedboat Tour:** Pier 16 (at South Street Seaport). Tel 212-563 3200.

Open May to October. Discount with your NYCard.

One of the best ways of admiring the Manhattan skyline is from the water. There's always the free Staten Island Ferry, but *The Beast* isn't just less time-consuming (half an hour), it zips you around the harbour at high, jet-lag-defeating speeds – great fun. See page 48 for further details.

★★★★ INSIDE TRACK ★★★★
★ The queues for visiting the Statue ★
★ of Liberty and the Ellis Island ★
★ Immigration Museum can be ★
★ enormous. The Lower East Side ★
★ Tenement Museum (see Lower ★
★ East Side Itinerary) offers an ★
★ excellent look at the immigration ★
★ story. ★

7 South Street Seaport: Fulton and Front Streets. Tel 212-732 7678 for programme of free events.

South Street Seaport Museum: 207 Front Street. Tel 212-748 8600

Back on land there's some browsing to be done: shops, including the city's original J Crew and a branch of the famous Strand Bookstore, bars and restaurants, great views of the Brooklyn Bridge and the old buildings and warehouses. The museum has a good children's programme, collections of artefacts and one of the best collections of tall-masted historic ships anywhere. See also page 40.

8 Souperman: 77 Pearl Street at Broad Street. Tel 212-269 5777

or **8a Vine:** 25 Broad Street at Exchange Place. Tel 212-344-8463

Time for a lunch break. Stroll down Pearl Street (once much closer to the shore and named for the abundance of mother-of-pearl shells). At the intersection with Broad Street, you'll find this sit-at-the-counter or take-away seller of some of New York's best soups. (Did you know Vichyssoise is not French but a New York invention?) If the weather is fine, order 'to go' and eat on the steps of the Stock Exchange or on one of Trinity Church's benches. For those who want a bit more comfort, try Vine just up the road.

DOWNTOWN TOUR 2

1 New York Stock Exchange: 20 Broad Street at Wall Street. Tel 212-656 3000.

Entrance to the gallery is free. The self-guided tours are timed to start at a quarter to each hour. By the way, the walkway over the exchange floor was glazed in after hippies in the late 1960s caused pandemonium by throwing handfuls of dollar bills on to the floor below. See also page 47.

2 Federal Hall: 26 Wall Street at Nassau Street. Entrance on Pine Street. Tel 212-825 6888.

Before strolling along Wall Street towards the slender spire of Trinity Church, notice the Greek Revival solidity of Federal Hall (1842) opposite the Stock Exchange. This site has always served the city or the nation. George Washington was inaugurated as the first president in an earlier building on the same spot.

3 Trinity Church: Broadway and Rector Street. Tel 212-602 0872.

This Anglican church was founded in 1697, though the current structure was built in 1839. There's a tiny 'museum' inside, and a delightful churchyard for summer musings. Several prominent figures are buried here and those that know such things say that Alexander Hamilton, America's first secretary of the treasury, shot in a duel by political rival Aaron Burr, haunts the graveyard to this day.

4 National Museum of the American Indian: Smithsonian Institution, 1 Bowling Green. Tel 212-668 6624. Free admission.

Before you, came the immigrants; before the immigrants, came the traders; before the traders, were the Indians. This museum covers tribes throughout the western hemisphere. It is located in New York's stately former Customs House. Note the two museum shops for interesting gifts and souvenirs. See also page 64.

5 Battery Park Promenade: Just behind the museum lies Battery Park. Walk towards the Promenade at the very tip of the island. You'll pass the red sandstone Castle Clinton which, before landfill, was 100 yards offshore. Though it never saw military action, it found use as an entertainment hall, then as an immigration centre (before Ellis Island) and later became the New York Aquarium. Stroll along the Promenade for some first-rate views of the harbour with Governor's Island to your left, the Statue of Liberty slightly to the right, the New Jersey shore at hard right.

6 Museum of Jewish Heritage:
18 First Place at Battery Place. Tel
212-968 1800.

Walk west past the Korean War
Memorial and a few steps north up
Battery Place to this hexagonal
building (think Star of David) with a
tiered roof. One of New York's
newest and perhaps most
worthwhile cultural attractions. The
museum shows a darker shade of the
human condition (spot the snakes-
and-ladders-like children's board
game called 'Jews Out!') but, as you
reach the top floor and a stunning
panoramic view of the Statue of
Liberty, the message goes beyond
regret and sect to hope and the
possibility of renewal. See also
pages 57–8.

7 Battery Park Esplanade: A gentle
10-minute salt-in-the-air stroll with
great views. See also page 46.

**8 World Financial Center/Winter
Garden:** Tel 212-945 0505 for
programme of free events.

Merrill Lynch, Amex, Lehman
Brothers – world-class financial
power houses are located in these
Cesar Pelli-designed towers right
next to the North Cove marina and
the huge glazed public space of the
Winter Garden. The 16 palm trees are
real and come from the Mojave
desert. As workers begin leaving their
offices you might be lucky enough to
catch one of the free concerts held
here. See also page 45. Sit and relax
a while – but don't forget to pick up
any packages you left with the shops
earlier.

Useful numbers
Alliance for Downtown NY (120
Broadway between Cedar and Pine
Streets, tel 212-566 6700) and
Lower Manhattan Cultural Council
(5 World Trade Center, tel 212-432
0900) for details of forthcoming
events.

LOWER EAST SIDE
It has been called the greatest
experiment on earth. Millions of
people from every corner of the
globe, living together, trading
together, dealing with one another in
a single city. The latest arrivals are
gradually forged into something new,
something unique by the strangeness
and the excitement of this melting
pot. Each wave of immigration –
from Italy, Ireland, Russia and points
beyond – slowly becomes established
in its new home, but the bubbling
cauldron is constantly refreshed with
new blood, new ideas, new
influences.

★★★★ **INSIDE TRACK** ★★★★

**Don't choose a Saturday to
explore the Lower East Side.
Many shops and even the
Visitor Center are closed for the
Jewish Sabbath.**

The history of America is to a great
extent the history of its immigrants.
New York City has always been the
major gateway for that immigration.
Everyone has heard of Ellis Island,
and the processing of those 'huddled

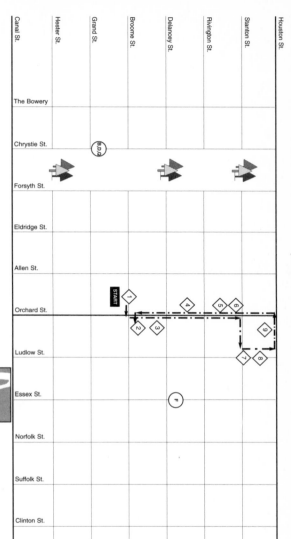

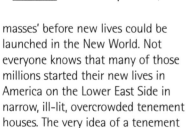

masses' before new lives could be launched in the New World. Not everyone knows that many of those millions started their new lives in America on the Lower East Side in narrow, ill-lit, overcrowded tenement houses. The very idea of a tenement

house on the Lower East Side remains to this day an important part of the American psyche. 'Everyone ought to have a Lower East Side in their lives,' wrote Irving Berlin, the famous New York songwriter. Like a badge, some family connection to the Lower East

Side marks you out as having honourably arrived.

There are still powerful remnants of this history. The older eastern European Jewish community (see how much of the area closes early on Friday in preparation for the Saturday Sabbath) lives side by side with the more recent Hispanic arrivals. If you want to locate the most unwashed Brit you have ever seen or smelt, you'll have a good chance of finding him here (probably tattooed and pierced). People, whether designers, artists or young adventurers, are still attracted by what until recently were Manhattan's cheapest rents.

Apart from history, the area is known for its shopping, sometimes cheap, sometimes cutting edge, sometimes both at the same time. So, you shop here for two reasons: either, because like many New Yorkers, you hate paying retail or, also like many New Yorkers, you want to find something that nobody else has. Either way, if you want to get a real feel for what makes New York tick, spend a little time on the Lower East Side.

Only 15 people at a time are able to go on the Tenement tour recommended below. Either book in advance or begin this itinerary at about 11am when they begin accepting reservations in person for tours later the same day.

1 Lower East Side Visitor Center: 261 Broome Street between Orchard and Allen Streets. Tel 212-226 9010. Open 10 am to 4 pm. Closed Saturdays.

Housed in a shop space, the Visitor Center has a small but helpful staff and more leaflets than you can shake a stick at.

2 Lower East Side Tenement Museum: 90 Orchard Street at Broome Street. Tel 1-800 965 4827 for reservations. Discount with your NYCard.

The houses are visited by guided tour only. Tours start at 1 pm, departing approximately every 20 minutes. They last about 1 hour. Book your place now for a tour later in the day. Then, get a feel for the area's development by watching one or both of the 25-minute films in the baby theatre before hitting the streets. See also page 56.

★★★★ INSIDE TRACK ★★★★

If you're travelling in a group, pick a spot on the itinerary as a 'base' in advance. Anyone late, bored or lost can regroup with the rest of the party there.

The rest of this itinerary (depending on how fast a shopper you are, what nose you have for your own discoveries and how long you linger over lunch) should take about 2–3 hours.

3 Bridge 1: 98 Orchard Street between Broome and Delancey Streets. Tel 212-979 9777.

The leather industry has been big business in this part of New York since 1680. Bridge is an example of the many leather clothing stores that dot the neighbourhood.

4 Giselle: 143 Orchard Street between Delancey and Rivington Streets. Tel 212-673 1900.

Many stores on Orchard Street offer discounts; this one specialises in classically tailored women's clothing. If you're used to paying many hundreds for fine clothes, you'll love this place for cutting the 'many' out of the equation.

5 Alik Singer Rubin Singer: 163 Orchard Street between Rivington and Stanton Streets. Tel 212-473 5922.

Alik is Russian and a classically trained designer. Who knows how soon we'll see his women's couture on Madison Avenue?

6 Zao: 175 Orchard Street between Stanton and Houston Streets. Tel 212-505 0500.

A very sleek clothing/art gallery, where you can lounge in the concrete garden, surf the web and even buy things (latest coin holder from Japan?) that the store may have just one example of.

★★★★ **INSIDE TRACK** ★★★★

The city that never sleeps is doziest before mid-morning – many shops don't open until about 10.30. Use those earlier hours for sightseeing.

7 Amy Downs Hats: 103 Stanton Street at Ludlow Street. Tel 212-598 4189.

Ascot? Henley? The back garden? Of course you get your hats from Amy in New York. She's often on the premises.

8 TG-170: 170 Ludlow Street between Houston and Stanton Streets. Tel 212-995 8660.

This store has a reputation for discovering soon-to-be-hip designers.

9 Katz's Deli: 205 Houston Street between Orchard and Ludlow Streets. Tel 212-254 2246.

Lunchtime. The décor here hasn't changed in years. You might be hungry now, though not as hungry as the immense portions suggest. (Those stacks of brown paper bags throughout the cafeteria are meant for you to take your uneaten portion home.) Order the pastrami sandwich: it's a taste that was born in this neighbourhood.

Lower East Side Tenement Museum: 90 Orchard Street at Broome Street.

Back here for the tour you booked earlier. This is a must-see for an understanding not only of this neighbourhood, which continues to function as a launching pad for fresh generations of artists and retailers, but also of the 'American success story'. It's a good alternative to the Ellis Island Immigration Museum (see page 39), and popular with children (they're allowed to try on the turn-of-the-century clothes).

4

CHINATOWN AND LITTLE ITALY

There are only a couple of streets left in the area known as Little Italy to give a flavour of what was once a huge Italian community. Perhaps the true Little Italy, certainly in terms of food, has moved to Arthur Avenue, between the New York Botanical Gardens and the Zoo in the Bronx. Still, thousands of Italian Americans visit the streets around Mulberry to point out to children and grand-children the way things were. And there's still the street feast of San Gennaro (see page 26) offering Italian colour, nourishment and above all atmosphere, in the third week of September from Mulberry Street to Worth Street.

As for Chinatown, it has grown immensely over the years and as it has grown it has diversified. Most original inhabitants were from Guangdong Province in China proper; many more recent arrivals however have come from communities in Malaysia, Vietnam and elsewhere. The area is a riot of sensation. This is where you come for those truly fake gen-u-wyne brand-name luxury pens and watches; for some of the tastiest and cheapest food, for silk-slipper bargains and world-class tat, for karaoke bars with laser disc screens, for street hawkers and art shops, plumbing goods stores and all manner of mysterious eastern merchandise!

1 Pearl River Mart: 277 Canal Street at Broadway, 2nd and 3rd floors. Tel 212-431 4770.

Start here, at the corner of Broadway and Canal. All of the hustle and bustle of the pavements and streets makes this intersection one of Manhattan's busiest. Everyone is buying and selling, delivering and collecting. Join in with a short climb upstairs to Chinatown's version of the department store. There's definitely going to be something here that you need.

★★★★ **INSIDE TRACK** ★★★★

★
★ **2001 is the year of the snake.**
★ **Head for Chinatown on**
★ **29 January and join in the**
★ **New Year celebrations**
★
★★★★★★★★★★★★★★★★★★★★★★

2 Kam Man: 200 Canal Street between Mulberry and Mott Streets. Tel 212- 571 0300.

Walk east along Canal Street, but take your time. There are so many things to seduce your attention, from 'Gucci' watches and wind-up toys to porcelain and luggage. Both children and adults will find the sights, sounds and smells fascinating.

Kam Man is one of the most comprehensive of Chinatown's umpteen grocery stores. They speak very little English here, so you'll have a hard time identifying a good portion of what you see. And you'll see a lot, all crazily juxtaposed, from Ovaltine to ginger jars.

From Canal Street, turn right on to Mott Street and then left when you come to tiny Pell Street.

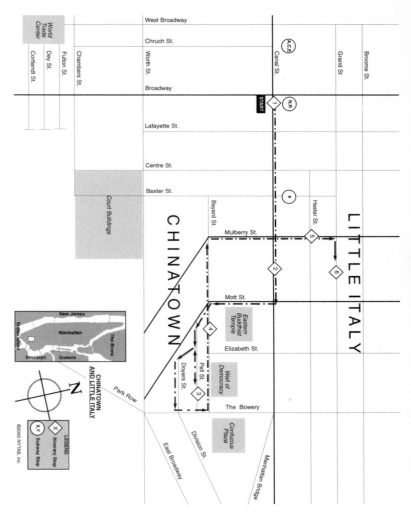

3 Joe's Shanghai: 9 Pell Street between Doyers Street and Bowery. Tel 212-233 8888.

Snack suggestion: it's impossible to walk through Chinatown without feeling hungry. We're not the only ones who think the dumplings here are delicious, so it's a good idea to come at off-peak hours to avoid the queues. Just be careful, they're very hot inside.

Backtrack along Pell Street and turn left on to Doyers Street. Pell and Doyers Streets mark the boundaries of the original Chinatown. They are today among the most picturesque streets in the area and as you look around it's easy to feel you've been transported to an entirely different cultural planet. Walk all the way along Doyers Street, then turn left on to the Bowery, passing Confucius Plaza (spot his statue). Turn left on to Bayard Street past the Wall of Democracy where you can theoretically keep up with the latest developments in, or criticisms of, Beijing.

4 Chinatown Ice Cream Factory: 65 Bayard Street between Mott and Elizabeth Streets. Tel 212-608 4170.

Pop your head in and check out the flavours. This place supplies most of the city's Japanese restaurants with green tea ice cream and has other equally exotic varieties.

Follow Bayard Street to Mulberry Street, and turn right.

As you head north, China magically transforms into Italy.

5 Forzano Italian Imports: 128 Mulberry Street at Hester Street. Tel 212-925 2525

Maybe you didn't come to New York for a picture of the Pope or an espresso machine – on the other hand, maybe you did.

6 Ferrara Pastries & Café: 195 Grand Street between Mulberry and Mott Streets. Tel 212-226 6150.

Little Italy is a bit of an artefact; a few blocks around Mulberry Street now suffice to contain it.

This pastry shop is also a relic, one of the oldest in the country, and a good place to rest at the end of your tour. They send their nougat and biscotti all over the world.

TriBeCa

To the west of Broadway and Chinatown lies a rough-chic wedge of Manhattan named after its shape. **Tri**angle **Be**low **Ca**nal Street. In the 1970s the real estate agents who named it decided TriBeCa was ripe for gentrification. It took only ten years for many of the area's factories and warehouses to be converted into cavernous artists' lofts. By the 1990s, the district was able to boast Robert de Niro as a resident, restaurateur (the TriBeCa Grill) and entrepreneur – his TriBeCa Film Center at 325 Greenwich Street offers facilities to local and visiting film-makers. Today, when friends of local celebrities visit, they can stay at the sleek new (and triangular) TriBeCa Grand Hotel and even rent its private screening room.

SOHO

SoHo stands for South of Houston (pronounced 'house-tun') Street. Its huge cast-iron lofts were earmarked for demolition in the 1960s. They were saved by the protests of artists who had discovered the buildings' big spaces and low rents. The use of cast iron (first developed in Britain) for buildings was a huge innovation, allowing classic styles to be mass-produced, sold by catalogue, and assembled on site. The result is an architecture that has inspired not just artists, but successive waves of galleries, interior and fashion design firms and multimedia start-ups. The area has moved from cutting-edge to chic, and the inevitably rising rents have forced out many of the original pioneers and today, SoHo is more design than art. It has a sleek style visible in people's dress, in shop displays, even in restaurant menus.

You can take your time and do the whole tour, or split this into two mini tours.

★★★★ **INSIDE TRACK** ★★★★

If you've decided to split your day between two areas of Manhattan, for example the Financial District and SoHo, then try being chauffeured by pedal power rather than taking a taxi. Ponycabs' bicycle rickshaws keep you at street level, and really a part of it all. Lovely when the weather is fine, and cosy for two under a blanket in winter. Arrange with them in advance where you should be picked up. Ponycabs, 517 Broome Street (at Thompson Street). Tel 212-766 9222 (212-PONYCAB).

1 Balthazar: 80 Spring Street between Broadway and Crosby Street. Tel 212-965 1414.

SoHo has a different, calmer feeling in the mornings than at other times, and undergoes a slow, almost continental wake-up. So we suggest you have breakfast, or better yet, Saturday brunch, in the neighbourhood. This place is one of the city's hottest restaurants in the evening, and it's a celebrity – therefore a celebrity-spotter – favourite.

You'll find masses of shops and galleries in SoHo, and it's a lot of fun just following your nose. The next two shops are very well known, and we've chosen them to flank your browse along Broadway.

2 Canal Jean Co.: 504 Broadway between Spring and Broome Streets. Tel 212-226 1130.

Those whose mission is to shop will find seemingly infinite racks of basics at basic prices here: jeans, T-shirts, etc., and quite a selection of vintage gear.

3 Avirex: 595 Broadway between Prince and Houston Streets. Tel 212-925-5455.

Just south of Houston Street you'll find this well-known source for aviator and varsity jackets.

As you walk back to Prince Street, you'll pass what has become known as Museum Row. Many of the artists that once made SoHo a hotbed of creativity have been priced out, but the museums this talent attracted remain. Take a look in one – or more if you have time.

4 Museum for African Art: 593 Broadway between Prince and Houston Streets. Tel 212-966 1313.

This is a lovely space with an interior designed by the talented Maya Lin whose Washington Memorial wall to the fallen in Vietnam is so moving. Its exhibitions draw on some remarkable private collections. Note the bookshop and museum store. See also page 63.

5 New Museum of Contemporary Art: 583 Broadway between Prince and Houston Streets. Tel 212-219 1355.

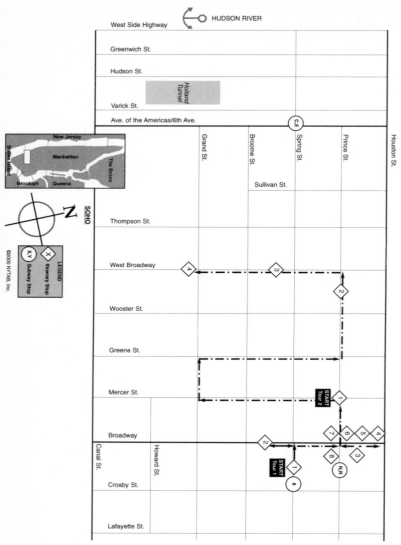

They really mean 'contemporary' here: every artist shown is alive. And every one has something to say, whether or not you agree with the message (often socially conscious) or the medium (for example, pebbles, light, computers). See also page 65.

6 Guggenheim Museum SoHo:
575 Broadway between Prince and Houston Streets. Tel 212-423 3500.

The downtown outpost of the uptown classic. See page 63 for more details.

7 Kate's Paperie: 561 Broadway at Prince Street. Tel 212-941 9816.

If you want to report your New York discoveries on hand-made paper, this is the spot to find it. Note the building the shop is in, the Little Singer Building, with its pretty cast-iron balconies decorated with porcelain.

8 Dean and DeLuca: 560 Broadway at Prince Street. Tel 212-226 6800.

If you cross the street directly opposite, you'll see this very swish grocery store, a good reflection of SoHo's particular style: food as art. And an astonishing display it is, too.

9 and 1 Fanelli's: 94 Prince Street at Mercer Street. Tel 212-431 5744.

Here's where to take a break at the end of Tour 1, or kick off Tour 2. The pub-like bar is easily the oldest in SoHo. If you're ready for a bite to eat, their burgers are delicious and the atmosphere is completely unpretentious and real. This isn't a tourist joint.

Mercer Street and Greene Streets: Although Broadway is a major thoroughfare and West Broadway has the best shopping, it's the cobbled streets between them that hold the most charm.

Take the time to stroll down Mercer and up Greene. (Note how New Yorkers leave off the word 'avenue' or 'street' when giving addresses or directions, eg 'I live on Park.') Greene Street is rich in the cast-iron facades the area is so famous for. Number 72, with its many columns and pedimented entrance, is known as

'the King of Greene Street.' The 'Queen', by the way, is the one at number 30 with the Second Empire façade.

2 Phat Farm: 129 Prince Street between Wooster Street and West Broadway. Tel 212-533 7428.

Hip-hop fashion was invented in New York. Richard Simmons' shop is one of the original sources of those drop-crotched pants. Now installed in high rent glory, it is an amazing contrast to its street-corner vendor beginnings of just a few years ago.

3 Robert Lee Morris: 400 West Broadway between Spring and Broome Streets. Tel 212-431 9405.

West Broadway (not to be confused with Broadway) has great shops. Take your time! This store belongs to one of the very few American jewellery designers who have an international reputation.

4 SoHo Grand Hotel: 310 West Broadway between Grand and Canal Streets. Tel 212-965-3000

If you've followed both SoHo tours, you're going to enjoy and deserve a cocktail in the Grand Bar, up the iron staircase, of this converted industrial space. It, and its clientèle are very stylish, very SoHo.

★★★★ **INSIDE TRACK** ★★★★
★   ★
★ **Had enough of shopping? Take a** ★
★   **15-minute stroll west to 278** ★
★ **Spring Street (between Hudson** ★
★   **and Varick Streets). The tiny NYC** ★
★   **Fire Museum is full of polished** ★
★   **nostalgia.** ★
★★★★★★★★★★★★★★★★★★★★★★★★★

GREENWICH VILLAGE

In the higgledy-piggledy maze of streets that makes up the delightful confusion of Greenwich Village, it is the solidity of Washington Square's triumphal arch that marks the district in people's minds. The arch commemorates George Washington's inauguration as the first president, and freedom from colonial rule.

The area has long represented one form of freedom or another. Initially, this countryside haven north of the city offered a retreat from cholera and yellow fever epidemics. Later, it was freedom from conformity that attracted avant garde artists, the Beat movement, Off Off Broadway, and a myriad of alternative lifestyles. The results have sometimes had world-wide repercussions, like the Stonewall Rebellion on Christopher Street in 1969, which is credited with having launched the gay rights movement. The Village today has an air of settled prosperity, but it still offers freedom from the city's famous towering heights and frantic pace. Its shops and its inhabitants range from the outright weird to the charmingly old-fashioned.

The Village is one of the few parts of New York City in which it's possible to get lost. Don't worry if you do, you'll soon find your way out. If you stick to the itinerary below, you'll spend between 2½ to 3 hours walking through some of the most picturesque streets and popping into a few of our many favourite shops.

★★★★ **INSIDE TRACK** ★★★★
Directory inquiry operators in New York are helpful for more than telephone numbers. If you're meeting someone, or trying to find a particular shop or restaurant, simply dial 411 on any pay phone and ask for the street address. It won't cost you a penny.

1 Washington Square Park:
Washington Square functions as a village playground: chess players, skateboarders, performance artists, there's always something to see. Both the original 1889 wooden arch and the current marble replacement were designed by Stanford White, one of the city's most famous architects and a native of the Village.

Note the elm tree in the north-east corner. It is possibly the oldest tree in Manhattan (well over 300 years), and the local executioner found its branches ideal for hangings between 1797 and 1819.

Washington Mews: Glance along here on your way north up University Place. These were the stables for the pretty Greek Revival houses along the northern side of the park.

2 Untitled: 26 West 8th Street between 5th and 6th Avenues. Tel 212-505 9725.

8th Street is home to a large number of edgy shoe and fashion shops. Poke

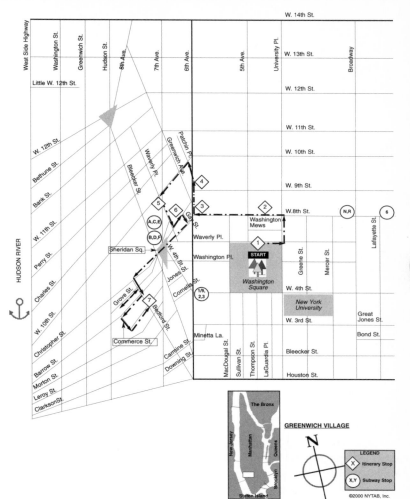

around for something daring. This shop includes some top international names as well as local discoveries.

3 C O Bigelow Chemists: 414 6th Avenue between West 8th and West 9th Streets. Tel 212-533 2700.

Jet lag? Stomach upset? This, the oldest traditional chemist in the country, has also long been respected as a source for homoeopathic medicines.

4 Balducci's: 424 6th Avenue at West 9th Street. Tel 212-673 2600.

Despite the crowds and the New York crush, this is an institution you definitely do want to be locked up in. One of the city's best food shops and a riot of smells, colours and tastes.

Patchin Place: Cross 6th Avenue at West 10th Street and follow West 10th as it angles south. Glance up Patchin Place on your right – a tiny street of just 10 houses. Number 4 was home to poet e.e. cummings for 40 years.

5 Three Lives Bookstore: 154 West 10th Street at Waverly Place. Tel 212-741 2069.

Everything a bookshop should be. A great selection, a knowledgeable staff and an atmosphere that encourages you to browse. Find a novel set in the neighbourhood.

6 Aedes de Venustas: The basement at 15 Christopher Street between 6th and 7th Avenues. Tel 212-206 8674.

You've travelled thousands of miles to be in New York. The least you can do is have the folks here help choose a scent that is truly you, a statement of your individuality – tomato leaf, perhaps? Very Village!

Take a tiny detour through Gay Street, New York's second shortest street (after nearby Weehawken Street). As you exit on to Waverly Place, turn right and look at the street sign. You're at the cross streets of Waverly Place and Waverly Place – what a tangle!

St Luke-in-the-Fields: Head along Christopher Street's bustle to quiet Bedford Street. Note the wood-frame house on the corner of Grove Street, perhaps the best-preserved in Manhattan.

If you take a step down Grove Street towards Hudson Street, you will see St Luke-in-the-Fields (1822) whose first warden, Clement Clarke Moore, wrote a poem for his children: 'Twas the night before Christmas and all though the house …'.

75½ Bedford Street: Stepping back into Bedford Street you will find the city's narrowest house. Number 75½ is just 9½ feet wide. Some say its neighbour, at number 77, is the oldest Greenwich Village house still standing.

Commerce Street and The Cherry Lane Theater: 38 Commerce Street. Tel 212-727 3673.

This backwater, where Barrow meets Commerce Street, is one of the most nostalgic parts of the Village. There's even a gaslight burning at the street's elbow. The Cherry Lane Theater just beyond the bend has hosted many a star. One actor who did not perform there but lived in a bachelor pad above the theatre in the 1920s was Archie Leach – he later became much better known as Cary Grant.

7 Chumley's: 86 Bedford Street off 7th Avenue. Tel 212-675 4449.

Depending on the time of day, this is an atmospheric lunch or casual dining spot. The fact that you won't find its name outside hints at its past and certainly the interior has hardly changed at all since 1928, when it began life as a speakeasy. It's also served as a drinking club for dozens of writers including Hemingway, Steinbeck and Faulkner. Spot the wall-mounted dust jackets that Lee Chumley encouraged authors to bring him.

MIDTOWN: 34th STREET

If you're only in town for a very short time, and need to work your way through a serious shopping list, you'll find most things in the three shops listed, and still have time for a major attraction, a civilised museum and a wonderful secret lunch-spot.

1 Macy's: 34th Street at Broadway. Tel 212-695 4400.

'The largest store in the world', they shout to everyone. And they're right. You can get just about anything here. By the way, in this megashopolis, we think The Cellar kitchen department is particularly good. See also page 115.

★★★★ **INSIDE TRACK** ★★★★
★ ★
★ Take advantage of all the NYCard ★
★ sightseeing discounts (see pages ★
★ 193–4 for details). $2 here, $3 ★
★ there and $5 somewhere else ★
★ soon adds up to a serious chunk ★
★ of change – which should come ★
★ in handy as you tour the shops! ★
★★★★★★★★★★★★★★★★★★★★★★★★

2 Daffy's: 1311 Broadway at West 34th Street. Tel 212-736 4477.

Let's face it, you're unlikely to come out of Macy's where you expected to – it's just too huge. But find your way back to the corner of Broadway and 34th, and opposite you'll see Daffy's. There are several branches in town, all stocking the finds of agents sent out scouting world-wide. Hunt through the racks for bargains galore, from top-name designers to everyday necessities to one-off

samples. Their slogan is apt: 'Clothing bargains for millionaires'.

3 Manhattan Mall: 6th Avenue between West 32nd and West 33rd Streets. Tel 212-465 0500.

Malls, though very popular in the rest of America, are rare in Manhattan. This 11-storey block is worth exploring for the sheer diversity of products offered.

4 Empire State Building Observatories and Skyride: 350 5th Avenue at 34th Street. Tel 212-736-3100 for the Observatories and 888-SKYRIDE for the Skyride.

Without a shadow of a doubt, the Empire State Building (see page 37) is the most famous skyscraper in the world: a hang-out for King Kong, 102 storeys of sheer New York exuberance – it was built in the face of the Great Depression. A B-25 bomber once crashed into the 79th floor, but did only minimal damage to the structure. Though we think the best overall views are from the World Trade Center (see page 37), the two decks here on the 86th and 102nd Floors are truly romantic.

The building also contains a popular attraction, NY Skyride, in which Scotty from the Starship *Enterprise* pilots you around and between the city's skyscrapers with hair-raising and entertaining results.

5 Morgan Library: 29 East 36th Street at Madison Avenue. Tel 212-685 0610. Discount with your NYCard.

You end this tour at a true insider's secret. Your NYCard gives you

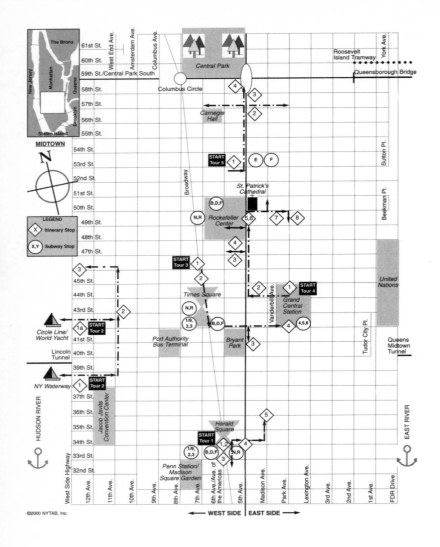

membership for a day, which entitles you to free admission and a discount in the shop. Wander around the museum (it was once a house). Have lunch in the peaceful courtyard café. It's glazed in and wonderful all the year round. J Pierpont Morgan

collected like a Renaissance prince, and you'll see Michelangelo, Durer, not one but three Gutenberg Bibles, and the original manuscript of Charles Dicken's *A Christmas Carol*. See also page 63.

MIDTOWN: HUDSON RIVER

New York's harbour is the finest on the Atlantic – and the reason that the city developed into one of the most important commercial centres on the planet. To get a true feel for this fact, and to see one of the world's most stunning skylines, it's essential to get out on to the water. Two companies offer a selection of cruises – lower harbour cruises, sunset cruises, dinner cruises and music cruises. For this itinerary, we suggest you take a cruise around the entire island of Manhattan. You'll not only see the famous landmarks, but also the winding upper reaches of the East and Harlem Rivers.

1 NY Waterway Cruises: Pier 78, West 38th Street and 12th Avenue. Tel 800-533 3779. Open May to November. Discount with your NYCard.

This high-speed catamaran will whisk you around the whole of Manhattan in just 2 hours. See also page 48.

1a Circle Line Cruises: Pier 83, West 42nd Street and 12th Avenue. Tel 212-563 3200. Open all the year round. Discount with your NYCard.

This is the more leisurely option. Circle Line has been showing the city to visitors and locals alike since 1945. Many of the boats are fully restored landing craft and tender ships used in the Second World War. The full Island Cruise takes 3 hours. See also page 48.

2 Market Diner: 572 11th Avenue at West 43rd Street. Tel 212-695 0415.

You'll find diners all over America, but not many in New York. This one is a classic – nondescript building, truck drivers, and an endless menu (including our favourite, pancakes, bacon and syrup). Of course it's open 24 hours a day.

3 *Intrepid* **Sea-Air-Space Museum:** Pier 86, West 46th Street and 12th Avenue. Tel 212-245 2533. Discount with your NYCard.

After lunch, return to the water across the West Side Highway. Moored just a few blocks up is one of the city's most popular attractions. And when you see the serious hardware you're allowed to clamber over and generally play with, you'll understand why. This museum is a Second World War aircraft carrier. Berthed next to it is a nuclear submarine. The deck is crammed with fighters, and there's a flight simulator inside. See also page 58.

MIDTOWN: TIMES SQUARE

Although all these Midtown tours can be done in any order, this is the one we think you should reserve for the evening. The energy and neon of the area is best experienced starting at dusk.

1 Times Square Visitor Center: 1560 Broadway between West 46th and West 47th Streets. Open until 8pm.

Situated in the old and very pretty Embassy Theater, this is the place to meet friends out of the heat, the cold or the crowds. And if you have to wait a few minutes, send a few free e-cards back home.

Times Square: Open 24-hours a day. Broadway slices through the Theater District with so many lit hoardings that it became known as The Great White Way. Stroll southwards and get the full neon feel. Enough souvenir mugs to fill a black hole, enough tourist traffic to populate a medium-sized nation. It's loud, it's brash, it's a must-see.

★★★★ INSIDE TRACK ★★★★

★ One evening, take to the water
★ for a spectacular dinner and
★ dancing cruise on *World Yacht*.
★ Board at 6.30pm at Pier 81 (West
★ 4th Street and Hudson River). The
★ boat leaves at 7pm and returns
★ at 10pm. Stupendous views. Call
★ 212-630 8100 for a reservation.
★ Jackets required. Discount with
★ your NYCard.

★★★★★★★★★★★★★★★★★★★★★★

2 Virgin Mega Stores: 1540 Broadway between West 45th and West 46th Streets. Tel 212-921 1020. Open until 1am.

Richard Branson's emporium shouts at you from the east side of the street. Branson realised a few years ago that it was cheaper to open a store than rent the space for an advertisement in this most famous of 'squares'. A *big* selection – and although the prices of CDs are not as keen as they once were, you'll still find a bargain or two.

Bryant Park: 42nd Street between 5th and 6th Avenues.

Walk east along 42nd Street and the most important thing to notice is how *clean* everything is compared to, say, 10 years ago. There's hardly a peep show left in the area. Even if you believe the area has become too sanitised – as some locals do – one undeniable improvement is the restoration of this open space to the public. Once full of bums and drug dealers, the park is now a wonderful retreat from the hustle and bustle of the streets and offers a range of free evening films during the summer months.

3 New York Public Library: 5th Avenue between 40th and 42nd Streets. Tel 212-930 0830. Open Mon to Thurs, Fri until 6pm; Tues, Wed until 7:30pm.

The public library is housed in 80 to 90 buildings, but it's this one, guarded by the lions, Patience and Fortitude, that everyone thinks of as the *real* library. Why should you go in? For the main reading room, where up to 700 can sit in splendid study, and for the exhibitions – usually very good, and free. See also page 47.

4 Grand Central Terminal: 42nd Street between Lexington and Vanderbilt Avenues. Open until 1am.

The uprising mass of this public palace is yet another example of New York's love affair with the *beaux arts* style. The main hall is truly spectacular: 375 feet long; 125 feet high; glass, marble, brass, and a vast starry night of painted ceiling. The entire station sports a just-finished cleaning and renovation. Only one small rectangle at the edge of the ceiling was left uncleaned: can you spot it? See also page 46.

Michael Jordan's Steakhouse: Gallery Level, Grand Central Terminal. Tel 212-655 2300. Open until 12:30am.

Have lunch, dinner or drinks here. The famous basketball player's restaurant overlooks the main floor of the station and is known for its immense porterhouse steaks.

Campbell Apartment Bar: Gallery Level, Grand Central Terminal. Tel 212-953 0409. Open until 1am.

The Campbell Apartment – only recently rediscovered – has been refurbished as a bar. It's up the narrow stairs on the other side of the gallery, and offers a cosy place for a drink.

MIDTOWN: ROCKEFELLER CENTER

If you are a conservative male, or travelling with someone who is, take this tour. Great men's clothiers are interspersed with great landmarks, and the tour ends with the promise of a drink.

1 Grand Central Terminal: 42nd Street between Lexington and Vanderbilt Avenues.

The food options in this temple to travel are truly amazing: from top-flight restaurants to the market. If you begin this itinerary in the afternoon you can treat yourself to a scrumptious frozen custard dessert at Custard Beach, tucked into the

northern side of the station's lower level. See also pages 46 and 90.

Once you've explored the station, head up the main stairs towards the gallery level and exit on to Vanderbilt Street, past Michael Jordan's restaurant.

2 Brooks Brothers: 346 Madison Avenue at East 44th Street. Tel 212-682 8800.

For 'button-down', read: East Coast Establishment. The phrase refers to button-collared shirts and denotes smartness, steadiness and conservatism. Time was, if you had any aspirations to any of those qualities, your shirts (and much more besides) probably came from this iconic men's clothier. Today, believe it or not, its parent company is Marks & Sparks and it has a full-scale women's department. Nevertheless, it's still a window on the American soul.

The shops on the Madison Avenue blocks immediately surrounding this store have traditionally dressed the American professional male: from Worth and Worth (hats) to Johnston and Murphy (shoes) to Paul Stuart (for everything in between).

3 Diamond Row: 47th Street between 5th and 6th Avenues.

As you walk north on 5th Avenue, sneak a peek into this, one of the world's most important diamond trading centres. Of all the diamonds in the United States, 80 per cent are cut, set, sold or prepared for sale here. Except for a couple of large retail stores, the action takes place in small stores and workshops, and the business is dominated by Orthodox Jews. You can feel the atmosphere of 'the deal' in the streets.

4 Osh Kosh B'Gosh: 586 5th Avenue between 47th and 48th Streets. Tel 212-827 0098.

Having loaded up with men's clobber, here's the place for boys and girls. Famous for its denim overalls, this iconic American brand is much cheaper here than back home.

5 Saks Fifth Avenue: 611 5th Avenue between 49th and 50th Streets. Tel 212-753 4000.

One of the world's most famous department stores, and still one of 5th Avenues' busiest (see page 115). Whatever you buy here, note two insider secrets: 1) there are lavatories (or restrooms, as they're known in America) on the sixth floor for men and the fourth floor for women; and 2) the eighth floor restaurant has great views of St Patrick's Cathedral and the Rockefeller Center ice rink. Standing outside this store gives you a near perfect view of 'Rock Center' across the street.

6 Rockefeller Center: West 48th to West 51st Streets between 5th and 6th Avenues. Tel 212-632 3975.

A total of 19 buildings make up this phenomenal city within a city. Building began in 1929 and – remarkably – continued throughout the Great Depression. Turn into the garden walkway, known as the Channel Gardens, directly opposite Saks. At the end, is the golden statue of Prometheus who holds his torch

over winter's ice-skating couples and summer's lunching lovers. Behind him, at Christmas, 5 miles of lights are strung on New York's favourite (and massive) tree. Radio City Music Hall, also part of the Center, is famous for its Christmas Spectacular and the legendary Rockettes.

Radio City Music Hall: 1260 6th Avenue at West 60th Street. Tel 212-247 4777 for show tickets and tours.

★★★★ INSIDE TRACK ★★★★
★ ★
★ Want a break? Search out one of ★
★ the two secret terraces above the ★
★ shopping atrium in Trump Tower ★
★ on the east side of 5th Avenue ★
★ between 56th and 57th Streets. ★
★★★★★★★★★★★★★★★★★★★★★★★

St Patrick's Cathedral: 5th Avenue between 50th and 51st Streets. Tel 212-753 2261.

This is America's largest Catholic church. Surrounded by skyscrapers, you need to go inside to realise its true scale – it seats 2,400.

7 The Villard Houses: 457 Madison Avenue between East 49th and East 50th Streets. Tel 212-935 3960 for Municipal Art Society and 212-935 3595 for Urban Center Books.

This wonderful amalgam of old and new comprises six brownstone houses and the soaring Palace Hotel. The left wing contains the Municipal Art Society, which offers some of the best architectural walking tours of the city, and a bookshop dedicated to architecture and urban planning - sounds boring, but in this city, it simply isn't. The right wing houses the stylish restaurant, Le Cirque.

8 The Cocktail Terrace/Sir Harry's/ Peacock Alley or The Bull and Bear: Waldorf-Astoria Hotel, 301 Park Avenue between East 49th and East 50th Streets. Tel 212-355 3000.

End your tour at the Waldorf-Astoria, with a well-deserved cocktail. The Cocktail Terrace overlooks the main lobby, has a piano, and is great for people-watching. Another possibility is Sir Harry's (a useful tip for night-owls is that it's open until 2:30 am). Peacock Alley has a lounge next to its fine restaurant. The Bull and Bear pours a decent drink and serves a decent steak.

MIDTOWN: PLAZA HOTEL

From 53rd Street to Central Park South lies the heart of Midtown. After visiting one of the world's most famous museums, you could bend your credit card seriously out of shape strolling up 5th Avenue. Note the jewellers at the corner of 5th Avenue and 56th Street, Harry Winston: they dressed Madonna in $20-million-worth of diamonds for the Oscars in 1991.

1 Museum of Modern Art (MoMA): 11 West 53rd Street between 5th and 6th Avenues. Tel 212-708 9480.

The museum is known to many as MoMA, but to the old guard as The Modern. It views itself as an attraction and, like many New York museums, sets out to entertain as well as educate. Incidentally, art

museums in New York are often what we would call galleries, whereas galleries in New York are shops that sell art. See also page 52.

2 University Club: 54th Street and 5th Avenue.

If you're at all interested in architecture, it will soon dawn on you that the firm of McKim, Mead & White was responsible for many of the city's most prized buildings, including The Morgan Library (see page 63) and the Villard Houses (see page 92). This 'small Renaissance palace' is a private club, but you can see some of the best interiors in New York from the pavement as the lights go on at dusk.

3 Tiffany & Co.: 727 5th Avenue at 57th Street. Tel 212-755 8000.

Passing the polished brass and bronze-tinted mirrors of Trump Plaza at 56th Street, you come to the much more sedate Tiffany's. You can't get breakfast here but you can find one or two things that are surprisingly affordable in this world-famous 5th Avenue store. And, boy, do they gift-wrap well. See also page 115.

57th Street: Many of the top brands in the world are here. You'll find the boutiques of Hermes, Chanel and Prada, and new retailing concepts like the temple to Nike, or the arcade of Warner Brothers. The Levis' store will even custom-cut your jeans. As you walk along 57th Street, don't forget to look up. You'll be rewarded by architecture like the remarkable ski-slope façade of 9 West 57th

Street, the number itself a hard-to-miss red sculpture smack in the middle of the sidewalk.

4 FAO Schwartz: 767 5th Avenue at 58th Street. Tel 212-644 9400.

Just past the very upmarket department store, Bergdorf Goodman (women's store on the west side, men's on the east side), you'll come to the best toy shop. If you are here with a child, you have to visit under pain of death. This is the place to buy the craze of the moment, or something so spectacular you'll reap Brownie points galore.

5 Plaza Hotel: 768 5th Avenue at 59th Street. Tel 212-759 3000.

Feeling foot-sore? Spent too much? Time for tea in the very gilt-laden lobby.

UPPER EAST AND UPPER WEST SIDES: MUSEUMS AND CENTRAL PARK

The Upper West Side is primarily a residential district. Unlike the Upper East Side, with its Madison Avenue shopping and Museum Mile, it has no immediately obvious, up-front lure for the visitor. But upon closer inspection, this area has a charm that would be sad to miss. And if it's any part of your plan to know the real Manhattan, then you need to understand that the Upper West Side is as affluent as the Upper East Side, but a tad more youthful, more liberal and less married. Certainly it's true that a person living on one side of Central Park would find it almost impossible to be transplanted to the

other. For the visitor, this area has the obvious mega-attractions, such as the American Museum of Natural History and the Lincoln Center. But there's also an atmosphere to absorb – the bars, the cafes, the slightly continental boulevard feel – and the following tour gives you an experience of both.

★★★★ **INSIDE TRACK** ★★★★

The fanfare surrounding the opening of the Museum of Natural History's Hayden Planetarium has resulted in long ticket lines. You can order tickets in advance for the Space Show at the planetarium, or for a specific IMAX film, lecture or event on 212-769-5200.

1 American Museum of Natural History: West 79th Street and Central Park West. Tel 212-769 5100.

This is the real thing – the kind of place that sends researchers through swamps, up mountains, and across deserts to discover such things as 80-million-year-old dinosaur eggs. It's the largest natural history museum in the world, with some 35 million objects and specimens, and an IMAX theatre, all crammed into 22 buildings sprawled over three city blocks. See page 55 for more details. The brand new Rose Center Hayden Planetarium is a multimedia spectacular, and one of the finest examples of the American trick of converting learning into entertainment.

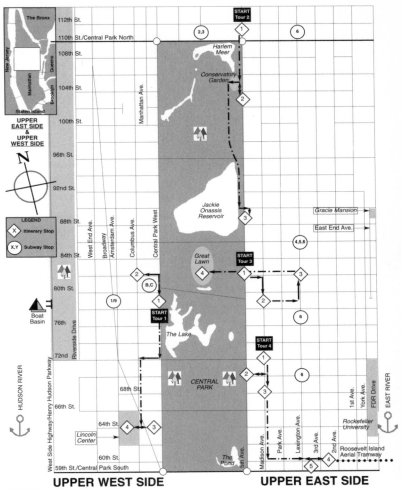

Legend:
- ⊗ X — Itinerary Stop
- ⊗ X,Y — Subway Stop

©2000 NYTAB, Inc.

UPPER WEST SIDE   **UPPER EAST SIDE**

4

2 Maxilla and Mandible:

451 Columbus Avenue between West 81st and West 82nd Streets. Tel 212-724 6173.

You can buy a real fossil here – a bone of your own. A most unusual shop, worth the small detour for that hard-to-please someone on your gift list.

Central Park West: Though it's easy to take a taxi to lunch, you can also walk the 15 blocks, following Central Park West.

Just below the Natural History Museum (at West 77th Street and Central Park West) is the neoclassical building of the New York Historical Society which, apart from being the city's oldest museum, has two collections of note: 150 Tiffany lamps and 432 original Audubon watercolours from *Birds of America*.

At the corner of West 72nd Street and Central Park West is the Dakota, one of the first, and certainly one of the most famous, apartment buildings in the city. When it was built, it was so far north of the city's boundaries that someone joked it was like living in Dakota – hence the name. Designed by Hardenberg, who later designed the Plaza Hotel (see page 172), the building's apartments are massive, and have housed many artists, such as Leonard Bernstein, Boris Karloff and Judy Garland. It was also the location for Roman Polanski's film, *Rosemary's Baby*.

One famous resident, John Lennon of the Beatles, was shot dead in front of this building in December 1980 by a deranged fan. His widow, Yoko Ono, still lives here. Just opposite, in Central Park, is the garden she created as a memorial, Strawberry Fields. It is shaped like a tear. Sadly, the original 25,000 strawberry plants were quickly eaten by birds. But 161 different varieties of plants and trees (representing the number of countries in the world at the time) remain.

Columbus Avenue: Turn right from Central Park West and continue down Columbus Avenue. Along with Broadway and Amsterdam, this street is one of the neighbourhood's main boulevards, lined with shops, bars, cafés and other local haunts for you to discover.

3 Picholine: 35 West 64th Street between Broadway and CPW. Tel 212-724 8585.

This is one of the finest restaurants in the city, worth every penny in every way. At lunch, your pennies go very far indeed with the $24 *prix fixe* menu, so treat yourself. By the way, the chef, Terrance Brennan, is famous for his love of cheeses (see page 153 in Restaurants chapter), and the cheese selection is consequently huge. Dress: smart casual.

4 Lincoln Center: Broadway between West 62nd and West 66th Streets. Tel 212-769 7020 (for Visitor Services guided tours), 212-769 7406 (for Juilliard School of Music) and 212-875 5030 (for New York Philharmonic).

This is the largest performing arts complex in the country and houses some of the best talent in the world, from opera to orchestral and from ballet to jazz. Even if you have no plans to attend a performance, take a tour. There are sculptures by Rodin and Henry Moore, paintings by Chagall and the New York State Theater was designed by the 94-year-old architectural aristocrat, Philip Johnson.

If you're skipping lunch, the world-famous Julliard School offers a free, and calorie-free, alternative: 1-hour chamber music concerts on Wednesdays at 1pm in Alice Tully Hall. This is during term time only, so call ahead to double check.

Alternatively, reverse this itinerary and sit in on the New York

Philharmonic's rehearsals at 9.45am Thursday (and, occasionally Wednesday) mornings for $12.

★★★★ **INSIDE TRACK** ★★★★

You don't have to shell out the big bucks to experience the marvel that is the Metropolitan Opera. Family circle tickets sell for just $25 and though you practically need binoculars from that height, many say the sound quality is the best in the house.

UPPER EAST AND UPPER WEST SIDES: 5TH AVENUE

The solid facades of the apartment buildings that march up 5th and Park Avenues are known as 'white glove' buildings, after the livery of their doormen, and conceal some of the most opulent and expensive real estate on earth. Between these two residential avenues, Madison Avenue caters to almost every shopping whim. Because of the area's wealth, it is sometimes known as the 'silk stocking district'.

★★★★ **INSIDE TRACK** ★★★★

Don't attempt these tours on a Monday, as you'll find several museums closed. Also remember when visiting museums (as well as shops) that the ground floor is called the first floor in America; the first floor is called the second, etc.

Many of the city's museums are to be found along 5th Avenue. Most face Central Park, although the

mighty Metropolitan (see page 53) is *in* it. The itineraries below combine this richness of couture and culture with the green, restful assets of the park. Each also includes a place for a bite to eat.

1 Emily's: 1325 5th Avenue between 111th and 112th Streets. Tel 212-996 1212.

We suggest you start this tour on a Friday or Saturday, preferably with a late lunch. This insider's secret has perhaps the best Southern fried chicken in town. Oh, and the ribs! Good at any time of year, but if you're travelling in winter, lunch here will stoke up the furnace nicely for the walk ahead.

2 Museum of the City of New York: 1220 5th Avenue at East 103rd Street. Tel 212-534 1672. Discount with your NYCard.

If New York and its history is beginning to intrigue or even fascinate you, then this museum is one not to miss. The constant battle with fire, notable interiors, great toy and Broadway and silver collections, thousands of photographs – it's the detail that creates the big and accurate picture. See also page 64.

★★★★ **INSIDE TRACK** ★★★★

Not only will you get two for one admission with your NYCard at the Museum of the City of New York, but, if you're travelling in a group, take advantage of their 'family entrance price' of $9. They interpret 'family' very loosely and any friendly group of under six people qualifies.

4

Conservatory Garden: 5th Avenue at 105th Street.

Cross 5th Avenue and enter Central Park through the Vanderbilt Gate at 105th Street. This is one of the few formally laid-out areas of the park. Stroll southwards towards the reservoir. A little known fact (just in case you are nervous of getting lost) is that the lampposts all have a plate with a four-digit number on them. The first two digits indicate the approximate cross street. So, 9712 would mean you have reached the level of 97th Street near the top end of the reservoir. If you prefer not to walk, catch a cab the 15 or so blocks to the Guggenheim Museum.

★★★★ ★★★★
★ **The New York Road Runners Club** ★
★ **has an all-season schedule and** ★
★ **welcomes visiting joggers.** ★
★ **Tel 212-860 4455.** ★
★ ★
★★★★★★★★★★★★★★★★★★★★★★

The Reservoir: Between 86th and 96th Streets.

Central Park consists of 843 acres of 'pastoral scenery' in the English romantic tradition. 20,000 workers blasted, dug and planted what has become Manhattan's lung. It opened in 1859 and, today, it would only qualify as pastoral if you're used to the countryside being full of roller-bladers, skateboarders, bicyclists, joggers, the sports-inclined, the tai chi-inclined and the simply reclined. And yet, with all the activity, the place is still a restful retreat. The reservoir stopped being a part of the city's water supply in 1993. The 106-acre expanse of water (40 feet deep and a billion gallons of it) is a favourite backdrop for joggers.

3 Guggenheim Museum: 1071 5th Avenue at East 89th Street. Tel 212-535 7710. Discount with your NYCard.

Leave the park via Engineers Gate at 90th Street and head for one of the most recognisable gallery buildings in the world. Designed by Frank Lloyd Wright, this remarkable spiral has important permanent collections of modern art (eg over 200 Kandinskys). It also mounts some stellar shows like last year's highly acclaimed motorcycle exhibition. In other words, though 'cutting edge' it does not use intellectual snobbery to push you off the cliff. See also page 59.

★★★★ ★★★★
★ **You will see that we suggest** ★
★ **visiting the Guggenheim late on a** ★
★ **Friday or Saturday afternoon.** ★
★ **Note, however, that this is the first** ★
★ **museum to open (at 9am), so if** ★
★ **you're jet-lagged and up early,** ★
★ **take advantage of the calm.** ★
★★★★★★★★★★★★★★★★★★★★★★

If you followed our suggestion and are taking this tour on a Friday or Saturday, you are in for a treat. On those nights from 5pm to 8pm, the museum turns into a world-jazz club. There's a full bar and snacks, and it's free with museum admission.

Above: Hansom cab ride

Right: West Village

Below: Greenwich Village

Bottom: Midtown 57th Street

Views of Central Park including a summer concert (right) and dining at the Central Park boathouse (below)

Above left: Metropolitan Museum of Art

Above right: The Intrepid Sea, Air, Space Museum

Below right: The Frick Collection

Below left: Lower East Side Tenement Museum

Bottom: The Time Warner Center at the Children's Museum

Above: Fashion Avenue

Above right: Fifth Avenue

Right: Trump Tower

Below right: Macy's

Bottom right: Bloomingdale's

Below: The Garment District

UPPER EAST AND UPPER WEST SIDES: METROPOLITAN MUSEUM

This tour takes in one of the most important museums in the world, the Metropolitan.

1 Metropolitan Museum of Art: 5th Avenue and East 82nd Street. Tel 212-879 5500.

Millions of objects covering 5,000 years of history spread over 1.5 million square feet – you do not 'do' this museum, you'd die trying. We have set out one suggested plan of attack below, but the trick is to know what you want to see, and learn how to get there. Pick up a museum map at the entrance and formulate your planned itinerary in advance. You can strategise on the balcony above the Great Hall, there are concerts on Friday and Saturday evenings, and a bar, from 4pm to 8pm. See also page 53.

A must is the Temple of Dendur on the ground floor. The Egyptian section is renowned and this temple, given by the Egyptian government and rebuilt here stone by stone, is truly superb.

Perhaps then, you could pick out some single (magnificent) object, like *The Harp Player,* which dates from the third century BC, in the Greek and Roman Antiquities section, also on the ground floor.

The delightful Costume Institute on the lower level, with its 45,000 costumes, and the American Wing on the ground floor, are both reached through the Egyptian section. American art (except for a couple of biggies like Sargent) is often given short shrift in European museums, but here it really shines. Our two favourites are the reconstruction of the living room of Frank Lloyd Wright's Little House, and the bucolic paintings of the Hudson River School – very New York. There are Sargents here too, notably *Madame X.*

In the comprehensive European art section, choose just one or two pictures from one or two countries. How about Vermeer's *Woman With A Jug* or Cézanne's *Cardplayers* on the first floor?

Take it as a given that the museum has examples of everything, but head straight for things that interest you: musical instruments (first floor), medieval art (first floor), African, American Indian and Oceanic art (ground floor), Asian art (first floor), Oriental antiquities (first floor) – it's all here, and will still be here the next time you visit.

2 Serafina Fabulous Pizza: 1022 Madison Avenue at East 79th Street. Tel 212-734 2676.

Stroll across to the corner of Madison Avenue and 79th Street. This is super quality pizza. There are beautiful people and the glazed-in roof terrace (walk up one more floor) is the place to head for. Try the Margherita Pizza and its ultra-thin crust. You may find another international traveller, but you won't find a tourist in this chic spot.

3 Big City Kite: 1210 Lexington Avenue at East 82nd Street. Tel 212-472 2623.

Now, you have a mission – and you don't need children to fulfil it. Go fly a kite! Big City Kite is a treasure trove of designs. Finding one that suits your character and whim, and flying it (or attempting to fly it) in one of the world's great urban open spaces will be a real and treasured New York memory. As a souvenir it isn't hard to pack, either. Trust us on this.

Great Lawn: This is where you fly your kite, in the centre of over 800 acres of green.

As you head south out of the park, spend a few minutes to find one oddity that most people never discover but which has been known to startle the occasional jogger: the bronze cat that lurks without pedestal or warning in the high foliage above the East Drive at about East 76th Street. It's been here since 1881, sculpted by a man called Edward Kemeys who worked for the Parks Department. He had a love for native animals, especially felines. This sculpture (called *Still Hunt*) represents an American mountain lion.

★★★★ INSIDE TRACK ★★★★
If you'd like to picnic in Central Park, Grace's Marketplace, 1237 3rd Avenue at East 71st Street, is the place to go for a really gourmet spread.

UPPER EAST AND WEST SIDES: MADISON AVENUE

Madison Avenue may mean advertising to some, but on the Upper East Side, it's pure shopping. High quality, high style, and often (but not always) high price. You'll find the very tip-top international and American designers, and this tour walks you down Madison's prime stretch. The time you take poking in and out of the shops depends on your own stamina and interest, but whatever your timing preference, do take the detour to the Frick Collection, one of the most enjoyable museums in the city.

★★★★ INSIDE TRACK ★★★★
The Roosevelt Island Aerial Tramway is in no way a tourist attraction, but does give some wonderful views of the East Side's skyscrapers. All you pay is the standard subway or bus fare of $1.50. It departs every 15 minutes from 2nd Avenue at 60th Street. Tel 212-832 4543.

1 Ralph Lauren: 867 Madison Avenue at East 72nd Street. Tel 212-606 2100.

Ralph Lauren may have based much of his lines and lifestyle ideas on old English themes, but he has by now made them all his own. This shop, his flagship, was once a private house, and the clothing, mixed in with silver snuff boxes, walking canes and linens, is draped on and around fireplaces, old leather armchairs and deep-pile rugs. You might find something you actually want here. And in terms of merchandising, this is a clever, class act.

2 Frick Collection: 1 East 70th Street at 5th Avenue. Tel 212-288 0700.

The American experiment has proved highly successful in creating individuals of great wealth and influence. Astor, Rockefeller, Carnegie, Morgan and Frick are some of the names that built much of New York's landscape and its culture. You'll find their names on libraries, universities, concert halls, museums and art galleries all over New York.

Henry Clay Frick may have made his millions in coal, but he's remembered for the oils he left behind (a world-class collection of Fragonard, Turner, Rembrandt, etc.) – and the furniture and the porcelains and the sculpture. The joy of the Frick Collection is that it is still housed in the mansion he had built for himself when he moved to the city in 1900. This not only gives you a sense of the scale on which these people lived, but also makes the collections more accessible and more personal. For a break, sit a while near the peaceful indoor reflecting pool. See also page 59.

3 Billy Martin's Western Wear: 810 Madison Avenue at East 68th Street. Tel 212-861 3100.

If anyone can upmarket the cowboy, it's Madison Avenue. This is a very American shop, and a great place for getting in touch with your inner Wild West self.

4 Serendipity 3: 225 East 60th Street between 2nd and 3rd Avenues. Tel 212-838 3531.

Don't be fooled. Make your way through the toy shop (you'll have time for it later) to one of the round tables in the back. Order a caviar omelette, or maybe a foot-long hot dog, or maybe a Forbidden Broadway sundae (Blackout Cake, hot fudge, and oh, so much more). You might even spot Mariah Carey or some other Upper East Side celebrity, brought here as a child and unable to break the habit.

5 Bloomingdale's: 1000 3rd Avenue between East 59th and East 60th Streets. Tel 212-705 2000.

★★★★ **INSIDE TRACK** ★★★★
Even though its address is on 3rd Avenue, Bloomingdale's is a full block wide, so you can enter on both Third and Lexington Avenues. On the mezzanine just above the Lexington Avenue entrance is the Visitors' Services Desk, where you can get a free gift with any purchase if you show your NYCard.

Bloomingdale's has been a part of city life since April, 1872. Just about every New Yorker finds a need to visit here at one time or another, and many on the Upper East Side treat it as their all- purpose general store, for everything from kettles to evening gowns. If you haven't yet found that perfectly off-beat gift for your nieces, you'll find knickers here with 'Bloomie's' printed across the front. See also page 114.

UPPER MANHATTAN

Harlem's reputation as being unsafe is very out of date. In fact, the area is undergoing something of a boom. There's a lot to do and see north of Central Park, and it's not possible to string everything comfortably together in a single walking tour. The area we're covering here is, in fact, very large, and is made up of several neighbourhoods from Inwood, at the very north of Manhattan, to Morningside Heights just above Central Park. There are at least two Harlems: Black Harlem centres around 125th Street and Lenox Avenue, and Spanish Harlem is on the east side of Central Park. We suggest you either choose one point of interest or one 'mini tour' at a time, or take an organised bus tour of the whole area. We've provided a map with more detail to guide you.

1 The Cloisters: Fort Tryon Park. Tel 212-923 3700.

The number 4 bus (which runs on Madison Avenue) takes you directly to the Cloisters and gives you quite a nice sightseeing trip on the way. Alternatively, the number A subway train stops at 190th Street and Fort Washington Avenue, with the museum a few minutes' walk through pretty Fort Tryon Park.

This is an outpost of the Metropolitan Museum and a true jewel – five French medieval cloisters melded together on a perch high above the Hudson River. There are herb gardens, tapestries and sculpture. It's simply beautiful. See also page 62.

2 Dyckman Farmhouse: West 204th Street and Broadway. Tel 212-360 8203 (call ahead for opening hours).

While you're in the area, drop by this small and free museum. It's the last remaining farmhouse in Manhattan and takes you straight back to Colonial times.

Harlem Spirituals: 690 8th Avenue (between West 43rd and West 44th Streets). Tel 212-391-0900. Discount with your NYCard.

This company – the only bus tour company that NYTAB recommends – offers gospel and jazz tours with guides that actually know what they're talking about. The various packages take in the things we list here and more. See also page 49.

3 Morris Jumel Mansion: 65 Jumel Terrace (between West 160th Street and Edgecombe Avenue). Tel 212-928 8008. Discount with your NYCard.

The oldest house in Manhattan (1765), it was briefly the headquarters of George Washington during the American's fight against the British. The big white clapboard house is just north of Sugar Hill, which extends from about 145th to 155th Streets, and which became the very comfortable neighbourhood of the black middle class. Duke Ellington, Count Basie, Cab Calloway and the boxer Sugar Ray Robinson all lived in this area, enjoying the 'sweet life'. See also page 47.

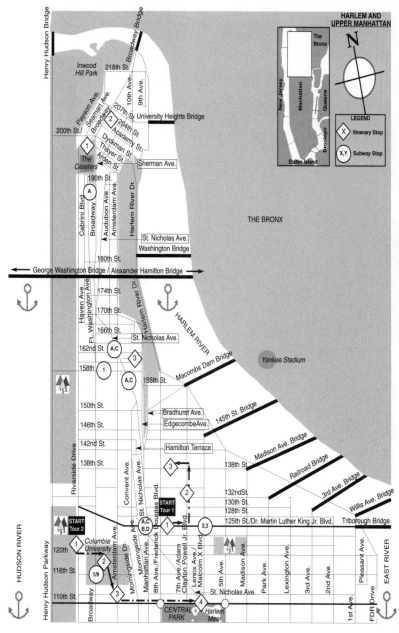

HARLEM AND
UPPER MANHATTAN

LEGEND

ⓧ Itinerary Stop

ⓍⓎ Subway Stop

Henry Hudson Bridge

Inwood
Hill Park

218th St.

Broadway Bridge

10th Ave.

9th Ave.

University Heights Bridge

207th St.

204th St.

Academy St.

Payson Ave.

Seaman Ave.

Broadway

200th St.

Dyckman St.

Thayer St.

Arden St.

Sherman Ave.

The
Cloisters

190th St.

Ⓐ

Cabrini Blvd.

Broadway

Audubon Ave.

Amsterdam Ave.

Harlem River Dr.

St. Nicholas Ave.

Washington Bridge

180th St.

← George Washington Bridge / Alexander Hamilton Bridge →

THE BRONX

Haven Ave.

Ft. Washington Ave.

174th St.

170th St.

166th St.

St. Nicholas Ave.

162nd St. Ⓐ,Ⓒ

③

HARLEM RIVER

Harlem River Dr.

158th ①

Ⓐ,Ⓒ 155th St.

Macombs Dam Bridge

Yankee Stadium

150th St.

146th St.

Bradhurst Ave.

EdgecombeAve.

142nd St.

Hamilton Terrace

145th St. Bridge

138th St.

③

Madison Ave. Bridge

Riverside Drive

Convent Ave.

St. Nicholas Ave.

138th St

132ndSt.

②

Railroad Bridge

3rd Ave. Bridge

130th St.

128th St.

START
Tour 1

Ⓐ,Ⓒ
Ⓑ,Ⓓ

①

②,③

125th St./Dr. Martin Luther King Jr. Blvd.

Willis Ave. Bridge

Triborough Bridge

HUDSON RIVER

Henry Hudson Parkway

START
Tour 2

①

Columbia
University

120th St.

②

116th St.

①/⑨

③

Broadway

Amsterdam Ave.

Morningside Dr.

Manhattan Ave.

Morningside Ave.

8th Ave./Frederick Douglas Blvd.

7th Ave./Adam
Clayton Powell Jr. Blvd.

Lenox Ave. /
Malcolm X Blvd.

5th Ave.

Madison Ave.

Park Ave.

Lexington Ave.

3rd Ave.

2nd Ave.

1st Ave.

Pleasant Ave.

FDR Drive

EAST RIVER

110th St.

St. Nicholas Ave.

CENTRAL
PARK

④ Harlem
Meer

New Jersey

Manhattan

Queens

Brooklyn

Staten Island

The
Bronx

N

©2000 NYTAB, Inc.

4

HARLEM MINI TOUR

1 Apollo Theatre: 253 West 125th Street between Adam Clayton Powell Jnr and Frederick Douglas Boulevards. Tel 212-531 5300 for tour information and show tickets.

This is now a television studio, but still holds the famous Amateur Nights on Wednesdays. For decades after it began putting on live shows in the 1930s, the Apollo could justly be called the world's showcase for black musical talent. Lena Horne, Sarah Vaughan and James Brown – among an astonishing list of greats – got their start here. Even today, if 125th Street is Harlem's High Street, then the Apollo is the Town Hall. Tours of the landmark are very entertaining.

INSIDE TRACK

★★★★ ★★★★
★ If you go to a baseball game, the
★ best way to get to Yankee
★ Stadium is by NY Waterway ferry.
★ Leave from South Street Seaport
★ and sail up the East and Harlem
★ Rivers. NY Waterway will even sell
★ you a complete package of
★ transport, game tickets plus
★ extras. Tel 800-533 3779.

2 Well's: 2247 Adam Clayton Powell Jnr Boulevard between West 132nd and West 133rd Streets. Tel 212-234 0700.

Famous for Mrs Well's crispy-fried-chicken-and-waffles-with-strawberry-butter dish, this place also has a popular Sunday gospel brunch.

3 Striver's Row: West 138th and West 139th Streets between Adam Clayton Powell Jnr and Frederick Douglas Boulevards.

After your stick-to-the-ribs fare, take a short stroll up to Striver's Row. Named, aptly enough, for those who had strived successfully for middle-class status, the block is one of the prettiest in Harlem.

MORNINGSIDE HEIGHTS MINI TOUR

1 Riverside Church: Riverside Drive between West 120th and West 122nd Streets. Tel 212-222 5974.

This church seems to shoot skywards using skyscraper, steel-framed technology. It's noted for its stone carving, stained glass and 74-bell carillon – the largest in the world. But it's actually the church's lofty position in Riverside Park by the Hudson River that makes this a really worthwhile destination. The observation platform, 108 metres (355 feet) up with stunning views, is a bit of a secret.

2 Grant's Tomb: Riverside Park at West 122nd Street.

The rather grand, tiered affair you may spot just north of Riverside Church was, until the First World War, one of New York City's most important attractions. Although Grant was elected President in 1868, it was his performance as a soldier and strategist in the Civil War that ensured his place in the memory of the nation. He's the only president to be buried in New York City.

3 Columbia University: Broadway and West 116th Street. Tel 212-854 1754.

This is the surprisingly peaceful campus of one of America's elite 'Ivy League' universities. There's a pretty main quadrangle and a very grand library building.

4 St John the Divine: 1047 Amsterdam Avenue at West 112th Street. Tel 212-316 7540.

The largest church in the US is still growing. The first stone was laid in 1891, but it will probably be another 20 years before the final piece of masonry is dressed! The main vault is 37 metres (124 feet) high and 183 metres (601 feet) long – impressive.

5 Make My Cake: 103 West 110th Street at Lenox Avenue. Tel 212-932 0833.

New York has some famous cheesecake bakers but the owners of this shop, the Baylor family, have put their own delicious spin on the classic. Their speciality is sweet potato cheesecake and it's a must-try.

CHAPTER 5

A Taste of the Outer Boroughs

or those with limited time in New York, you may not be able to get as far as the outer boroughs of the Bronx, Queens', Brooklyn and Staten Island. However, here is just a taste of some of the sights you can enjoy in the first three of these areas if you have just that bit extra time to spare. Of course, you can pick and choose if you are trying to cram a lot into your days in the city.

A TASTE OF THE BRONX

The Bronx has a scary reputation, but parts of it are very safe and have attractions that make a visit to the area well worthwhile. The Bronx history dates back to 1609 when Henry Hudson took refuge from a storm there. It is the northernmost borough of New York and the only one on the mainland. In 1639 Jonas Bronck, a Swedish captain from the Netherlands, settled here with his wife and servants. The story goes that when people left Manhattan to visit the family, they would say they were going to the Bronck's and the name stuck.

The really horrible part is the south Bronx, but even there things are slowly improving. The northern part is home to the famous **New York Yankees,** a beautiful botanical garden that includes a huge chunk

of the original forests that once covered all of New York, and **The Bronx Zoo** (see page 41), one of the leading wildlife conservation parks in the world. The best days to visit are Thursday or Friday when the Bronx Museum of Art opens at 10am. If you go any other day, arrive in time for the Yankee Stadium tour at noon.

Yankee Stadium: River Avenue at 161st Street. Tel 718-293 4300. Arrive via the 4 or D train. Tours start at noon daily Mon to Sat. No reservations needed. Tickets $8 adults, $4 under 15s.

Sporting aficionados will be delighted to see the tribute to past players, the field, dugout, clubhouse, locker room and press box.

New York Botanical Gardens: Southern Boulevard at 200th Street. Tel 718-817 8700. If going there direct, take the C, D or 4 subway to Bedford Park and then the BX36 bus. Entrance summer $3, under sixes free; winter $1.50.

Originally supported by magnates Cornelius Vanderbilt, Andrew Carnegie and JP Morgan, society folk still support it today. The iron and glass conservatory, which was modelled on the one at Kew Gardens, has recently been refurbished to shimmering perfection. The grounds include the stunning Bronx River Gorge where the meandering waterway tumbles over rocky outcroppings formed by the retreat of the Wisconsin Ice Sheet.

★★★★ **INSIDE TRACK** ★★★★

★ For thousands of years New York
★ was covered by a hemlock forest
★ and a 40-acre fragment remains
★ in the Botanical Gardens. Look
★ for the petroglyph rock carving of
★ a turtle drawn by the
★ Weckquasgeek Indians.

Little Italy: Take the D train to Tremont Avenue and walk east to Arthur Avenue. Treat yourself to lunch at one of the many restaurants where you can eat fresh pasta, nibble pastries and sip cappuccino. The old-world Belmont District is a charming area filled with shops selling every Italian delicacy plus the **Enrico Fermi Cultural Center** in the Belmont Library (610 East 186th Street, tel 718-933 6410) and the old **Belmont Italian American Theater** (2385 Arthur Avenue, tel 718-364 4700) which still shows films. Afterwards, walk north on Arthur, then east on Fordham Road past Fordham University to the **Bronx Park.**

The Bronx Zoo/Wildlife Conservation Society: Bronx River Parkway and Fordham Road. Tel 718-367 1010, or see their website at **www.wcs.org** Entrance $6.75 adults, $3 under 12s.

The largest urban zoo in America, it houses 4,000 animals – 650 species – in naturalistic habitats and has just completed a multi-million-dollar expansion of the ape and monkey environment. Here you can ride a camel, walk through the Congo to board the Bengali Express for an unforgettable train ride to the heart of Asia.

★★★★ **INSIDE TRACK** ★★★★

★ Note for anglers, don't miss City
★ Island – just one and three
★ quarter miles long, this little gem
★ is actually part of the Bronx,
★ though you'd hardly believe it.
★ It's filled with sail makers, wharf-
★ side tables serving calamari or
★ clam chowder and antique
★ boutiques. Here you can go
★ fishing for blackfish or flounder
★ in the Long Island Sound. Serious
★ anglers can charter the Apache
★ (tel. 718-885 0843) or the
★ Riptide (tel 718-885 0236).

For more information on attractions in The Bronx you can contact the **Bronx Tourism Council** on 718-590 3518 or look at their website at **www.ilovethebronx.com**

Bronx Museum of the Arts: 1040 Grand Concourse. Tel 718-681 6000. Entrance $3 adults, under 12s free.

Housed in an attractive glass building, the museum's collection consists of more than 700 contemporary works of art in all media by African, Asian and Latin American artists.

A TASTE OF QUEENS

The largest of all the New York boroughs, Queens has the highest percentage of first-generation immigrants. There are many distinct areas though the most important in terms of attractions are Astoria, Jackson Heights, Jamaica, Flushing and Corona.

Given the borough's suburban look, it is hard to imagine it as the densely forested area it was four centuries ago, inhabited by the Algonquian Indian tribes who fished in its freshwater streams and creeks, hunted game and gathered shellfish from its bays. It is also difficult to picture 17th-century Queens and its early Dutch and English farmers, along with Quakers, fighting for religious freedom.

Yet there remain places where such scenes can be easily reconstructed such as **The Jamaica Bay Wildlife Refuge** (tel 718-318 4340) with its open marshlands that were once the territory of Jameco Indians and which are now home to many species of birds and **The Queens County Farm House Museum** (73-50 Little Neck Parkway, Floral Park, tel 718-347 FARM). That has the largest tract of farmland left in New York and its colonial farmhouse is thought to date back to 1772.

Today Queens is as much about the ethnic diversity of the borough, though, and in each of the places you can visit with this itinerary, you will find many examples of the cultures of people from Asia, the West Indies, Latin America and Greece. To start your day, take the International Express – 7 subway train – from Times Square to the 74th Street-Broadway station.

Little India: 74th Street between Roosevelt and 37th Avenues at Jamaica Heights.

Here you can stroll through the cumin-infused streets looking at the intricately embellished gold and silk on display. Two stops should include the **Menka Beauty Salon** (37–56 74th Street, tel 718-424 6851) where traditional henna designs are drawn on the skin, and the **Butala Emporium** (37–46 74th Street, tel 718-899 5590), which sells everything from Southern Asian art and children's books in Punjabi to Ayurvedic medicine and religious items.

Lunch: Travel one stop to 82nd Street in Elmhurst for an Argentinian lunch at **La Fusta** (80–32 Baxter Avenue, tel 718-429 8222) or two stops to the 90th Street station for Peruvian fare at **Inti Raymi** (86–14 37th Avenue, tel 718-424 1938).

Queens Museum of Art: New York City Building, Flushing Meadows–Corona Park, tel 7198-592 9700. Subway 7 to Willets Point-Shea Stadium. Entrance $3.

Most famous exhibit here is the miniature scale model of the entire city of New York City, which turns dark every 15 minutes, complete with miniature lights, and also has aeroplanes flying into the airports. You can rent binoculars to check out

All that jazz ...

For jazz lovers there is a new tour, **The Queens Jazz Trail,** that shows you the homes of the jazz greats, their haunts and culture. Call Flushing Town Hall for information on 718-463 7700. It's a great tour even if you aren't a real jazz buff as it gives an insight into the lifestyles of another era. The tour includes a visit to the newly opened home of Louis Armstrong, the Louis Armstrong archives at Queen's University (watch out for the fantastic views of Manhattan's skyline) and the Addisleigh Park area, home to celebrated sports stars and top jazz and pop entertainers including Ella Fitzgerald, Lena Horne, Count Basie, Billie Holliday, Milt Hinton and Thomas 'Fats' Waller. Other famous musicians, who lived in different parts of Queens, include Dizzy Gillespie, Bix Beiderbecke, Glenn Miller and Tony Bennett. The tour includes a delicious traditional soul-food lunch or dinner and a jazz concert at the newly renovated concert hall at Flushing Town Hall.

If jazz really is your thing, then avoid the tourist-trap venues on Manhattan and head out to Queens for a cheap jazz night out. Underground clubs include **Carmichael's Diner,** 117–08 Guy Brewer Boulevard, Jamaica. Tel 718-224 1360. Entrance $10. Open 8-10.30pm on Wednesday nights. The action takes place in the basement. Be warned: there are no signs, but it definitely happens! You should also contact **Flushing Town Hall** (137-35 Northern Boulevard, Flushing, tel 718-463 7700) for details of forthcoming jazz concerts and the **Cultural Collaborative Jamaica** (Jamaica Avenue and 153rd Street, Jamaica, tel 718-526 3217). Not only is it cheaper to get into venues in Queens, but you can also usually stay for both 'sets' rather than being forced to leave after just one.

where you're staying. The museum is on the site of the 1964–65 World Fair and has had a recent $15-million renovation.

Shea Stadium: Tel 718-507 6387.

Stroll through Corona Park to the home of the Mets baseball team. On the way you will see huge remnants of both the 1939 and the 1964 World Fairs, plus a series of weird buildings including the New York Hall of Science. The park also has barbecue pits and boating on the lake. This is also the home of the US Open's Flushing Meadows.

Bowne House: 37–01 Bowne Street, Flushing. Tel 718-359 0528. Entrance adults $2, children $1.

You can walk to this NYC landmark from the park. Built in 1661 by John Bowne, it is a rare example of Dutch-English architecture with an unusual collection of decorative arts, painting and furniture, all of which belong to nine generations of the Bowne family. Bowne was a pivotal figure in the fight for religious freedom in the New World.

Queens Botanical Garden: 43–50 Main Street, Flushing. Tel 718-886 3800. Entrance free.

Walk back to the north-east corner of Corona Park to see the 39 acres that were created for the 1939 World Fair.

Little Asia: Roosevelt Avenue and Main Street. The nearby jumble of Chinese, Korean, Thai and Vietnamese markets and restaurants offer everything from soft-shell turtles, bentwood bows, kimchi and wire baskets. At 45–37 Bowne Street is the beautiful Hindu Temple Society of North America building, which is adorned with carvings of Hindu gods.

★★★★ **INSIDE TRACK** ★★★★

Cabs are not as plentiful in the outer boroughs as in Manhattan. If an unmetered taxi pulls up, make sure it is a TL&C registered vehicle and agree to the fare before getting in.

Dinner: Choopan Kabab House, 42–47 Main Street. Tel 718-539 3180.

A great place to try out Afghan fare. Alternatively, sample Korean food at **Kum Kang San**, 138–28 Northern Boulevard, tel 718-461 0909.

Nightclubs: Try **Chibcha**, 79–95 Roosevelt Avenue, tel 718-429 9033, subway 7 to 82nd Street, a Columbian nightclub and restaurant. Or, if you prefer, Sunday night is Irish music night at **Taylor Hall,** 45–15 Queens Boulevard, subway 7 to 46th Street. For something more exotic, there are operettas, flamenco and tango shows at the **Thalia Spanish Theater,** 41–17 Greenpoint Avenue. Tel 718-729 3880. Subway 7 to 40th Street. For more information contact the Queens Council on the Arts on 718-647 3377 or check the website at **www.queenscouncilarts.org**

STATEN ISLAND

With its picturesque scenery, Staten Island deserves its Indian name 'Monacnong', which means 'enchanted woods'. This is where New Yorkers go to relax and escape the hustle and bustle of the city, and it's easy to reach by ferry or bus.

If you only have a few days in New York, you may not be able to squeeze in a visit, although you should try to fit in a trip on the Staten Island Ferry, which leaves Manhattan Island from Battery Park (see page 44) and offers brilliant views of Downtown and the Statue of Liberty.

If you do get to the island, you can enjoy relaxing on the beaches or in the parks, or enjoy a round of golf. You might want to visit Staten Island's Children's Museum (see page 68), or Historic Richmond Town (Tel 718-351 1611) where you can get a glimpse of daily life on the island in a bygone era.

A TASTE OF BROOKLYN

Brooklyn Museum of Art: 200 Eastern Parkway at Washington Avenue, Brooklyn, tel 718-638 5000. Take subway 2 or 3 to Eastern Parkway. The museum is open from 10am to 5pm Wednesday to Friday, from 11am to 6pm Saturday and Sunday, so you can either go in the morning or afternoon depending on whether you'd like lunch or dinner at my restaurant choice that follows: the River Café. On the first Saturday of each month, it's open until 11pm with free musical entertainment. This museum, housed in a fabulous Beaux Arts building, is a little-known treasure of New York and, unlike the Metropolitan, won't be packed with crowds of tourists. Despite this, it has wonderful collections including the Rodin sculpture court, which is surrounded by works of art by Monet and Degas, the Egyptian Galleries, the African art and pre-Colombian textile galleries and a superb Native American collection.

River Café: 1 Water Street at Cadman Plaza West, tel 718-522 5200. Fine restaurant by the water's edge. The building is hardly imposing yet once inside it's a refined and elegant setting to soak up fantastic views of the Manhattan skyline. Night time is best – the twinkling lights in the skyscrapers look just like a picture postcard. Have a drink at the bar to enjoy the best views before tucking into a sumptuous supper. It is expensive and you will have to book in advance, but it's an experience you'll never forget. Jackets are essential after 5pm.

Brooklyn Bridge: Whether you've had lunch or dinner, a walk across the stunning Brooklyn Bridge will certainly help the digestive system. It's the most famous bridge in New York and was the world's largest suspension bridge when it was completed in 1883. The views are fantastic and strolling along the wooden pedestrian walkway gives an insight into why it took 16 years to build.

CHAPTER 6

Shopping

Well, it's one of the main reasons Brits cite for visiting New York and it definitely lives up to its reputation. Here you can get a taste of fantastic American service at any of the fabulous and famous department stores, and shop until you drop for cheaper CDs, clothes, shoes, cameras, books and a thousand and one novelty items that you didn't know you needed until you saw them. Although New York City does have real American malls like the one at the South Street Seaport, it is better known the hundreds of boutiques selling everything from designer clothes to retro vintage items, household goods and antiques.

Just as each New York neighbourhood has its own distinct atmosphere, so that is reflected in the type of shopping available in the different areas. The upper section of **5th Avenue** in the Midtown area is where you will find all the top department stores and other posh shops. Even posher – well, exclusive, actually – is **Madison Avenue,** which is home to all the top American and many of the top European designers including Prada, Valentino and Versace.

The Villages are excellent for boutique shops that tend to open late but stay open late too. In **Greenwich** you'll find jazz records, rare books and vintage clothing and **West Village's** tree-lined streets are full of fine and funky boutiques and popular restaurants that cater to a young, trendy crowd. On the major shopping streets of **Bleecker, Broadway** and **8th,** you'll find everything from antiques to fashion and T-shirt emporiums. There are plenty of up-and-coming designers and second-hand shops in the **East Village.** Try 9th Street for clothes and 7th for young designers.

The **Flatiron District** around 5th Avenue from 14th to 23rd Streets is filled with wonderful old buildings that are brimming with one-of-a-kind shops and designer boutiques. **SoHo** is filled with boutiques selling avant-garde fashion and art, plus restaurants and art galleries, all housed in handsome cast-iron buildings dating from the 1850s. **West Broadway** is the main drag, but other important streets include Spring, Prince, Green, Mercer and Wooster.

TriBeCa is another area that takes its name from the street that contains it – triangle below Canal in this case. Here you will find trendsetting boutiques, art galleries and restaurants including Robert de Niro's, in an area that combines loft living with commercial activity.

Last but not least is the **Lower East Side,** which is to bargains what Madison Avenue is to high-class acts. Many of the boutiques offer fashion by young designers, some of whom go on to open outlets in the posher areas of New York, and famous-name gear at huge discounts. This whole area reflects the immigrant roots of New York and stands out as a bargain hunter's paradise on Sundays. Orchard Street from Houston to Delancey Streets is famous for leather goods, luggage, designer clothes, belts, shoes and fabrics. Ludlow Street is famous for trendy bars, and boutiques filled with clothes by up-and-coming designers.

★★★★ INSIDE TRACK ★★★★
★ A sales tax of 8.25 per cent ★ always used to be added on to all ★ label prices. Now, following the ★ success of tax-free shopping ★ weeks, New York City has abol- ★ ished the sales tax on all clothing ★ and footwear under $110.

TOP TIPS FOR SHOPPING

There are some useful tips to follow when shopping in the Big Apple to save yourself time and money:

• If you're on a really tight schedule time-wise, call ahead and book appointments with the **personal shoppers** of major stores. They're very helpful and a free service. Bargain! Call Macy's on 212-695 4400 and Bloomingdale's on 212-705 2000.

• Alternatively, you can arrange to go on a shopping tour of everything from Saks Fifth Avenue to discount-hunting at Century 21. Joy Weiner of **Shopping Tours of New York** plans customised shopping tours for groups of one to 15 or more by taxi, limo or minivan. Call 212-873 6791 for more information. Another personal shopping service is provided by **Intrepid New Yorker,** phone 212-534 5071.

• You have a right to a **full refund** on goods you return within 20 days with a valid receipt unless the shop has signs saying otherwise. Always check, though, especially if the item is in a sale.

• Call in advance for **opening hours.** Smaller shops downtown – in SoHo, The Villages, Financial District and Lower East Side – tend not to open until noon or 1pm, but are often open as late as 8pm. Many of them are also closed on Mondays.

• You can **put items on hold** for a day or two until you make a decision – and if you're still thinking about it the next day you should buy it or you'll be kicking yourself all the way back on that flight home.

• You can **avoid sales tax** if you arrange to have your purchases shipped outside of New York State – a facility that is available at larger stores and those that are more tourist orientated.

• Watch out for **'Sale'** signs on the Midtown section of 5th Avenue in the 30s and 40s. Here most of the shop windows are filled with signs that say 'Great Sales!', 'Going Out Of Business!' - yet they have been around for years and are still going strong. Most of what is on sale can be bought cheaper elsewhere and with a guarantee.

DEPARTMENT STORES

Just as London has its Harrods, New York has its big-name department stores that are as much a sight as a shop. If you want to experience more than one, give yourself plenty of time for browsing in each, carry a bottle of water with you to stop yourself getting dehydrated and take plenty of tea or coffee breaks – there's nothing worse than attempting a shopping trip when you're too tired. All of the following are in the Midtown area either in or near 5th Avenue. Standard opening times are Monday to Friday 10am to 8pm, Saturday 10am to 7pm and Sunday noon to 6pm. The notable exception is Bergdorf Goodman, which doesn't open on a Sunday.

Barneys: 660 Madison Avenue at 61st Street. Tel 212-826 8900. Subway N, R to 5th Avenue; 4, 5, 6 to Lexington Avenue. Open until 9pm every night.

A truly up-to-the-minute fashion outlet, largely aimed at bright young things, this store is filled with all the top designers and a good selection of newer ones. There is a branch called **Coop** on 18th Street in Chelsea, and there's a branch at the World Financial Center downtown, but this is the $100-million megastore. Miss it and miss out!

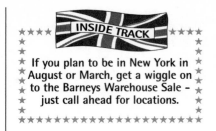

★★★★ INSIDE TRACK ★★★★
★   ★
★   ★
★ If you plan to be in New York in   ★
★ August or March, get a wiggle on   ★
★ to the Barneys Warehouse Sale –   ★
★ just call ahead for locations.   ★
★   ★
★★★★★★★★★★★★★★★★★★★★★★★★★★

Bergdorf Goodman: 754 5th Avenue at 57th Street. Tel 212-753 7300. Subway N, R to Fifth Avenue; B, Q to 57th Street.

An air of understated elegance pervades every department – not surprising, given that it has been around for generations of New Yorkers. It is not only still going strong, but positively booming and has even opened a Bergdorf Goodman Men on the opposite side of the street.

Bloomingdale's: 1000 3rd Avenue at 59th Street. Tel 212-355 5900. Subway 4, 5, 6 to 59th Street; N, R to Lexington Avenue.

After Saks, this is probably the most famous of all 5th Avenue's department stores. You can't go wrong with anything you buy from here. A truly glitzy shop filled with all the right designers.

Lord and Taylor: 424 5th Avenue at 39th Street. Tel 212-391 3344. Subway B, D, F, Q to 42nd Street; 7 to Fifth Avenue.

Good service but at much cheaper prices. The store is famous for its animated window displays at Christmas time.

Macy's: Herald Square at West 34th Street, 6th Avenue and Broadway. Tel 212-695 4400. Subway B, D, F, N, Q, R to 34th Street.

This is a beast of a gigantic store, filling as it does an entire city block, so you can be forgiven for getting yourself lost. And thanks to the Macy's sponsored Thanksgiving Day parade and Fourth of July fireworks, it appears even larger in people's minds than its physical presence.

Saks Fifth Avenue: 611 5th Avenue at 50th Street. Tel 212-753 4000. Subway E, F to 5th Avenue.

Not only is this one of the finest shopping institutions in New York, it also has fabulous views of the Rockefeller Center (see page 38) and is right next door to the beautiful St Patrick's Cathedral (see page 47). If you overspend in Saks, you can always light a candle next door and pray the money will arrive in time to pay all the bills! Seriously, though, Saks is a classic and has all the big names. Women should note there is a fabulous beauty area on the ground floor where you can get a personal consultation and a makeover.

Takashimaya: 693 5th Avenue between 54th and 55th Streets. Tel 212-350 0100. Subway N, R to 5th Avenue; 4, 5, 6 to 59th Street.

Hugely expensive, but filled with truly gorgeous things laid out in a six-storey townhouse building. For a quick and light refreshment, don't miss the tea shop in the basement.

Tiffany & Co.: 727 5th Avenue at 57th Street. Tel 212-755 8000. Subway N, R to 5th Avenue.

Audrey Hepburn's shop in *My Fair Lady*, it not only equals all expectations, but surpasses them. One of the few stores that still has lift attendants, who are very happy to explain exactly where everything is. Drool over the golden counters downstairs before taking the lift up to the first floor ('elevator to second' in American-speak) where the more moderately priced silver wing may be able to tempt you to part with wads of cash. And why not? It's well worth it for the exquisite wrapping of each purchase and the divine blue Tiffany drawstring bags!

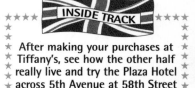

★★★★ INSIDE TRACK ★★★★
★   ★
★ After making your purchases at ★
★ Tiffany's, see how the other half ★
★ really live and try the Plaza Hotel ★
★ across 5th Avenue at 58th Street ★
★   for an afternoon tea.   ★
★   ★
★★★★★★★★★★★★★★★★★★★★★★★

FASHION

You can get everything from top designers to up-and-coming newcomers. The main shopping areas for fashion are the Upper East Side (for posh), SoHo (for designer), The East Village and Lower East Side (for cheap designer). It is advisable generally to call ahead for opening times as many shops do not open until late – but they stay open late, too.

Hints and Tips

Sizes: Clothes sizes are one size smaller in America, so a dress size 10 in the US is a size 12 in the UK. It means you can travel out a size 12 and come back a size 10! It is the same for men – a jacket size 42 is the English size 44. But it's the opposite with shoes – an American size 10 is our size 9.

Measurements: The Americans still work in feet and inches, which is great for anyone over the age of 30!

Taxes: You will have to add local taxes on to the cost of your purchases – this can add anything from 7 to 9 per cent on to the price, depending on where you are buying. (New York sales tax is 8.25 per cent, though it has now been dropped on clothes and shoes costing under $110).

UK shopping allowances: Your duty-free allowance is just £145 and, given the wealth of shopping opportunities, you're likely to exceed this, but don't be tempted to change receipts to show a lesser value as, if you are rumbled, the goods will be confiscated and you'll face a massive fine. In any case, the prices for some goods in America are so cheap that, even once you've paid the duty and VAT on top, they will still work out cheaper than buying the same item in Britain. Duty can range from 3.5 to 19 per cent depending on the item: for example, computers are charged at 3.5 per cent, golf clubs at 4 per cent, cameras at 5.4 per cent and mountain bikes at a massive 15.8 per cent. You pay this on goods above £145 and then VAT of 17.5 per cent on top of that.

Duty free: Buy your booze from US liquor stores – they're better value than the airports – but remember your allowance is 1 litre of spirits and two bottles of wine.

Videos: US video tapes are not compatible with our machines.

agnès b: 116 Prince Street between Wooster and Green Streets. Tel 212-925 4649. Subway N, R to Prince Street. Area: SoHo.

Superb designs for women – simple but stunning.

Amy Downs Hats: 103 Stanton Street at Ludlow. Tel 212-598 4189. Subway F to 2nd Avenue or Delancey Street. Area: Lower East Side.

A designer who gives as much attention to her clients as she does to her unusual, individual designs. Will make up a hat to personal order.

Anna Sui: 113 Greene Street between Prince and Spring Streets. Tel 212-941 8406. Subway C, E to Spring Street. Area: SoHo.

Get the glamour-with-a-hint-of-grunge look with Anna's dresses, skirts, blouses, platform boots and scarves. The small collection for men includes trousers, shirts and jackets from the outrageously loud to the positively restrained.

Avirex: 595 Broadway between Houston and Prince Streets. Tel 212-925 5456. Area: SoHo.

Great for flight and varsity jackets.

Banana Republic: 552 Broadway between Spring and Prince Streets. Tel 212-925 0308. Subway N, R to Prince Street. Area: SoHo.

A fairly classy and reputable chain. Best buys are in the frequent sales.

Betsey Johnson: 138 Wooster Street between Houston and Prince Streets. Tel 212-420 0169. Subway C, E to Spring Street. Area: SoHo.

A wonderful combination of party and working clothes.

Billy Martin's Western Wear: 645 Madison Avenue at East 68th Street. Tel 212-861 3100. Subway 6 to 68th Street. Area: Upper East Side.

Everything for the posh cowboy.

Calvin Klein: 654 Madison Avenue at 60th Street. Tel 212-292 9000. Subway N, R to Lexington Avenue; 4, 5, 6 to 59th Street. Area: Upper East Side.

CK's leading outlet seems to have enjoyed as much attention from the designers as the clothes themselves!

Canal Jeans: 504 Broadway between Spring and Broome Streets. Tel 212-226 1130. Subway N, R to Prince Street. Area: SoHo.

An excellent place to find jeans and casual co-ordinates at great prices. Also vintage clothes and accessories.

Diesel: 770 Lexington Avenue at 60th Street. Tel 212-308 0055.

Subway N, R to Lexington Avenue; 4, 5, 6 to 59th Street. Area: Upper East Side.

A massive store in which you'll find everything from denim to vinyl clothing, shoes and accessories.

D&G: 434 West Broadway between Prince and Spring Streets. Tel 212-965 8000. Subway N, R to Prince Street. Area: SoHo. Also at 825 Madison Avenue between 68th and 69th Streets. Tel 212-249 4100. Subway 6 to 68th Street. Area: Upper East Side.

Shop for jeans, suits, bags and dresses to a background of (loud) pop music.

Dollhouse: 400 Lafayette Street at 4th Street. Tel 212-539 1800. Subway N, R to Prince Street. Area: Greenwich Village.

As the name suggests, it's all very much for young girls or those who are young at heart. Nicole Murray specialises in gear for the body-conscious, and prices are excellent.

Emporio Armani: 601 Madison Avenue between 67th and 68th Streets. Tel 212-317 0800. Subway 6 to 68th Street. Area: Upper East Side.

Armani's line for younger people.

Gianni Versace: 647 5th Avenue between 51st and 52nd Streets. Tel 212-759 3822. Subway E, F to 5th Avenue. Area: Midtown.

A beautiful shop, housed in the former Vanderbilt mansion, selling beautiful clothes for the rich and famous.

Giorgio Armani: 760 Madison Avenue at 65th Street. Tel 212-988 9191. Subway 6 to 68th Street. Area: Upper East Side.

A huge boutique, which sells all three of Armani's lines. Come here to find well-tailored classics.

Gucci: 685 5th Avenue at 54th Street. Tel 212-826 2600. Subway E, F to 5th Avenue. Area: Midtown.

So you may not be able to afford anything on display, but it's essential to know what 'look' you are trying to achieve when you browse through the copy-cat shops downtown.

J Crew: 99 Prince Street between Mercer and Greene Streets. Tel 212-966 2739. Subway N, R to Prince Street. Area: SoHo.

American-style men's and women's clothes plus shoes and accessories.

Keiko: 62 Green Street between Spring and Broome Streets. Tel 212-226 6051. Subway N, R to Prince Street. Area: SoHo.

Designer swimwear for all tastes – and you may recognise the odd super model here, too.

Levi's: 3 East 57th Street between 5th and Madison Avenues. Tel 212-838 2125. Subway E, F to 5th Avenue. Area: Midtown.

If you've ever had trouble getting a pair of jeans that fit you perfectly, you can get yourself measured and your jeans custom-cut and sent to you ten days later. Sadly, women only.

Liquid Sky: 241 Lafayette Street between Prince and Spring Streets. Tel 212-343 0532. Subway N, R to Prince Street. Area: SoHo.

T-shirts with the shop's trademark alien, army print shorts and dresses, baggy jeans and skirts in a marijuana leaf print.

★★★★ **INSIDE TRACK** ★★★★
★ ★
★ While at Liquid Sky check out ★
★ Temple Records downstairs and ★
★ pick up the many invites to raves ★
★ and clubs from the front. ★
★ ★
★★★★★★★★★★★★★★★★★★★★★★★★

Lingerie & Company: 1217 3rd Avenue at 70th Street. Tel 212-737 7700. Area: Upper East Side.

A very user-friendly shop for gorgeous undies.

Liz Claiborne: 650 5th Avenue at East 52nd Street. Tel 212-956 6505. Subway 6 to 51st Street; E, F to Lexington Avenue. Area: Midtown.

Career and sportswear with style for women.

Marc Jacobs: 163 Mercer Street between Houston and Prince Streets. Tel 212-343 1490. Subway N, R to Prince Street. Area: SoHo.

Minimalist and luxury garments displayed in a renovated garage.

Mark Montano: 434 East 9th Street between 1st Avenue and Avenue A. Tel 212-505 0325. Subway 6 to Astor Place. Area: East Village.

Drew Barrymore, Johnny Depp and Kate Moss are all fans of the funky designer who uses bright, often vintage fabrics to create designs with style.

Old Navy Clothing: 610 6th Avenue at 18th Street. Tel 212-645 0663. Subway F to 14th Street. Area: Flatiron District.

If it looks like the Gap, that's because they own it. The good news is it's 30 per cent cheaper.

Patricia Field: 10 East 8th Street between 5th Avenue and University Place. Tel 212-254 1699. Subway A, B, C, D, E, F, Q to West 4th Street. Area: Greenwich Village. Also **Hotel Venus:** 382 West Broadway between Spring and Broome Streets. Tel 212-966 4066. Subway C, E to Spring Street. Area: SoHo.

The two outlets of Patricia Field are filled with her trend-setting club and streetwear that is so outrageous it attracts a large following amongst the drag-queen and stripper crowd. But don't let that put you off if you fancy a corset, fake fur coat, bodysuit or bikini that's completely OTT.

Phat Farm: 129 Prince Street between West Broadway and Wooster Street. Tel 212-533 7428. Subway C, E to Spring Street. Area: SoHo.

If you're into hip-hop baggies, you'll find everything you need here.

Prada: 841 Madison Avenue at 70th Street. Tel 212-327 4200. Subway 6 to 68th Street. Area: Upper East Side.

Check out the season's look before you head for the bargain basement stores.

Ralph Lauren: 867 Madison Avenue at East 72nd Street. Tel 212-606 2100. Subway 6 to 68th Street. Area: Upper East Side.

Worth a visit just to see the store – it's in an old Rhinelander mansion and is decorated with everything from Oriental rugs to riding whips, leather chairs and English paintings. The clothes are excellent quality too.

Religious Sex: 7 St Mark's Place between 2nd and 3rd Avenues. Tel 212-477 9037. Subway 6 to Astor Place. Area: East Village.

If you're feeling outrageous (sequinned thong, anybody?) you'll find the clothes you want here.

Sears and Robot: 120 East 7th Street between 1st Avenue and Avenue A. Tel 212-253 8719. Subway 6 to Astor Place. Area: East Village.

Japanese-inspired designs that include skirts, trousers, Lycra tops and T-shirts.

Stüssy Store: 104 Prince Street between Mercer and Green Streets. Tel 212-274 8855. Subway N, R to Prince Street. Area: SoHo.

Everything you could want for if you're after a West Coast look.

Trash and Vaudeville: 4 St Mark's Place between 2nd and 3rd Avenues. Tel 212-982 3590. Subway 6 to Astor Place. Area: East Village.

You'll get the East Village look in no time if you step into this punk/grunge paradise. Here you'll find outrageous creations by Gaultier, Todd Oldham jeans, rubber dresses and shirts, black leather outfits and plenty of studded gear. There's footwear to match in the back room.

Todd Oldham: 123 Wooster Street between Prince and Spring Streets. Tel 212-219 3531. Subway C, E to Spring Street. Area: SoHo.

Bold prints in cotton, satin or nylon for men and women. You can also pick up jackets, trousers and skirts in denim, plus some of the sexiest gowns for women.

Untitled: 26 West 8th Street between 5th and 6th Avenues. Tel 212-505 9725. Subway A, B, C, D, E, F, Q to West 4th Street. Area: Greenwich Village.

Contemporary clothing and accessories from exclusive New York designers as well as the likes of Vivienne Westood and Rifat Özbek.

Urban Outfitters: 682 Broadway between Houston and Bleecker Streets. Tel 212-475 0009. Subway B, D, F, Q to Broadway/Lafayette Street; 6 to Bleecker Street. Area: Greenwich Village.

The last word in trendy, inexpensive clothes. Also has vintage urban wear.

X-Large: 267 Lafayette Street at Prince Street. Tel 212-334 4480. Subway N, R to Prince Street. Area: SoHo.

Get your urban street clobber here. Sized for boys, but good for girls, too.

VINTAGE

Arkle and Sparkle: 216 Lafayette Street between Spring and Broome Streets. Tel 212-925 9699. Subway N, R to Prince Street. Area: SoHo.

Never-worn vintage, pre-worn vintage and retro designs all from the 1960s and 1970s. The wide range of sizes and styles on offer is particularly good. You'll also find marked-down Prada, Gaultier and Versace.

Domsey's Warehouse: 496 White Avenue at South 9th Street. Tel 718-384 6000. Subway J to Marcie Avenue Station. Area: Brooklyn.

Well worth the trip for an excellent selection.

Gentlemen's Resale: 322 East 81st Street between 1st and 2nd Avenues. Tel 212-734 2739. Subway 6 to 77th Street. Area: Yorkville.

Top-notch designer suits at a fraction of the original price.

Out Of Our Closet: 136 West 18th Street between 6th and 7th Avenues. Tel 212-633 6965. Subway 1, 9 to 18th Street. Area: Chelsea.

Used designer fashions in excellent condition at a fraction of the price.

Screaming Mimi's: 382 Lafayette Street between 4th and Great Jones Streets. Tel 212-677 6464. Subway N, R to NYU 8th Street. Area: Greenwich Village.

Everything from polyester dresses to denim shirts and tropical prints from the 1960s. There is also jewellery, sunglasses and other accessories plus a home department upstairs.

Tokyo Joe: 334 East 11th Street between 1st and 2nd Avenues. Tel 212 473 0724. Subway 6 to Astor Place. Area: East Village.

The pre-worn designer offerings are advertised on a blackboard outside.

Tokio: 7 64 East 7th Street between 1st and 2nd Avenues. Tel 212-353 8443. Subway 6 to Astor Place; N, R to 8th Street. Area: East Village.

Plenty of vintage and downtown designer gear.

★★★★ **INSIDE TRACK** ★★★★
★ ★
★ ★
★ Balducci's at 424 6th Avenue ★
★ between West 9th and 10th in ★
★ Greenwich Village offers Fortnum ★
★ and Mason quality food but a lot ★
★ cheaper. While Dean and Deluca ★
★ at 560 Broadway at Price Street, ★
★ SoHo is an excellent introduction ★
★ to SoHo's style: food as art. ★
★★★★★★★★★★★★★★★★★★★★★★★

Transfer International: 594 Broadway, Suite 1002, between Prince and Houston Streets. Tel 212-355 4230, website at **www.transferintl.com** Subway N, R Prince Street. Area: SoHo.

Specialises in Gucci, Prada, Chanel and Hermès – one of the best places to buy post-worn designer clothes and the accessories you need to really carry them off. They also carry **agnès b** and **Betsey Johnson.**

DISCOUNT STORES

Century 21: 22 Cortlandt Street at Broadway. Tel 212-227 9092. Subway N, R, 1, 9 to Cortlandt Street. Area: Financial District.

Excellent discounts on everything from adult and children's clothing to goods for the home. Arrive early to avoid the lunchtime rush.

Daffy's: 111 5th Avenue at 18th Street. Tel 212-529 4477. Subway L, N, R, 4, 5, 6 to 14th Street/Union

How to find a real bargain

Goods at normal prices in New York are cheaper than here in Britain, but it is possible to find whatever you are looking for at even better prices. Here is your guide to getting the best bargains around.

• Consult **Insider Shopping,** a phone- and internet-based service designed to help you zero in on bargain opportunities. Either dial 212-55-SALES or go to the website at **www.inshop.com** to find out about sales and promotional events at exclusive Manhattan retailers such as Bloomingdale's and Barneys.

• If shopping bargains are your main reason for visiting New York, then bear in mind that the **major sales** are held in March and August. The December sales seem to start earlier and earlier and may even begin before Christmas.

• Check out the **Sales and Bargains** section of *New York* magazine, the ads in the *New York Times* and the Check Out section of *Time Out.*

• Get a copy of **S&B Report** from 108 East 38th Street, Suite 2000, New York, NY 10016. Call 212-683 7612 for information on designer sample sales and cheap and chic clothes, or contact the Bargain Hotline on 212-540 0123.

• Bear in mind that many of the **vintage clothing outlets** are excellent for barely worn designer clothes and some even specialise in never-worn-before sample sales.

Square. Area: Flatiron District. Also at 33 Madison Avenue at 44th Street. Tel 212-557 4422. Subway S, 4, 5, 6, 7 to 42nd Street/Grand Central. Area: Midtown. 1311 Broadway at West 34th Street. Tel 212-736 4477. Subway B, D, F, N, Q, R to 34th Street. Area: Midtown. 135 East 57th Street between Lexington and Park Avenues. Tel 212-376 4477. Subway 4, 5, 6 59th Street; N, R Lexington Avenue. Area: Midtown.

You'll find an amazing range of designer stock from all over the world at these four outlets, and if you're prepared to hunt through the rails you may find a real bargain.

Dollar Bill's: 32 East 42nd Street between Madison and 5th Avenues. Tel 212-867 0212. Subway 4, 5, 6, 7, S to 42nd Street/Grand Central. Area: Midtown.

Specialising in Versace and Byblos, designer clothes for men and women plus accessories and underwear.

Loehmann's: 101 7th Avenue between 16th and 17th Streets. Tel 212-352 0856. Subway 1, 9 to 18th Street.

A five-storey building filled with bargains for men and women. Head straight for the top floor for designer labels such as Donna Karan, Calvin Klein and Versace. The other floors feature accessories, bags, casual clothing and shoes all at great prices.

BOOKS

Books are big business in New York and book readings are also a popular form of entertainment. If you want to get a real slice of the New York lifestyle, there are a number of places that specialise in readings and you can check them out on **www.bookwire.com**

Here are a few regular spots: **The Drawing Center** (35 Wooster Street, tel 212-219 2166) sponsors monthly readings; **The Poetry Project** at St Mark's Church (131 East 10th Street, tel 212-674 0910) has three evening readings a week on Mondays, Wednesdays and Fridays; **The 92nd Street Y** (1395 Lexington Avenue, tel 212-996 1100) also has a great series of lectures and readings, as does **The Dia Center for the Arts** (548 West 22nd Street, tel 212-989 5912). Also check out **Barnes & Noble** (see below) for another great selection.

Barnes & Noble: 105 5th Avenue at 18th Street. Tel 212-675 5500. Subway L, N, R, 4, 5, 6 to 14th Street/ Union Square. Area: Flatiron District.

This is the original store of one of the largest chains of bookstores in America and as well as a massive selection of books, it also has CDs and videos. Barnes & Noble are responsible for putting many independent bookstores out of business, but are well worth a visit. Many have coffee shops and seating areas for you to look through books before buying. You'll see them everywhere.

Borders Books & Music: 461 Park Avenue at 57th Street. Tel 212-980 6785. Subway N, R to Lexington Avenue; 4, 5, 6 to 59th Street. Area: Midtown. Also at 5 World Trade

Antiques and Flea Markets

In balmy weather, nothing beats strolling through the treasure trove of antiques, collectibles and one-off pieces that can be found at any of New York's outdoor markets. The **Annex Antiques Fair & Flea Market** (26th Street and 6th Avenue, tel 212-243 5343) is where hordes of weekend browsers head year-round to pick through several parking lots full of vintage clothing, furniture, pottery, glassware, jewellery and art. Get there early for the best finds. **The Showplace** (40 West 25th Street, tel 212-633 6010) is like an indoor extension of the outdoor market, with a small café downstairs. Weekends only. **The Garage** (112 West 25th Street, tel 212-647 0707) is exactly that – a two-storey parking garage that transforms into another bustling venue at the weekend. Nearby, the 12-storey **Chelsea Antiques Building** (110 West 25th Street, tel 212-929 0909) houses 90 galleries of antiques and collectibles with merchandise ranging from Japanese textiles to vintage phonographs and radios. **The SoHo Antiques Fair** (Broadway and Grand Street, tel 212-682 2000) is a good general market for antiques and collectibles all the year round. Uptown there's **Green Flea Indoor/Outdoor Market,** which is held on Saturdays on the East Side at East 67th Street between 1st and York Avenues and on Sundays on the West Side at Columbus Avenue and 77th Street (tel 212-721 0900). You'll find antiques, collectibles, bric-a-brac, handmade pottery and discount clothing. Good antique shops include **Irreplaceable Artifacts** (14 2nd Avenue at Houston Street, tel 212-777 2900) for actual architectural bits and bobs; **Lillian Nassau** (220 East 57th between 2nd and 3rd Avenues, tel 212-759 6062) for art nouveau lamps and glassware especially original Tiffany; **Manhattan Arts & Antiques Center** (1050 2nd Avenue between East 55th and East 56th Streets, tel 212-355 4400); **Old Print Shop** (150 Lexington Avenue between East 29th and East 30th Streets, tel 212-683 3950) for Americana up to the 1950s; and **Susan Parrish Antiques** (390 Bleecker Street between Perry and West 11th Streets, tel 212-645 5020) for American quilts from the 1800s to 1940.

Center between Vesey and Church Streets. Tel 212-839 8049. Subway A, C to Chambers Street; N, R, 1, 9 to Cortlandt Street.

Excellent outlets for books, CDs and videos. Good for more obscure books, too.

Shakespeare & Co.: 716 Broadway at Washington Place. Tel 212-529 1330. Subway N, R to 8th Street; 6 to Astor Place. Area: Greenwich Village.

The name, of course, instantly makes us Brits feel at home and the good news is that it is an excellent bookstore. Unlike many a Barnes & Noble, where the staff sometimes don't appear to be able to recognise joined-up writing, all the assistants here are graduates and have probably heard of the book you're looking for. If in any doubt at all, ask at the counter where a member of staff will be genuinely helpful.

St Mark's Bookshop: 31 3rd Avenue between 8th and 9th Streets. Tel 212-260 7853. Subway 6 to Astor Place. Area: East Village.

An excellent bookstore with a broad range of books. The bulletin board in the front gives details of local literary events.

Strand Book Store: 828 Broadway at 12th Street. Tel 212-473 1489. Subway L, N, R, 4, 5, 6 to 14th Street/Union Square. Area: Union Square.

The whole area used to be famous for antiquarian booksellers, but the Strand is the only one left. This store has over two million secondhand and new books on any subject you'd care to name – all at around half the published price.

Three Lives Bookstore: 154 West 10th Street off 7th Avenue. Tel 212-741 2069. Area: Greenwich Village.

A delightful shop with a charming ambience, known for attentive staff with encyclopaedic knowledge.

Tompkins Square Books and Records: 111 East 7th Street between Avenue A and 1st Avenue. Tel 212-979 8958. Subway F to 2nd Avenue; L to 1st Avenue; 6 to Astor Place. Area: East Village.

Known for its good selection of secondhand books and vintage records. You can even try out your choices before you buy them.

Tower Books: 383 Lafayette Street at 4th Street. Tel 212-288 5100. Subway B, D, F, Q to Broadway/Lafayette; 6 to Bleecker Street. Area: Greenwich Village.

Contemporary fiction and a huge magazine section.

Urban Center Books: 457 Madison Avenue, between East 50th and East 51st Streets. Tel 212-935 3595. Subway 6 to 51st Street or E, F to 5th Avenue. Area: Midtown.

Housed in the pretty Villard Houses, this bookstore is a treasure trove for anyone interested in architecture and buildings.

Smokers' Corner

Amazingly, the best shop to buy your fags from is a chain of chemists called **Duane Reade** – the New York equivalent of our Boots! Because of the large volume they sell, they are the cheapest outlet and also frequently do three for the price of two offers. A word of caution, though, if you ask for 20 cigarettes they are likely to think you want 20 packets of cigarettes! Also ask for a pack, not a packet – they just don't understand you otherwise!

MUSIC

Tower Records: 692 Broadway at 4th Street. Tel 212-505 1500. Subway N, R to 8th Street. Area: Greenwich Village. Also at 1961 Broadway at 66th Street. Tel 212-799 2500. Subway 1, 9 to 66th Street/Lincoln Center. Area: Lincoln Center.

Diamonds are forever

Want a true sparkler? Then look no further than the **47th Street Diamond District** where the little gems are traded, cut and set. More than 2,600 independent businesses are to be found in a single block between 5th Avenue and the Avenue of the Americas (6th Avenue). Many have booths in jewellery exchanges such as the **World's Largest Jewelry Exchange** at 55 West 47th Street (tel 212-354 5200). Clustered near the Diamond District are a prestigious group of internationally renowned jewellers including **H Stern** (645 5th Avenue, tel 212-688 0300) and **Martinique Jewellers** (1555 Broadway between 46th and 47th Streets, tel 212-869 5765). Other jewellers of note include **Wempe** (700 5th Avenue at 55th Street, tel 212-397 9000) and **Tourneau** (Madison Avenue at 52nd Street, tel 212-758 6098), which are both famous for fine watches. **Fortunoff** (681 5th Avenue at 54th Street, tel 212-758 6660) offers discounts on a large variety of jewellery items, including engagement rings, pearls, name-brand watches and gold bracelets and necklaces. **Robert Lee Morris** (400 West Broadway) in SoHo is one of only two or three American jewellery designers with an international reputation.

An excellent range of CDs and tapes. Around the block from the Village shop on Lafayette Street is the knockdown **Tower Clearance** shop.

Virgin Megastore: 1540 Broadway between 45th and 46th Streets. Tel 212-921 1020. Subway N, R, S, 1, 2, 3, 9, 7 to 42nd Street/Times Square. Area: Theater District.

A huge emporium with everything from CDs to tapes and vinyl.

CAMERAS and ELECTRONICS

Have a clear idea of what you're looking for before buying – it's a good idea to pick up a copy of Tuesday's *New York Times* to check out prices in the Science section before buying. Of course, you could always pick up electrical items at really cheap prices in the Chinatown stretch of Canal Street, but you won't get a guarantee!

B&H Photo & Video: 420 9th Avenue between West 33rd and West 34th Streets. Tel 212-444 6600. Subway A, C, E to 34th Street/Penn Station. Area: Midtown.

This store stocks every conceivable piece of electronic imaging, audio, video and photo equipment you've ever heard of. A shop for the professionals.

Fotografica: Room 300, 27 West 20th Street between 5th and 6th Avenues. Tel 212-929 6080. Subway F to 23rd Street. Area: Madison Square Gardens.

A vast stock of used camera equipment at trade prices. Owner Ed Wassel will be happy to order anything they don't have in stock.

J&R Music World: 33 Park Row at Center Street. Tel 212-732 8600. Subway 4, 5, 6 to City Hall; J, M, Z to Chambers Street. Area: Financial District.

Check out the weekly ads in the *New York Post* and *Village Voice* to get an idea of what's on offer. Also sells jazz, Latin and pop music.

Nobody Beats the Wiz: 726 Broadway between Washington and Waverly Places. Tel 212-677 4111. Subway N, R to 8th Street; 6 to Astor Place. Area: Greenwich Village.

For the last word in bargain-basement buys, this is your best bet. Phone ahead for other locations.

Willoughby's: 136 West 32nd Street between 6th and 7th Avenues. Tel 212-564 1600. Subway B, D, F, Q, N, R to 34th Street. Area: Herald Square.

Reputedly the largest collection of cameras and all things audio in the world, but the service isn't brilliant so make sure you know what you want before you go.

CHILDREN

FAO Schwarz: 767 5th Avenue at 58th Street. Tel 212-644 9400. Subway N, R to 5th Avenue.

The most famous children's store in the whole wide world, it's not only huge, but is also an entertainment centre in its own right with giant, oversized displays that take your breath away. This store has every conceivable toy your child could want – go without the kids if you plan on having any money left for your own purchases!

★★★★ **INSIDE TRACK** ★★★★

If you haven't time to get down to FAO Schwarz, you can still send a gift from there to anywhere in the world. The store's personal shopper will advise, choose, wrap and ship it for you.

The Disney Store: 711 5th Avenue at 55th Street. Tel 212-702 0702. Subway E, F at 5th Avenue. Also at 210 West 42nd Street. Tel 212-221 0430. Subway 1, 2, 3, 9, N, R to Times Square/42nd Street. 39 West 34th Street. Tel 212-279 9890. Subway B, D, N, F, Q, R to 34th Street (adjacent to the Empire State Building).

If it comes with a pair of ears, then you'll find it here!

Warner Brothers Studio Store: 1 East 57th Street at 5th Avenue. Tel 212-754 0300. Subway N, R to 5th Avenue.

The last word in items that feature Bugs Bunny, Daffy Duck, Tweety and Sylvester. You have eight floors to walk around and will find clothes for adults as well as children, toys and original cartoon cels.

CHAPTER 7

Shows, Bars and Nightlife

BROADWAY SHOWS

One of the first things you discover about Broadway is that it is just one tiny stretch of almost the longest thoroughfare on the island of Manhattan. The Theater District (see page 40), as it is known, is actually a congregation of theatres between Broadway and 8th Avenue from about 44th to 52nd Streets (take the N, R, 1, 2, 3, 7, 9, S lines to 42nd Street/Times Square). This is Broadway. You'll also see and hear the terms 'Off Broadway' and 'Off Off Broadway' (yes, really), which generally refer to Uptown and Downtown, particularly in Greenwich Village, East Village and Soho.

Of course shows change all the time, but many of the big shows – the ones that most Brits are interested in – have been around for some time and I have included reviews of these. For a completely up-to-date guide to what's on at the theatre, pick up the *New York Times,* which has complete listings of dance, classical music, opera, Broadway, Off Broadway and Off Off Broadway every day. Other papers and magazines you can check out include the *New Yorker, Village Voice* and *New York Press.*

You can book tickets in advance in the UK through either your travel agent or **Keith Prowse** (tel 01232

232425). An alternative is to use the **Ticketmaster** website at **www.ticketmaster.com**

If you decide to leave your booking until you arrive in New York, then there are plenty of options for buying tickets in town – including directly from the theatre, of course! They are: **Theatre Direct** (tel 800-334 8457, website at **www.theatredirect.com**); **Broadway Line** (tel 212-302 4111); **Americana Tickets & Travel** (tel 212-581 6660); and **Premiere Ticket Service** (tel 212-643 1274).

★★★★ INSIDE TRACK ★★★★

Queues for the Times Square TKTS booth start long before it opens, so arrive early to get a good choice.

If money is tight, then there is a way to get tickets at a cheaper rate – sometimes up to half-price – and that is through the two **Theater Development Fund/TKTS** booths in town. The most popular is the one in the middle of Times Square at 47th Street, which is open Mon, Tues, Thurs and Fri 3pm to 8pm, Wed and Sat 10am to 2pm and Sun 11am to 7pm. The other booth is at 2 World Trade Center, which is open Mon to Fri 11am to 5pm and Sat 11am to 3pm. The latter is much quieter, but in both cases arrive early for the best selection, then spend the day either in Midtown or the Financial District/Downtown area (see Chapter 4, Getting to the Core of the Big Apple). In both cases bear in mind that the booths only accept cash or travellers' cheques. Have plenty of options ready in case there are no tickets for your first show choice.

CURRENT PRODUCTIONS

Beauty and the Beast: Lunt-Fontanne Theater, 205 West 46th Street between Broadway and 8th Avenue. Tel 212-307 4747. Tickets $22.50 to $80. Wed to Sat 8pm, matinées Wed and Sat 2pm, Sun 1pm and 6.30pm.

The award-winning Disney version with music by Alan Menken and lyrics by Tim Rice and the late Howard Ashman. It tells the age-old story of how a young woman falls in love with a stubborn, but charming beast and is sure to captivate adults as well as children.

Cabaret: Studio 54, 524 West 54th Street between Broadway and 8th Avenue. Tel 212-239 6200. Tickets $45 to $90. Tues to Sat 8pm, Sun 7pm, matinées Sat and Sun 2pm.

★★★★ INSIDE TRACK ★★★★
★   ★
★ **Same-day rear mezzanine tickets** ★
★ **for *Cabaret* are available at the** ★
★ **box office for $25 Tues to Thurs** ★
★ **and Sun.** ★
★   ★
★★★★★★★★★★★★★★★★★★★★★★

The place is Berlin and the time is just before the outbreak of the Second World War. While the world outside the theatre doors is preparing for war, inside the cabaret must go on. What makes it so special are the characters, who include Sally Bowles, a tragic British singer desperate for glamour, Fraülein Schneider, the innkeeper and a true survivor, and the Master of Ceremonies, who watches over all the madness.

Chicago: Schubert Theater, 225 West 44th Street between Broadway and 8th Avenue. Tel 212-239 6200. Tickets $30 to $80. Tues to Fri 8pm, matinées Sat 2pm and 8pm, Sun 2pm and 7pm.

★★★★ INSIDE TRACK ★★★★
★   ★
★ **$20 day-of-performance tickets** ★
★ **for *Chicago* are available at** ★
★ **the box office from 10am.** ★
★ **First come, first served.** ★
★   ★
★★★★★★★★★★★★★★★★★★★★★★

This great musical with wonderful dancing is the winner of six 1997 Tony Awards and has other productions throughout the world, but many still consider this production to be the best. *Chicago* tells the story of a chorus girl who kills her lover and then escapes the noose and prison with the help of a conniving lawyer. If greed, corruption, murder and treachery are your bag, then this is the musical for you!

★★★★   ★★★★
★   ★
★   Watch out for ticket touts   ★
★   outside theatres – an increasing   ★
★   number of the tickets they sell   ★
★   are actually fake.   ★
★   ★
★★★★★★★★★★★★★★★★★★★★★★★

Jekyll and Hyde: Plymouth Theater, 236 West 45th Street between Broadway and 8th Avenue. Tel 212-239 6200. Tickets $45 to $80. Tues to Sat 8pm, matinées Wed and Sat 2pm, Sun 3pm.

Dr Jekyll was the toast of London society, who spent his days in pursuit of medical advances, but after one experiment too many, he created an evil alter-ego known as Edward Hyde. This musical production uses fiery special effects to evoke a London of the nineteenth century, when every lamp cast a foggy shadow.

★★★★   ★★★★
★   ★
★   Look for discount coupons at   ★
★   various Neighborhood   ★
★   Information stands and street   ★
★   information barrows throughout   ★
★   Manhattan.   ★
★   ★
★★★★★★★★★★★★★★★★★★★★★★★

Les Misérables: Imperial Theater, 249 West 54th Street between Broadway and 8th Avenue. Tel 212-239 6200. Tickets $20 to $80. Tues to Sat 8pm, matinées Wed and Sat 2pm, Sun 3pm.

A long-running musical adaptation of Victor Hugo's classic novel about Jean Valjean. Spectacular sets and heartrending music are used to bring to life the story of thief Jean and his redemption as a result of saving an orphan girl.

Rent: Nederlander Theater, 208 West 41st Street between 7th and 8th Avenues. Tel 212-307 4100. Tickets $35 to $80. Mon to Sat 8pm, matinées Wed and Sat 2pm, Sun 2pm and 7pm.

★★★★   ★★★★
★   ★
★ $20 day-of-performance *Rent*   ★
★   tickets are sold by lottery,   ★
★   starting two hours before the   ★
★   show. Limit one pair per person.   ★
★★★★★★★★★★★★★★★★★★★★★★★

The Tony Award- and Pulitzer Prize-winning musical is based on Puccini's opera *La Bohème,* but is set in New York's East Village. It tells the story of struggling young artists living on the edge in the search for glory.

The Lion King: New Amsterdam Theater, 214 West 42nd Street at Broadway. Tel 212-307 4100. Tickets $25 to $90. Wed to Sat 8pm, matinées Wed and Sat 2pm, Sun 1pm and 6.30pm.

With the original music from Elton John and Tim Rice combined with new music from Hans Zimmer and Lebo M, Disney tells the story of a young lion cub named Simba who struggles to accept the responsibilities of adulthood and his destined role as king. Winner of six Tony Awards in 1998.

The Phantom of the Opera:
Majestic Theater, 245 West 44th
Street between Broadway and 8th
Avenue. Tel 212-239 6200. Tickets
$15 to $75. Mon to Sat 8pm,
matinées Wed and Sat 2pm.

Set in 19th-century Paris, this is
Andrew Lloyd Webber's famous
musical of Gaston Leroux's novel. It
tells the timeless story of a
mysterious spectre, who haunts the
Paris opera house, spooking the
owners and falling in love with a
beautiful singer.

MAJOR MUSIC VENUES

Apollo Theater: 253 West 125th
Street between Adam Clayton Powell
Jnr and Frederick Douglas
Boulevards. Tel 212-749 5838.
Subway A, C, B, D, 2, 3 to 125th
Street. Area: Harlem.

Past its heyday, but once the
launching pad for stars like Ella
Fitzgerald and Michael Jackson.
Nowadays it's most famous for
Wednesday's Amateur Night which is
taped for *Showtime at the Apollo* on
television.

Carnegie Hall: 154 West 57th Street
at 7th Avenue. Tel 212-247 7800.
Subway A, C, B, D, 1, 9 to 59th
Street/Columbus Circle. Area:
Midtown West.

Built in the *beaux arts* style under
the patronage of Andrew Carnegie,
this is perhaps one of the most
famous classical concert venues in
New York and a real Broadway
landmark. Check the listings sections
of newspapers or *Time Out* for details
of visiting artists. If you don't fancy

any of the concerts on offer, you can
see the hall on a guided tour by
phoning the number above.

Madison Square Garden: 7th
Avenue at 32nd Street. Tel 212-465
6741. Subway A, C, E, 1, 2, 3, 9 to
34th Street/Penn Street Station.
Area: Herald Square.

New York's biggest and most famous
rock venue, which is also used as a
sports stadium. Also the Theater at
Madison Square Garden, which is
under Madison Square Garden, plays
host to big-name stars who want to
share some intimacy with their
audience.

Radio City Music Hall: 1260 6th
Avenue at 50th Street. Tel 212-247
4777. Subway B, D, F, Q to 47th to
50th Street/Rockefeller Center. Area:
Midtown.

Recently renovated, this home to the
Rockettes in its art deco splendour
also plays host to some big-name
stars. See also page 39.

Lincoln Center: 65th Street at
Columbus Avenue. Tel 212-875 5400.
Subway 1, 9 to 66th Street/Lincoln
Center. Area: Upper West Side.

The major venue for classical music
in New York, the Lincoln Center, a
collection of buildings that include
the home to the Metropolitan Opera,
was built on slums that were
featured in the film *West Side Story*.
There is the **Alice Tully Hall** (tel
212-875 5050), which houses the
Chamber Music Society of Lincoln
Center; the **Avery Fisher Hall** (tel
212-875 5030), home to the New
York Philharmonic; the **Metropolitan**

Left: Beauty and the Beast

Above: The Lincoln Center

Below: The Lion King

Bottom left: Metropolitan Opera at the Lincoln Center

Below left: Rent 2000

Above: Rooftop restaurant at the Bentley

Below: Europa Grill

Bottom left: American Park at the Battery

Left: Serafina Fabulous Pizza

Above: Matthew's

Right: Park View at the Boathouse

Below: World Yacht

Above: Yankee Stadium

Below: New York Yankees

Bottom: Shea Stadium

Below left: Madison Square Garden

Left: Flushing Meadow

1986 WORLD CHAMPS!

Opera House (tel 212-362 6000); the **New York State Theater** (tel 212-870 5570), home to New York City Opera; and the **Walter Reade Theater** (tel 212-875 5601), which is home to the Film Society of Lincoln Center.

BARS

East Village

Alphabet Lounge: 104 Avenue C at Lafayette Street. Tel 212-780 0202.

This pastel-coloured lounge effortlessly attracts a lively crowd of locals, artists and other cool folk to listen to a rotating roster of DJs and live bands.

Angel: 74 Orchard Street between East Houston and Stanton Streets. Tel 212-780 0313.

Live music nightly. No cover charge.

It was originally founded as a jazz club but has since diversified into different styles and sounds on different evenings. Call ahead. A great place for a fun night out.

Barmacy: 538 East 14th Street between Avenues A and B. Tel 212-228 2240.

Arrive very, very late, because the uptown-goes-downtown crowd loves it too. Once a pharmacy, it is now a very cool joint run by Deb Parker with good DJs at weekends.

Beauty Bar: 231 East 14th Street between 2nd and 3rd Avenues. Tel 212-539 1389.

Deb Parker's theme bar is equipped with 1960s-style hairdryers and chairs, great drinks and a heavy dose of the hip and beautiful.

Joe's Pub: 425 Lafayette Street between 4th Street and Astor Place. Tel 212-539 8770.

This promises to continue to be a real hot-spot for some time to come. An extension of the Public Theater, Joe's brings you live music, spoken-word performances and a crowd jam-packed with the trendiest types around.

KGB: 85 East 4th Street between 2nd and 3rd Avenues. Tel 212-505 3360.

As the name suggests, it is decorated with deep-red walls, portraits of Lenin and Brezhnev, propaganda posters and an oak bar preserved from the time when the place was a front for the Communist party. The crowd is a mix of actors, writers and drunks who love the private-parlour feel of the place.

Korova Milk Bar: 200 Avenue A between 12th and 13th Streets. Tel 212-254 8838.

The Milk Bar is decorated in a wacky retro-futuristic style that pays homage to Stanley Kubrick's *A Clockwork Orange*. It attracts a sci-fi crowd, who love its surreal quality.

Lower East Side

Baby Jupiter: 170 Orchard Street at Stanton Street. Tel 212-982 2229.

This storefront-turned-bar, restaurant and performance space is a big hit, so there's little chance of finding a seat, but it's fun if you like crowds.

bOb: 235 Eldridge Street between Houston and Stanton Streets. Tel 212-777 0588.

Standing room only as the place gets packed with lovers of the Latin, funk and hip-hop classics, who are also drawn by the cheap drinks. bOb doubles as an art gallery.

Idlewild: 145 East Houston Street between Eldridge and Forsyth Streets. Tel 212-477 5005.

Designed to look like an aircraft, it is equipped with aeroplane toilets, reclining seats, bartenders in pilot uniforms and busboys posing as ground-traffic controllers. Great fun.

Kush: 183 Orchard Street between Houston and Stanton Streets. Tel 212-677 7328.

Get a taste of paradise by sipping a few cocktails in this Moroccan oasis. The décor is fab with wonderful tiling and whitewashed walls lit by candles.

Lansky Lounge: 104 Norfolk Street between Delancey and Rivington Streets. Tel 212-677 9489.

Once the former boardroom of infamous 1920s gangster Meyer Lansky, the Jewish genius who masterminded many of Bugsy Siegal and Lucky Luciano's biggest moves, the Lansky Lounge has a real speakeasy vibe. The prices can be a bit steep, though, and in observance of the Jewish Sabbath it is closed on Friday nights.

Max Fish: 178 Ludlow Street between Houston and Stanton Streets. Tel 212-529 3959.

A bit of an institution; you'll get cheap drinks here, yet it still has one of the best jukeboxes in town.

Orchard Bar: 200 Orchard Street between Houston and Stanton Streets. Tel 212-673 5350.

One of the best lounges on the Lower East Side, its décor is very different (think rocks for seats). Cutting-edge DJs and a trendy crowd of artists and musicians mean it gets packed at the weekends.

SoHo and TriBeCa

Botanica: 47 East Houston Street between Mott and Mulberry Streets. Tel 212-343 7251.

One of the best spots for drinks at decent prices in *très chic* SoHo, this is a favoured watering hole of artists and locals.

Café Noir: 32 Grand Street at Thompson Street. Tel 212-431 7910.

With its delectable grape leaves, extensive wine list and soothing décor, this little Moroccan tapas bar is an urban oasis. Stop by for the live jazz.

Spring Street Lounge: 48 Spring Street at Mulberry Street. Tel 212-965 1774.

This bar is the New York version of the British pub, with its wooden benches, constantly refilled pints and classics-only jukebox.

Spy Bar: 101 Greene Street between Prince and Spring Streets. Tel 212-343 9000.

Another haunt of models and the super stylish, it is filled with sofas and chandeliers.

Velvet Restaurant and Lounge: 223 Mulberry Street between Prince and Spring Streets. Tel 212-965 0439.

A truly discreet lounge bar that takes darkness to new depths. The giant sofas add to the chilling-out factor.

Void: 16 Mercer Street at Canal Street. Tel 212-941 6492.

Once the preferred watering hole of cybergeeks and short-film-and-video nerds, Void has since matured into a mellow neighbourhood bar. A giant video screen fills one wall, while either a DJ spins the grooves or a jazz band plays.

Midtown

Russian Vodka Room: 265 West 52nd Street between Broadway and 8th Avenue. Tel 212-307 5835.

A brilliant vodka bar that doesn't require you to take out a second mortgage. There are cheap smoked fish platters, delicious cocktails and marvellous vodka infusions. It tends to attract the publishing crowd.

Russian Samovar: 256 West 52nd Street between Broadway and 8th Avenue. Tel 212-757 0168.

Down shots of infused vodka, nibble blini with caviar and groove to the broken English of the cabaret singer.

Russian Tea Room: 150 West 57th Street between 6th and 7th Avenues. Tel 212-974 2111.

A great late-night lounge in the beautiful environs of Warner LeRoy's over-the-top gilded décor.

Upper East Side

Rooftop at the Met: 5th Avenue and 81st Street. Tel 212-535 7710.

It's a stunning view and you'll get to admire the exhibits at the Metropolitan Museum along the way. Known as a great singles pick up joint, the best time to go is at sunset. The terrace is open during the summer months.

The Village

Madame X: 94 West Houston Street between Thompson Street and La Guardia Place. Tel 212-539 0808.

There's a real London Soho den-of-iniquity feel to this joint, bathed as it is in red and lit by the glow of lanterns. Known for serving pretty potent cocktails and rare imported beers. Best of all, you'll probably be able to find a little corner for your group.

Marylou's: 21 West 9th Street between 5th and 6th Avenues. Tel 212-533 0012.

Famous for its midnight all-you-can-eat chicken, pasta and potatoes if you buy one single drink on a Sunday, it's still worth a visit any day of the week.

Moomba: 133 7th Avenue South between West 10th and Charles Streets. Tel 212-989 1414.

The inside of this triple level restaurant and bar is filled with celebs of all kinds – which explains why it's so tough to get in.

HOTEL BARS

There are plenty of hotel bars, but these stand out from the crowd. For a spot of living like the other half do, check them out.

Bull & Bear: Waldorf-Astoria, 301 Park Avenue between 49th and 50th Streets. Tel 212-872 4900. Subways 6 to 51st Street; E, F to Lexington/3rd Avenue. Area: Midtown East.

Filled with bronze images of bulls and bears (funnily enough), this popular wood-panelled spot focuses on the rounded mahogany bar encircling a towering selection of wines and spirits. Specialities include great cigars and port.

C3 Lounge: Washington Square Hotel, 103 Waverly Place at MacDougal Street. Tel 212-254 1200. Subway A, B, C, D, E, F, Q to West 4th Street/Washington Square. Area: The Village.

The small, cosy basement space's classic bar and luxurious red leather chairs are a reminder of another era, while beautifully-stencilled windows offer a glimpse of the current street scene. It attracts a large European crowd, who find it the perfect spot to pore over a map and a martini, but locals – as well as occasional celebs – can also be found enjoying the laid-back scene.

Fantino: Central Park Inter-Continental Hotel, 112 Central Park South between 6th and 7th Avenues. Tel 212-757 1900. Subway N, R, B, Q to 57th Street. Area: Midtown.

Formerly known as The Bar at the Ritz, this is still an institution for wealthy world travellers, who come for the excellent martinis prepared by Norman, bartender extraordinaire.

Gramercy Park Hotel Bar: 2 Lexington Avenue, Gramercy Park at 21st Street. Tel 212-475 4320. Subway 6 to 23rd Street. Area: Gramercy Park.

A home from home for media types from around the world. The bar is narrow and maybe a little dark, but for all that is friendly and unpretentious. Notable for reasonably priced drinks and the cheese snacks that are served with boundless generosity.

The Grand Bar and Salon: SoHo Grand Hotel, 310 West Broadway between Grand and Canal Streets. Tel 212-965 3000. Subway C, E to Canal Street. Area: Soho.

A chic gathering-place ever since the hotel opened a few years ago. The multilingual crowd – mostly dressed very smartly in black – creates an energetic buzz that makes you feel like you're at the centre of things. The Grand Bar was at the forefront of the lounge-as-living-room trend and is filled with a mix of comfy, retro-chic furnishings that serve as great perches for drinking, people watching and nibbling on snacks.

The Grotto: Michelangelo Hotel, 152 West 51st Street between 6th and 7th Avenues. Tel 212-765 1900. Subways S, R to 49th Street; B, D, F, Q to 47th to 50th Street/Rockefeller Center. Area: Midtown.

A refined hideaway for sophisticated evenings out in one of the city's more inviting cigar bars. With its tan leather couches, The Grotto has a more casual atmosphere than the upstairs Limoncello Restaurant but offers the same assortment of gourmet cuisine to those looking for a tasty snack or a full meal.

Halcyon Lounge: RIGHA Royal Hotel, 151 West 54th Street between 6th and 7th Avenues. Tel 212-468 8888. Subway N, R to 57th Street. Area: Midtown West.

An elegant setting for pre-theatre cocktails and nightly entertainment.

Istana: New York Palace Hotel, 455 Madison Avenue between 50th and 51st Streets. Tel 212-303 7788. Subway E, F to 5th Avenue. Area: Midtown East.

A stylish refuge offering something unique in addition to its extensive wine and cocktail list – a 30-variety olive bar to accompany its comprehensive selection of Spanish sweet and dry sherries. Enjoy!

Jack's Bar: Le Parker Meridien, 118 West 57th Street between 6th and 7th Avenues. Tel 212-245 5000. Subway N, R to 57th Street; B, D, E to 7th Avenue. Area: Midtown West.

With a wall full of black and white photos of famous Jacks, this bar sets a classic tone with martinis served in your own personal shaker. Jack's offers a cosy environment and a refined selection of beers, wines and sprits and the 25-ounce Belgian Duvel beer, which comes capped with a champagne cork. Anyone named Jack (who can prove it) drinks for free between 8pm and 10pm.

Mark's Bar: Mark Hotel, 25 East 77th Street at Madison Avenue. Tel 212-744 4300. Subway 6 to 77th Street. Area: Upper East Side.

This bar has been described as a cosy tea room that feels like a luxury train car. It never gets too noisy and patrons, who perch on forest-green sofas and floral slipper chairs, are treated like guests in an elegant private home. The bar attracts a youngish fashion set, but the crowd can be diverse depending on the evening.

The Oak Bar: Plaza Hotel, 5th Avenue at Central Park South. Tel 212-546 5330. Subway N, R to 5th Avenue. Area: Midtown West.

This bar is perhaps most famous for its wall murals by painter Everett Shinn – Cary Grant sat beneath one in a scene from Hitchcock's *North by Northwest*. Today, the bar attracts a mature, business-like crowd, although recent sightings of Kevin Costner and Al Pacino have been reported. Specialities are the views of Central Park, and the world's largest raisins for nibbling with drinks.

The Oak Room: Algonquin, 59 West 44th Street between 5th and 6th Avenues. Tel 212-840 6800. Subway B, D, F, Q to 42nd Street; 7 to 5th Avenue. Area: Midtown West.

Once world-famous as the New York literary set's salon of choice, this handsome room provides an intimate and civilised setting for some of the country's leading jazz and cabaret artists, who are usually booked for extended runs. The clientèle is clubby and patrician, but anyone can buy dinner or drinks and hold their own.

Oasis: West New York, 541 Lexington Avenue at 49th Street. Tel 212-755 1200. Subway 6 to 51st Street. Area: Midtown East.

An oasis of tranquillity, things heat up when the fashion, art and music crowd descends for cocktails before dinner at the hotel's Heartbeat restaurant. The ambience is Californian and casual with clever touches that include a waterfall and backgammon tables disguised as tree stumps. Also at the hotel is the **Whiskey Blue,** overseen by Rande Gerber, otherwise known as Cindy Crawford's husband. The hip clientèle enjoy cosy sofas that are great for people-watching and a top-notch sound system that plays until the wee small hours of the morning.

Royalton: 44 West 44th Street between 5th and 6th Avenues. Tel 212-869 4400. Subway B, D, F, Q to 42nd Street; 7 to 5th Avenue. Area: Midtown West.

The first of the Philippe Starck-designed hotels holds its own against all newcomers and its long, narrow bar is still a place to see and be seen. The loos are wonderful, too. By the way – a tip: it's incredibly easy to walk past the Royalton, or '44' as it's known – there is no signpost outside, just large wooden doors. You have been warned!

Skybar: Best Western Manhattan, 17 West 32nd Street between Broadway and 5th Avenue. Tel 212-736 1600.

Subway N, R to 28th Street. Area: Midtown.

A cross between a backyard deck and a funky beach bar, this partially enclosed rooftop watering hole is packed year-round with international visitors who appreciate the casual atmosphere and towering views of the Empire State Building.

The View: Marriott Marquis Hotel, 1535 Broadway at Times Square. Tel 212-704 8900. Subway N, R, 1, 2, 3, 7, 9 to 42nd Street/Times Square. Area: Times Square.

As the title suggests, this bar has a magnificent view of the city as seen from Times Square. It is a huge space with ceiling-to-floor windows. The bar itself rotates very slowly to give a 360-degree panorama of the city.

NIGHTCLUBS

This category includes live music venues as well as mainly dance clubs. Hours vary with the event at most clubs, so check out the listings in the *Village Voice, Paper, New York Press* and *New Yorker.* **Liquid Sky** has a popular phone line for rave parties: 212-343 0532, as does **Mello:** 212-631 1023. There are two useful websites to check out the parties at different venues on different nights and they are: **www.papermag.com** and **www.clubnyc.com**

There are a few rules for making sure you get a good night's clubbing:

• On Friday and Saturday nights, clubs get packed out with the borough's crowds who come in from out of Manhattan. For a quieter night, try Thursday or Sunday.

• Call ahead early in the evening to find out if there's a cover charge, when to arrive and how to dress.

• The real nightlife doesn't get going until after midnight, so get some zeds in before you go out.

• Carry some ID with you just in case – it would be horrible if you couldn't get a drink.

• Big groups of men don't stand much chance of getting into straight clubs – you'll have more chance if you're with a woman.

Cheetah: 12 West 21st Street between 5th and 6th Avenues. Tel 212-206 7770. Subway F, N, R to 23rd Street. Area: Flatiron District.

An intimate venue with attractive animal print décor and snuggly booths. Not a place for wannabees, just for people chilling out with their friends.

Copacabana: 617 West 57th Street between 11th and 12th Avenues. Tel 212-582 2672. Subway A, C, B, D, 1, 9 to Columbus Circle/59th Street. Area: Midtown West.

A mostly Latin clientèle who go for the live bands playing salsa and merengue. Everyone is fairly well dressed, not casual but not overdone. It's great but it does get packed.

Exit: 610 West 55th Street at 11th Avenue. Tel 212-582 8282. Subway A, B, C, D, 1, 9 to Columbus Circle/59th Street; C, E to 50th Street. Area: Midtown West.

Formerly the Mirage, then Carbon, it has three levels including a massive main dance floor, five lounges and a large roof deck. It has gay, straight and mixed nights.

Flamingo East: 19 2nd Avenue between 13th and 14th Streets. Tel 212-533 2860. Subway L to 3rd Avenue; N, R, 4, 5, 6 to 14th Street/ Union Square. Area: East Village.

The big night currently is the party called Salon Wednesday's, which attracts a pretty dressy, fashionable crowd. The venue also has a restaurant downstairs.

★★★★ ☆ INSIDE TRACK ★★★★
Keep an eye out for flyers in downtown clubs, bars and shops – you may even get a money-saving coupon for a club.

Float: 240 West 52nd Street between 8th Avenue and Broadway. Tel 212-581 0055. Subway 1, 9 to 50th Street; C, E to 50th Street; B, D, E to 7th Avenue. Area: Midtown West.

Be warned, if you choose this paradise of stockbrokers and models, you will part with wads of cash for a good night out, but the environment is beautiful. There is a main dance floor plus loads of VIP areas for those who think they're important, and plenty of side-rooms, small lounges and little cubby-holes to make everyone else feel at home. A nightspot for the beautiful people.

The Greatest Bar on Earth: 1 World Trade Center, West Street between Liberty and Vesey Streets. Tel 212-524 7000. Subway C, E to World Trade Center; N, R to Cortlandt Street. Area: Financial District.

Not particularly trendy, but an excellent spot because of its views – it's on the 107th floor! It mostly attracts Wall Street types and tourists looking for a good time. Check out the sushi bar, too.

★★★★ ★★★★
★ ★
★ **Many venues are both straight** ★
★ **and gay – just on different** ★
★ **nights or sometimes even** ★
★ **the same night.** ★
★★★★★★★★★★★★★★★★★★★★★★★

Latin Quarter: 2551 Broadway at 96th Street. Tel 212-864 7600. Subway 1, 2, 3, 9 to 96th Street. Area: Upper West Side.

As the name suggests, if Latin music's your thing, then you can salsa and merengue to your heart's content here. Be warned, though, it gets packed at weekends.

Limelight: 660 6th Avenue at 20th Street. Tel 212-807 7780. Subway F, N, R to 23rd Street. Area: North of The Village.

A good, mixed crowd who are very friendly and well dressed. There is also plenty of space to dance.

Nell's: 246 West 14th Street between 7th and 8th Avenues. Tel 212-675 1567. Subway A, C, E to 14th Street; L to 8th Avenue. Area: The Village.

Despite its location, it attracts a straight crowd who go for the jazz and funky soul upstairs and the reggae and R 'n' B downstairs.

Roxy: 515 West 18th Street between 10th and 11th Avenues. Tel 212-645 5156. Subway A, C, E to 14th Street; L to 8th Avenue. Area: The Village.

A huge venue with plenty of different themes on different nights. Single men beware, though, it's very hard to get in without a female partner!

★★★★ ★★★★
★ ★
★ ★
★ **Do make an effort to get dressed** ★
★ **up if you're going clubbing. Don't** ★
★ **wear trainers or jeans – you** ★
★ **won't get in.** ★
★★★★★★★★★★★★★★★★★★★★★★

Sapphire: 249 Eldridge Street between Houston and Stanton Streets. Tel 212-777 5153. Subway F to 2nd Avenue. Area: Lower East Side.

A very small dance club that plays a mix of hip-hop, reggae, acid jazz, R 'n' B and disco classics.

SOBs: 204 Varick Street at Houston Street. Tel 212-243 4940. Subway 1, 9 to Houston Street. Area: The Village.

The place to come for the last word in all Latin sounds from salsa to samba and even reggae.

Sound Factory: 618 West 46th Street between 11th and 12th Avenues. Tel 212-643 0728. Subway A, C, E to 50th Street. Area: Midtown West.

One of the better-known venues, it has a reasonable-sized dance floor that can get pretty packed on big party nights. Good for a visit, though, and the crowd is very well mixed. Call 212-489 0001 to get yourself on the guest list and save $5. Leave your name, the number of people in your group and don't forget to say which day's list you want.

Tunnel: 220 12th Avenue at 27th Street. Tel 212-695 4682. Subway C, E to 23rd Street. Area: Chelsea.

One of the oldest clubs around, it is absolutely huge. If you find the main dance floor too much, head for one of the smaller rooms. A mixed crowd with everything from businessmen in suits to transvestites in leopard-print dresses.

Twilo: 530 West 27th Street between 10th and 11th Avenues. Tel 212-268 1600. Subway C, E to 23rd Street. Area: Chelsea.

It has a huge dance floor, seating spaces around the floor and nice lounges. The last Friday of the month is Sasha and Digweed, who play techno/rave and trance.

★★★★ **INSIDE TRACK** ★★★★
★ ★
★ **Men in New York find it very** ★
★ **hard to get into nightclubs on** ★
★ **their own, but there is one way** ★
★ **round this – if you see a couple** ★
★ **of women by themselves ask if** ★
★ **you can team up with them just** ★
★ **to get into the club.** ★
★ ★
★★★★★★★★★★★★★★★★★★★★★★★

Vinyl: 6 Hubert Street between Greenwich and Hudson Streets. Tel 212-343 1379. Subway A, C, E to Canal Street; 1, 9 to Franklin Street. Area: TriBeCa.

A good, mixed crowd and a good mix of music, but not a huge space – and there's no alcohol, either.

Webster Hall: 125 East 11th Street between 3rd and 4th Avenues. Tel 212-353 1600. Subway L, N, R, 4, 5, 6 to 14th Street/Union Square. Area: East Village.

A fairly straight crowd from the suburbs, there are lots of different rooms playing different types of music. It's a fun place to go.

Westreet SoHo

There's a new term for the area that is west of SoHo, north of TriBeCa and south of Greenwich Village – and it's WeVar, which means west of Varick. Whether it will catch on is another matter, but there is a huge congregation of clubs in this particular area. To get there, take subway 1, 9 to Houston Street.

Don Hill's: 511 Greenwich Street at Spring Street. Tel 212-219 2850. Open seven days 9pm to 4am.

A Mecca for fashion and music celebs, this is a great place to find dance and live music nights. Even the mixed nights have a big gay crowd. The big night is BeavHer Thursdays, DJ Frankie Inglese's party that has been going since the club opened and is still full of energy.

Ice Bar: 528 Canal Street at Washington Street. Tel 212-226 2602. Open Tues to Sat 7pm to 4am.

A stylish club that has been drawing a steady local crowd who love the lack of a door policy, which is about creating an atmosphere without pretence or attitude. Inside white covers everything: the walls, furniture, curtains, ceiling and even the pumpkin seeds sitting on each table.

★★★★ **INSIDE TRACK** ★★★★
★   ★
★ Avoid the crowds at Manhattan ★
★ jazz clubs by going for the late ★
★ set. Also remember that stormy ★
★ weather puts off New Yorkers ★
★ from going out so you could get ★
★ a great seat if it's raining heavily. ★
★   ★
★★★★★★★★★★★★★★★★★★★★★★★★

Jet Lounge: 286 Spring Street between Varick and Hudson Streets. Tel 212-929 4780. Open Wed to Sat 9.30pm to 4am.

The zebra-striped bar is now a legal dancing den thanks to a recently-acquired cabaret licence. It's a great space and there is a dance floor, but drinks tend to be pricy.

NV: 289 Spring Street at Hudson Street. Tel 212-929 NVNV. Open Wed to Sun 10pm to 4am.

The crowd is trendy and friendly, while the music is a great mix of everything from house to disco to hits from the 1980s. The upstairs has dance-floor energy while the much larger downstairs keeps a mellow lounge atmosphere.

All that jazz

In some respects, a visit to New York City wouldn't be complete without a visit to one of the various jazz venues. I've listed the main ones on Manhattan, but for a cheaper jazz night out try **Queens,** where you can hear jazz much more cheaply (see page 109).

First and foremost is the **Blue Note** (131 West 3rd Street between MacDougal and 6th Avenue, tel 212-475 8592) in Greenwich Village, which considers itself the jazz capital of the world. Then there is **Iridium** (44 West 63rd Street at Columbus Avenue, tel 212- 582 2121), which is Midtown's answer to the Blue Note. Other good venues include **Birdland** (315 West 44th Street between 8th and 9th Avenues, tel 212-581 3080) in Midtown West; **The Jazz Standard** (116 East 27th Street between Park and Lexington Avenues, tel 212-576 2232) which is near Madison Square; and **Roulette** (228 West Broadway at White Street, tel 212-219 8242), which is in TriBeCa and has concerts from March to May and October to December.

Also in The Village are **Smalls** (183 West 10th Street at 7th Avenue, tel 212-929 7565); **Sweet Basil** (88 7th Avenue South between Bleecker and Grove Streets, tel 212-242 1785) and **Village Vanguard** (178 7th Avenue South at Perry Street, tel 212-255 4037).

Sway: 305 Spring Street between Hudson and Greenwich Streets. Tel 212-620 5220. Open seven days 9pm to 4am.

Moroccan-themed interiors have been fairly well done and this place is comfortable, though getting a table can be hard work. Sway has a DJ on most nights and for the most part the music reflects the mood of the crowd.

Veruka: 525 Broome Street between Thompson and 6th Avenue. Tel 212-625 1717. Open daily till 4am. Dinner Wed to Sat until 2am.

West SoHo's most élite nightspot, celebs include Mark Wahlberg, Robert de Niro, Sean Penn, Mariah Carey and Naomi Campbell. Weekends are huge so arrive early.

CHAPTER 8

Restaurants

N ew Yorkers take their restaurants very seriously – not surprising, given that many of them have tiny kitchens if they have one at all. In fact, eating out is such a huge pastime in the city that many local stores have deli counters selling freshly prepared hot foods that can be taken away and eaten at home. Of course, like everything American, big is best and in the case of restaurants big doesn't necessarily refer to size, but to the reputation of the chefs, many of whom have become celebrities in their own rights. And getting into their establishments is a well-nigh impossible task. If your heart is set on a meal at a landmark New York restaurant, you will need to book weeks ahead. At other restaurants in the speciality category you will still have to book ahead – especially if you want to eat out at the weekend. Obviously the number of restaurants in New York precludes me from giving all but a 'best of the best' kind of listing here. I have gone for the well-known, the excellent and the trendy and added a few neighbourhood joints for good measure.

$	under $25 per head
$$	under $50 per head
$$$	$50 and up!

SPECIAL RESTAURANTS

American Park at the Battery:
Battery Park opposite 175 State Street. Tel 212-809 5508. Subway 1, 9 South Ferry; 4, 5 Bowling Green. Area: Battery Park.

A superb restaurant in an elegant, glass-enclosed building that shows off the spectacular views of the Hudson and East Rivers and the Statue of Liberty. In good weather you can even eat outside on the terrace. Sumptuous American dishes include sautéed day-boat sea scallops, whole roasted black sea bass and free-range stuffed chicken breast. **$$$**

Aureole: 34 East 61st Street between Madison and Park Avenues. Tel 212-319 1660. Subway 4, 5, 6 to 59th Street; N, R to Lexington Avenue. Area: Upper East Side.

Always among the Top Ten Restaurants in New York, the courtyard garden is the restaurant's best-kept secret. Tucked behind the brownstone that houses Aureole, away from the hustle and bustle of the street, it's an idyllic spot for outdoor dining and always incredibly romantic when lit by candles at night. Celebrity chef Charlie Palmer's delicious concoctions include wood-grilled lamb mignons with lentil cakes, pan-seared foie gras steak and fricassee of lobster with Provençal artichokes. **$$$**

Barbetta Restaurant: 321 West 46th Street between 8th and 9th Avenues. Tel 212-246 9171. Subway A, C, East to 42nd Street. Area: Midtown West.

During the summer, the Barbetta garden is one of the city's most sought-after sites for dining with its century-old trees and the scented blooms of magnolia, wisteria, jasmine and gardenia. Barbetta is the oldest Italian restaurant in New York and features cuisine from Piedmont in the north-west region of Italy. **$$$**

★★★★ INSIDE TRACK ★★★★
★ ★
★ Check the dress code when ★
★ eating out, especially if heading ★
★ somewhere posh – they expect ★
★ formal clothes to match the ★
★ setting and men may need to ★
★ wear a tie or risk being turned ★
★ away. ★
★★★★★★★★★★★★★★★★★★★★★★★

Remi: 145 West 53rd Street between 6th and 7th Avenues. Tel 212-581 4242. Subway N, R to 49th Street; B, D, East to 7th Avenue. Area: Midtown West.

To New Yorkers, this restaurant is like a taste of Venice with its enchanting Atrium Garden that offers foreign films and live music to accompany dinner al fresco. It also has rotating art exhibits all year long in the Rialto Room. The food is delicious and you can even get Remi take-aways. **$$$**

River Café: 1 Water Street under the Brooklyn Bridge. Tel 718-522 5200. Subway A, C to High Street/Brooklyn Bridge. Area: Brooklyn Heights.

For unrivalled views of New York's magnificent Lower Manhattan skyline, this is the place to come and the food matches up. Superb dishes include braised Maine lobster, crisp black sea bass, seared diver sea scallops, grilled, aged prime sirloin of beef and pan-roasted chukar partridge. **$$$**

★★★★ INSIDE TRACK ★★★★
★ ★
★ It is possible to soak up the ★
★ fantastic views and exquisite ★
★ vibes of the River Café without ★
★ parting with huge wads of cash. ★
★ You can take a seat in the ★
★ cocktail bar and enjoy the ★
★ sparkling lights of the ★
★ skyscrapers opposite, while ★
★ sipping on whatever takes ★
★ your fancy. ★
★★★★★★★★★★★★★★★★★★★★★★★

SeaGrill: 19 West 49th Street between 5th Avenue and Rockefeller Plaza. Tel 212-332 7610. Subway B, D, F, Q to 47th–50th Streets/ Rockefeller Center. Area: Midtown.

Surrounded by lush greenery, the outdoor tables topped with striped umbrellas in summer, offer fine views of the Rockefeller Center. In winter, the outdoor seating is replaced by the famous skating rink. The seafood specialities include Chilean sea bass with wilted spinach, grilled lobster with home-made fettucine and coriander-crusted swordfish. Note that the newly-refurbished restaurant's dress-code has changed to exclude jeans, shorts and trainers. **$$$**

Supper Club: 240 West 47th Street between Broadway and 8th Avenue. Tel 212-564 8074. Subway 1, 9 to 50th Street. Area: Midtown West.

For fine dining combined with swing dancing and a cabaret – the show is a mix of Cab Calloway, the Blues Brothers and other swing acts. The food is also delicious, particularly the lobster and steak, and I defy anyone to hate the New York cheesecake – so much lighter than European cheesecake, it just melts in your mouth. Stupendous. **$$$**

Water Club: 500 East 30th Street at East River. Tel 212-683 3333. Subway 6 to 28th Street. Area: East River near Madison Square Garden.

Another delightful and special venue from the owner of the River Café, this restaurant also specialises in seafood. Although on the pricy side – though worth it for the fine cuisine – the weekend brunch option at a prix fixe of $20 is an excellent way to sample some delicious dishes while gazing out across the East River. **$$$**

Windows on the World: 1 World Trade Center, 107th floor at West Street between Vesey and Liberty Streets. Tel 212-524 7000. Subway 1, 9, N, R to Cortlandt Street. Area: Financial District.

The views, of course, are stunning and the food is also good. There is a prix fixe sunset supper. The bar is open for lunch and dinner daily and the restaurant is open for dinner each evening and Sunday brunch. **$$$**

World Yacht Dining Cruise: Pier 81, West 41st Street at Hudson River. Tel 212-630 8100. Subway A, C, East to 42nd Street. Area: Midtown West.

A beautiful, four-course dining experience with the best views of Midtown and Lower Manhattan plus the Statue of Liberty. Dishes include Chilean sea bass, rosemary-roasted chicken with scallions, bean purée and sweet garlic jus, red snapper with anchovy paste, topped with sweet and spicy cilantro-chipotle rouille, and herb-roasted rack of lamb served with arugula and couscous, and the chefs are some of the finest around New York. The prix fixe meal including a three-hour cruise and live music for dancing costs **$67** from Sun to Thurs, **$75** on Fridays and **$79** on Saturdays. NYCard-holders get a discount.

★★★★ **INSIDE TRACK** ★★★★
If you are up in Harlem, drop in for a cuppa and a delicious cake at Make My Cake, 103 West 110th Street at Lenox Avenue. Tel 212-932 0833.

LANDMARK RESTAURANTS

21 Club: 21 West 52nd Street between 5th and 6th Avenues. Tel 212-582 7200. Subway F to 5th Avenue. Area: Midtown East.

RESTAURANTS

A former speakeasy that is as famous for its burger and chicken hash, this attracts New York's élite, who treat the glamorous institution as a haunt for power lunches. Great for people-watching. **$$**

Carlyle: Carlyle Hotel, 35 East 76th Street at Madison Avenue. Tel 212-744 1600. Subway 6 to 77th Street. Area: Upper East Side.

It's an old establishment that attracts an older clientèle, but if you want to see how the other half lives, try the fine French cuisine for breakfast or brunch. Divine. **$$$**

★★★★ **INSIDE TRACK** ★★★★
If you want to experience one of these landmark restaurants without parting with your entire holiday spending money, opt to go for lunch – same delicious food, only cheaper, and you're far more likely to get in, too!

Four Seasons: 99 East 52nd Street between Lexington and Park Avenues. Tel 212-754 9494. Subway 6 to 51st Street; E, F to Lexington/3rd Avenues. Area: Midtown East.

You have a choice between the Grill Room or the Pool Room and whichever you opt for will make you feel like one of New York's movers and shakers – this is where they come for their power lunches. The continental dishes are exquisite, the setting elegant and the service impeccable. Pricy? You bet. **$$$**

Jean Georges: Trump International Hotel, 1 Central Park West between

60th and 61st Streets. Tel 212-299 3900. Subway A, B, C, D, 1, 9 to 59th Street/Columbus Circle. Area: Midtown West.

Celebrity chef Jean-Georges Vongerichten's exquisite French dishes are served in an elegant and subtle restaurant designed by Adam Tihany, with superb views of Central Park. It's an unbeatable combination, so get a rich uncle to take you pronto! **$$$**

La Caravelle: Shoreham Hotel, 33 West 55th Street between 5th and 6th Avenues. Tel 212-586 4252. Subway F to 5th Avenue; B, Q to 57th Street. Area: Midtown East.

Owned by the welcoming husband-and-wife team of André and Rita Jammet, this paragon of classic French cuisine has an elegant setting. Delicious dishes include truffled pike quenelles in a lobster sauce and crispy duck with cranberries. **$$$**

Le Cirque 2000: NY Palace Hotel, 455 Madison Avenue between 50th and 51st Streets. Tel 212-303 7788. Subway 6 to 51st Street. Area: Midtown East.

If you can actually get a table (book a few months ahead), you'll be rewarded with the best people-watching in town as this is the place for celebs and the local élite. Obviously, the haute cuisine matches expectations: mouth-watering dishes include sea bass in crispy potatoes with red wine sauce, veal with fresh morels and broiled salmon with lemon-grass crust. Simply divine. **$$$**

Oyster Bar: Grand Central Station, lower level, between 42nd Street and Vanderbilt Avenue. Tel 212-490 6650. Subway 4, 5, 6, 7 to Grand Central/42nd Street. Area: Midtown East.

This place was made famous by generations of connoisseurs consuming 1,000 dozen oysters every day at the counters and in the landmark restaurant and atmospheric saloon. **$$**

Russian Tea Room: 150 West 57th Street between 6th and 7th Avenues. Tel 212-974 2111. Subway B, Q to 57th Street. Area: Midtown.

Originally founded in 1927 by members of the Russian Imperial Ballet who fled to America following the revolution, this legendary restaurant has been reopened by Warner LeRoy, the creative force behind the Tavern on the Green. Now a tantalising mix of old and new, the clubby first floor is the best place to soak up the atmosphere of the good old days with the original carpet design, period Russian painting, bar and famous revolving door. **$$**

Tavern on the Green: Central Park West between 66th and 67th Streets. Tel 212-873 3200. Subway B, C to 72nd Street. Area: Central Park.

A landmark restaurant that gets packed out for Sunday brunch, it's not actually the American food that draws the crowds, but the over-the-top décor and divine setting. **$$**

THE BEST OF THE REST

44: Royalton Hotel, 44 West 44th Street between 5th and 6th Avenues. Tel 212-944 8844. Subway B, D, F, Q to 42nd Street. Area: Midtown.

A *très* trendy joint in the Philippe Starck-designed Royalton, serving new American cuisine. A favourite with posh magazine editors. **$$**

★★★★ **INSIDE TRACK** ★★★★
If you're heading to 44 then be warned that the entrance to the Royalton is so discreet, it's incredibly easy to walk past. Look out for a pair of wooden doors and go right in.

Alouette: 2588 Broadway between 97th and 98th Streets. Tel 212-222 6808. Subway 1, 2, 3, 9 to 96th Street. Area: Upper West Side.

This French bistro attracts the crowds despite having a very simple menu. **$$**

Asia de Cuba: Morgans Hotel, 237 Madison Avenue between 37th and 38th Streets. Tel 212-726 7755. Subway 6 to 33rd Street or 4, 5, 6, 7 to Grand Central/42nd Street. Area: Midtown East.

The Philippe Starck interior guarantees a trendy crowd for the fusion Asian and Cuban food. **$$**

Babbo: 110 Waverly Place between MacDougal and 6th Avenues. Tel 212-777 0303. Subway A, B, C, D, E, F, Q to Washington Square. Area: The Village.

A recent Italian newcomer that is already famous for its 'tasting' menu (a little bit of everything). **$$**

Balthazar: 80 Spring Street between Broadway and Crosby Streets. Tel 212-965 1414. Subway N, R to Prince Street. Area: SoHo.

A classy French brasserie serving up good food to a trendy crowd. **$$**

★★★★ **INSIDE TRACK** ★★★★
★ ★
★ ★
★ **To calculate your tip, double the** ★
★ **amount of sales tax added to** ★
★ **your bill – and add a little more** ★
★ **if you're very impressed.** ★
★ ★
★★★★★★★★★★★★★★★★★★★★★★★

Belgo Nieuw York: 415 Lafayette Street between Astor Place and 4th Street. Tel 212-253 2828. Subway 6 to Astor Place. Area: East Village.

A New York outlet based on London's top Belgian restaurant. **$$**

Blue Ribbon: 97 Sullivan Street between Prince and Spring Streets. Tel 212-274 0404. Subway C, East to Spring Street. Area: SoHo.

This place gets packed at any time of the day or night, but the eclectic and seafood dishes are worth the wait. **$$**

Bolivar: 206 East 60th Street between 2nd and 3rd Avenues. Tel 212-838 0440. Subway 4, 5, 6 to 59th Street; N, R to Lexington Avenue. Area: Upper East Side.

Serving the New York craze for Latin American fare, this recently opened restaurant has proved a big hit. **$$$**

Bond Street: 6 Bond Street between Broadway and Lafayette. Tel 212-777 2500. Subway B, D, F, Q to Broadway/Lafayette; 6 to Bleecker Street. Area: Nolita.

A new Japanese restaurant that has proved to be a big hit with the black-wearing in-crowd. **$$**

Bop: 325 Bowery Street at 2nd Street. Tel 212-254 7887. Subway 6 to Bleecker Street. Area: East Village.

Serves excellent Korean dishes to a trendy crowd. **$$**

Café de Bruxelles: 118 Greenwich Avenue at West 13th Street. Tel 212-206 1830. Subway A, C, East to 14th Street. Area: West Village.

A friendly Belgian bistro. **$$**

Café des Artistes: 1 West 67th Street between Columbus Avenue and Central Park West. Tel 212-877 3500. Subway 1, 9 to 66th St. Area: Upper West Side.

A reasonably-priced fine dining establishment that serves up wonderful French cuisine in a romantic setting. **$$**

Caviar Russe: 538 Madison Avenue, second floor, between 54th and 55th Streets. Tel 212-980 5908. Subway F to 5th Avenue. Area: Midtown East.

Posh caviar and cigar lounge where you can see how the other half live. **$$$**

Celadon: 1167 Madison Avenue at 86th Street. Tel 212-734 7711. Subway 4, 5, 6 to 86th Street. Area: Upper East Side.

A Californian–Asian fusion restaurant with a big, bright ground level and a more intimate first-floor level. **$$**

8

Chat 'n' Chew: 10 East 16th Street between 5th Avenue and Union Square West. Tel 212-243 1616. Subway L, N, R, 4, 5, 6 to Union Square/14th Street. Area: Union Square.

Classic 1950s American diner with huge servings of meatloaf *et al.* **$**

★★★★ **INSIDE TRACK** ★★★★
★   ★
★ **If you want to smoke, opt to eat** ★
★ **in the bar area if possible or** ★
★ **choose a restaurant with less** ★
★ **than 35 seats. Some restaurants** ★
★ **do allow smoking later in the** ★
★ **evening, so check in advance.** ★
★   ★
★★★★★★★★★★★★★★★★★★★★★★★★

Chez Es Saada: 42 East 1st Street between 1st and 2nd Avenues. Tel 212-777 5617. Subway 6 to Bleecker Street. Area: East Village.

Moroccan basement restaurant that gets packed with beautiful people. Open late. **$$**

China Grill: CBS Building, 52 West 53rd Street between 5th and 6th Avenues. Tel 212-333 7788. Subway B, D, F, Q to 47th–50th Streets/Rockefeller Center. Area: Midtown.

Classy establishment serving eclectic food in a fairly noisy setting. Has a bar that gets pretty crowded. **$$**

Chin Chin: 216 East 49th Street between 2nd and 3rd Avenues. Tel 212-888 4555. Subway 6 to 51st Street. Area: Midtown East.

One of New York's finest Chinese restaurants, it frequently plays host to the city's power crowd. **$$**

Docks Oyster Bar: 633 3rd Avenue at 40th Street. Tel 212-986 8080. Subway 4, 5, 6, 7 to Grand Central/42nd Street. Area: Midtown East.

This raw fish and seafood speciality restaurant also has a popular bar. **$**

Europa Grill: 599 Lexington Avenue at 53rd Street. Tel 212-755 6622. Subway E, F to Lexington/Third Avenues. Area: Midtown East.

A welcoming restaurant, which has been designed in natural elements of wood, stone and earth tones to create a soothing and tranquil environment. Lincoln Engstrom, formerly of the River Café, is the chef and he has created delicious Mediterranean dishes. They include poussin stuffed with ricotta salata and zucchini, peppers and sage, pomegranate-marinated lamb with crispy panisse and fresh mint, and lemon-cured pork loin served with soft polenta. **$$**

Fannelli Café: 94 Prince Street at Mercer Street. Tel 212-226 9412. Area: SoHo.

Contemporary crowds pack an old saloon-style bar and dining room. It does an excellent selection of sandwiches for lunch. **$**

Firebird: 365 West 46th Street between 8th and 9th Avenues. Tel 212-586 0244. Subway A, C, East to 42nd Street. Area: Theater District.

The classic, opulent Russian décor creates a fabulous setting for tucking into the caviar and blinis. There is a prix fixe pre-theatre dinner, which is excellent value at $20. **$$**

Florent: 69 Gansevoort Street between Greenwich and Washington Streets. Tel 212-989 5779. Subway A, C, East to 14th Street. Area: West Village.

Open 24 hours at the weekend, this is a popular late-night spot with club crowds. **$**

★★★★ INSIDE TRACK ★★★★
★   ★
★ **Weird but true: some smaller** ★
★ **restaurants don't take credit** ★
★ **cards. If it's important to you,** ★
★   **check in advance.**   ★
★★★★★★★★★★★★★★★★★★★★★★★★

Frank: 88 2nd Avenue between 5th and 6th Streets. Tel 212-420 0202. Subway 6 to Astor Place. Area: East Village.

A tiny Italian restaurant with a real parlour feel, it serves good Tuscan fare at reasonable prices. **$**

Frankie and Johnnie's: 269 West 45th Street between Broadway and 8th Avenue. Tel 212-997 9494. Subway A, C, E, N, R to 42nd Street. Area: Theater District.

In an excellent location, it's renowned for its steaks and grills. **$$**

Garage Restaurant: 99 7th Avenue South between Barrow and Grove Streets. Tel 212-645 0600) Subway 1, 2, 3, 9 to Christopher Street. Area: West Village.

A friendly spot in a great location; it also has live jazz. **$**

Gina & George's Restaurant: 169 East 106th Street between Lexington and 3rd Avenues. Tel 212-410 7292. Area: Harlem.

A great spot for Puerto Rican cuisine. **$$**

Globe: 373 Park Avenue South between 26th and 27th Streets. Tel 212-545 8800. Subway 6 to 28th Street. Area: Gramercy Park.

Classy, modern diner with bar seating for smokers, good American fare and a raw bar. The bar gets packed at night. **$$**

Gotham Bar and Grill: 12 East 12th Street between 5th Avenue and University Place Tel 212-620 4020. Subway L, N, R, 4, 5, 6 to Union Square/14th Street. Area: The Village.

Always highly rated by Zagat, the excellent American cuisine is served up in a superb environment to a trendy, stylish crowd. **$$$**

Gramercy Tavern: 42 East 20th Street between Broadway and Park Avenue South. Tel 212-477 0777. Subway N, R to 23rd Street. Area: Flatiron District.

Another real winner and again always highly ranked by the Zagat survey, this is another excellent American restaurant in a delightful setting. **$$$**

Grange Hall: 50 Commerce Street at Barrow Street. Tel 212-924 5246. Subway 1, 9 to Christopher Street. Area: West Village.

In one of the Village's prettiest streets, this serves American fare with an organic twist. **$$**

149

Grimaldi's: 19 Old Fulton Street between Front and Water Streets. Tel 718 858 4300. Subway A, C to High Street/Brooklyn Bridge. Area: Brooklyn Heights.

Considered the best place in New York to get a delicious pizza – and it won't cost you a small fortune, either. $

Indochine: 430 Lafayette Street between Astor Place and 4th Street. Tel 212-505 5111. Subway 6 to Astor Place. Area: Nolita.

A bit of a celebrity haunt, this serves delicious Vietnamese–French fusion food in tiny portions. $$

Istana: NY Palace Hotel, 455 Madison Avenue at 51st Street. Tel 212-303 6032. Subway 6 to 51st Street. Area: Midtown East.

A little-known but excellent place serving Mediterranean cuisine. $$

Joe's Shanghai: 9 Pell St between Bowery and Mott Street. Tel 212-233 8888. Subway J, M, N, R, Z, 6 to Canal Street. Area: Chinatown.

Known for the most fabulous soup dumplings in all of New York. $

John's Pizza: 278 Bleeker Street between 6th and 7th Avenues. Tel 212-243 1680. Area: East Village.

A great place for brick-oven pizzas. $

La Grenouille: 3 East 52nd Street between 5th and Madison Avenues. Tel 212-752 1495. Subway 6 to 51st Street. Area: Midtown East.

A sophisticated temple for francophiles, the exquisite food is well worth the money. If money's no object, go for dinner – otherwise go for the cheaper lunch. $$$

Katz's Delicatessen: 205 East Houston Street at Ludlow Street. Tel 212-254 2246. Subway F to Second Avenue. Area: Lower East Side.

A real institution – it's been there since 1888 – the sandwiches may sound pricy at around $9, but I defy you to finish one. Luckily, there are plenty of brown paper bags around to take your leftovers away with you as everybody else does. Stick to the sandwiches though – the soups are a bit disappointing. You get a ticket on the way in, order your food at the counter and get your ticket filled out, then you pay as you leave. If the canteen-style seating seems familiar to you, it's because that orgasm scene with Meg Ryan and Billy Crystal in *When Harry Met Sally* was filmed here! $

Lespinasse: St Regis Hotel, 2 East 55th Street between 5th and Madison Avenues. Tel 212-339 6719. Subway 4, 5, 6 to 59th Street. Area: Midtown East.

Fine Asian–French cuisine is served in the plush environs of the St Regis Hotel to the élite of New York. The restaurant has won numerous awards and is open for lunch and dinner. $$$

Les Pyrénées: 251 West 51st Street between Broadway and 8th Avenue. Tel 212-246 0044. Subway 1, 9 to 51st Street. Area: Theater District.

An old French classic that always comes up trumps. $$

L–Ray: 64 West 10th Street between 5th and 6th Avenues. Tel 212-505 7777. Subway F to 14th Street. Area: The Village.

A recently opened restaurant that serves up Gulf Rim cuisine from Louisiana, Cuba and Mexico. **$$**

Lucky Strike: 59 Grand Street between West Broadway and Wooster Street. Tel 212-941 0479. Area: SoHo.

Restaurateur Keith McNally's hot spot has become a watering hole for models, celebrities and club kids as well as SoHo's art crowd. The menu is French, chocolate and Lucky martini. **$$**

Mark's: The Mark, 25 East 77th Street at Madison Avenue. Tel 212-879 1864. Subway 6 to 77th Street. Area: Upper East Side.

Excellent French–American cuisine. The prix fixe lunch and pre-theatre deals are great value – just make sure you give yourself time to soak up the ambience. **$$$**

Markt: 401 West 14th Street at 9th Avenue. Tel 212-727 3314. Subway L to 8th Avenue; A, C, East to 14th Street. Area: West Village.

A stylish Belgian brasserie with a popular bar. **$$**

Match: 160 Mercer Street between Houston and Prince Steets. Tel 212-343 0020. Subway N, R to Prince Street. Area: SoHo.

American–Asian food that still attracts big crowds in the early hours. **$$**

Matthew's: 1030 3rd Avenue at 61st Street. Tel 212-838 4343. Subway 4, 5, 6 to 59th Street. Area: Upper East Side.

There's a real touch of Casablanca about this Moroccan restaurant with its ceiling fans and cool greenery. The delicious dishes are created by celebrity chef Matthew Kenney and include Moroccan spiced lamb shank with caramelised turnips, dates and couscous, sea-salt-crusted salmon with wild mushrooms, artichokes and arugula pistou, and crispy red snapper with orange zest, onions and pignoli. Divine. **$$**

Mercer Kitchen: Mercer Hotel, 99 Prince Street at Mercer Street. Tel 212-966 5454. Subway N, R to Prince Street. Area: SoHo.

Jean-Georges Vongerichten (he of Jean Georges fame) oversees the eclectic French-inspired cuisine that is served to a trendy crowd in a chic environment. **$$**

Mesa Grill: 102 5th Avenue between 15th and 16th Streets. Tel 212-807 7400. Subway L, N, R, 4, 5, 6 to Union Square/14th Street. Area: Union Square.

Delicious and inventive south-western cuisine from Bobby Flay. A real winner. **$$**

Metronome: 915 Broadway at 21st Street. Tel 212-505 7400. Subway N, R to 23rd Street. Area: Flatiron District.

The cheaper alternative to the Supper Club (see page 144), it serves Mediterranean food in a beautiful candle-lit setting and has great jazz from Wednesday to Saturday. **$$**

Montrachet: 239 West Broadway between Walker and White Streets. Tel 212-219 2777. Subway A, C, East to Canal Street. Area: TriBeCa.

One of the best French bistros in the city and well known for excellent service. **$$$**

Moomba: 133 7th Avenue South between Charles and West 10th Streets. Tel 212-989 1414. Subway 1, 9 Christopher Street. Area: West Village.

A star-spotter's paradise, the likelihood of getting in is not high, but if you make it, expect American food at pretty steep prices. **$$**

Nobu: 105 Hudson Street at Franklin Street. Tel 212-219 0500. Subway 1, 9 Hudson Street. Area: TriBeCa.

A wonderful Japanese restaurant serving excellent cuisine to mostly celebrities. If you can get in you'll enjoy the décor and dining ... As I said, if! **$$$**

Nobu, Next Door: Right next to the celebrity haunt is an outlet for mere mortals who can sample some of the food everyone is raving about. **$$**

Odeon: 145 West Broadway between Duane and Thomas Streets. Tel 212-233 0507. Subway 1, 9 to Chambers Street. Area: TriBeCa.

A *très* hip hangout that still attracts celebs for its cool vibe and the American–French cuisine. **$$**

O Padeiro: 641 6th Avenue between 19th and 20th Streets. Tel 212-414 9661. Subway F to 23rd Street. Area: Chelsea.

Excellent value Portuguese bakery-cum-café that serves light snacks all night. **$**

Orienta: 205 East 75th Street. Tel 212-517 7509. Subway 4, 5, 6 to 77th Street. Area: Upper East Side.

A great neighbourhood restaurant serving delicious fusion food. **$$**

Palm: 837 2nd Avenue between 44th and 45th Streets. Tel 212-687 2953. Subway 4, 5, 6, 7 to Grand Central/42nd Street. Area: Midtown East.

The place in New York to get a steak or tuck into a huge lobster. The trademarks of both this establishment and **Palm Too** across the road (840 2nd Avenue) are the simple décor and the grumpy waiters. **$$**

Petrossian: 182 West 58th Street at 7th Avenue. Tel 212-245 2214. Subway N, R to 57th Street. Area: Midtown West.

Take advantage of the $20 prix fixe lunch to tuck into caviar, foie gras and smoked salmon. **$$$**

Philip Marie: 569 Hudson Street at West 11th Street. Tel 212-242 6200. Subway 1, 9 to Christopher St. Area: West Village.

Hearty American fare. Try the newcomer's parsley salad with country ham, dried tomatoes and Wisconsin cheese. **$$**

RESTAURANTS

Picholine: 35 West 64th Street between Broadway and Central Park West. Tel 212-724 8585. Area: Upper West Side.

A beautiful restaurant serving exquisite Mediterranean dishes in a refined and elegant setting, this is now among the best restaurants in New York. Opt to make it one of your 'special' treats while in the city and you can partake of the amazing cheese trolley – yes trolley, not board. Each day more than 50 different cheeses out of a total of 70 varieties are displayed on the trolley and if you have any worries about what to choose, all the waiters have been given lessons in exactly what cheeses go well with what wines and for what kind of palates. A tradition to be savoured. **$$$**

Rao's: 455 East114th Street at Pleasant Avenue. Tel 212-722 6709. Subway 6 to 116th Street. Area: Harlem.

If you ever come across the handful of people who actually have access to this eight-table restaurant, then go with them otherwise you'll never get in! Famous for its sauces, which Sinatra used to have flown to him around the world. Now the jukebox plays all the crooner's favourites. **$**

René Pujol: 321 West 51st Street between 8th and 9th Avenues. Tel 212-246 3023. Subway C, East to 50th Street. Area: Theater District.

A great French bistro serving delicious food in a delightful setting. **$$**

Republic: 2290 Broadway between 82nd and 83rd Streets. Tel 212-579 5959). Subway 1, 9 to 79th Street. Area: Upper West Side. Also at 37 Union Square West between 16th and 17th Streets. Tel 212-627 7172. Subway L, N, R, 4, 5, 6 to Union Square/14th Street. Area: Union Square.

Specialists in excellent, quick, noodle-based Pan-Asian dishes in a canteen-style environment. **$**

Rock Center Café: 20 West 50th Street between 5th Avenue and Rockefeller Plaza. Tel 212-332 7620. Subway 47th–50th Streets/ Rockefeller Plaza. Area: Midtown.

A Mecca for tourists, thanks to the scenic setting, though the American dishes are a little disappointing. **$$**

Rosa Mexicana: 1063 1st Avenue at 58th Street. Tel 212-753 7407. Subway 4, 5, 6 to 59th Street. Area: Upper East Side.

Extremely popular Mexican eaterie that is known as much for its margaritas as for its food. **$$**

Ruby Foo's: 2182 Broadway at 77th Street. Tel 212-724 6700. Subway 1, 9 to 79th Street. Area: Upper West Side.

Beautiful, classic Asian décor with delicious Asian food. The dim sum is a speciality. **$$**

Serafina Fabulous Grill: 29 East 61st Street between Madison and 5th Avenues. Tel 212-702 9898. Subway 4, 5, 6 to 59th Street. Area: Upper East Side.

Famous for thin-crust pizzas that have been voted the best in the world by gourmets, this is a haunt of both Prince Albert of Monaco and Ivana Trump. Toppings include Al Porcini with porcini mushrooms, fontina cheese and mozzarella and Al Caviale with salmon caviar, potatoes and crème fraîche. The signature focaccias, two layers of stuffed dough with fillings, range from Scottish smoked salmon, asparagus and Italian Robiola cheese to truffle oil and Robiola cheese. **$$**

Spartina: 355 Greenwich Street at Harrison Street. Tel 212-274 9310. Subway 1, 2, 3, 9 to Chambers Street. Area: TriBeCa.

Steve Kalt's hugely popular Mediterranean restaurant. **$$**

Spazzia: 366 Columbus Avenue at West 77th Street. Tel 212-799 0150. Subway 1, 9 to 79th Street. Area: Upper West Side.

The sister restaurant to Spartina, this restaurant serves delicious Mediterranean food just a stone's throw from the American Museum of Natural History. **$$**

Stingy Lulu's: 129 St Mark's Place. Tel. 212-674 3545. Area: East Village.

Another great diner. **$**

Sylvia's: 328 Lenox Avenue between 126th and 127th Streets. Tel 212-996 0660. Subway 2, 3 to 125th Street. Area: Harlem.

Southern home-style cooking – otherwise known as soul food. Sylvia's place is a New York institution and famous for its Sunday gospel brunch. **$**

Tabla: 11 Madison Avenue at 25th Street. Tel 212-889 0667. Subway N, R to 23rd Street. Area: Madison Square.

Danny Meyer's bi-level restaurant serving American Indian cuisine is a big hit and attracts a trendy crowd. Downstairs is cheaper, you'll be pleased to know. **$$$**

Tapika: 950 8th Avenue at West 56th Street. Tel 212-397 3737. Subway N, R to 57th Street. Area: Midtown.

A superb restaurant serving delicious south-western cuisine in a divine setting. There's a pretty lively bar crowd too. **$$**

TriBeCa Grill: 375 Greenwich Street at Franklin Street. Tel 212-941 3900. Subway 1, 9 Franklin Street. Area: TriBeCa.

Robert de Niro and Drew Nierporent's popular new restaurant. The $20 prix fixe lunch attracts major crowds. **$$**

Veruka: 525 Broome Street between Thompson Street and 6th Avenue. Tel 212-625 1717. Subway C, East to Spring Street. Area: SoHo.

Hip and happening late-night joint. You don't have to eat here, you can just hang out in the lounge. Look out for Johnny Depp. **$$**

Vong: 200 East 54th Street at 3rd Avenue. Tel 212-486 9592. Subway E, F to Lexington/3rd Avenues. Area: Midtown East.

Another of Jean-Georges Vongerichten's masterpieces, this Thai–French restaurant has sunken tables and deep booths that keep the trendy crowd happy. **$$$**

Yaffa Café: 97 St Mark's Place between 1st and Avenue A. Tel 212-677 9000. Area: East Village.

A classic diner with a grungy East Village twist. **$**

THEME RESTAURANTS

Hard Rock Café: 221 West 57th Street between Broadway and 7th Avenue. Tel 212-459 9320. Subway B, D, East 7th Avenue. Area: Midtown.

Classic burger 'cuisine' in a noisy, rock 'n' roll environment. **$**

Harley Davidson Café: 1370 6th Avenue at 56th Street. Tel 212-245 6000. Subway B, Q to 57th Street. Area: Midtown.

Home-style American comfort foods like meatloaf and chicken pot pie. The memorabilia include a huge floor road map of Route 66. **$**

Motown Café: 104 West 57th Street between 6th and 7th Avenues. Tel 212-581 8030. Subway N, R, B, Q to 57th Street. Area: Midtown.

Has live musical acts and occasional karaoke nights that are fun. The soul food is okay. **$**

Official All Star Café: 1540 Broadway at 45th Street. Tel 212-840 8326. Subway N, R, 1, 2, 3, 7, 9 to

Times Square/42nd Street. Area: Theater District.

Designed to look like a huge sports stadium, it is filled with sporting memorabilia, but the American food is below par. **$**

Planet Hollywood: 140 West 57th Street between 6th and 7th Avenues. Tel 212-333 7827. Subway N, R, B, Q to 57th Street. Area: Midtown.

Brilliant Hollywood memorabilia with the standard American burger fare. **$**

Theater District

Have no fear if you're heading for a show in the Theater District – along with the many theatres, there are hundreds of restaurants and you'd be hard-pressed to go wrong. From 6th Avenue in the east to 9th Avenue in the west and from West 40th Street to West 53rd Street, the Theater District is as good a place as any to get a pre-theatre meal. The main drag for eateries is between 8th and 9th Avenues on West 46th Street and is known as Restaurant Row.

AREA GUIDE

It is worth noting that there are many more restaurants for the Villages and Chelsea in Chapter 9 – Gay New York. Also, many of the bars referred to in Chapter 7 serve meals too.

Battery Park

American Park at the Battery – American

Financial District

Windows on the World – American

TriBeCa

Montrachet – French
Nobu – Japanese
Nobu, Next Door – Japanese
Odeon – American–French
Spartina – Mediterranean
TriBeCa Grill – American

Chinatown

Joe's Shanghai – Chinese

SoHo

Balthazar – French
Blue Ribbon – Eclectic–seafood
Fannelli Café – American
Lucky Strike – French
Match – American–Asian
Mercer Kitchen – French
Veruka – International

Lower East Side

Katz's Delicatessen

West Village

Café de Bruxelles – Belgian
Florent – French
Garage Restaurant – American
Grange Hall – Organic
Markt – Belgian
Philip Marie – American

Greenwich Village

Babbo – Italian
Gotham Bar and Grill – American
John's Pizza – pizza
L-Ray – Gulf Rim

East Village

Belgo Nieuw York – Belgian

Bop – Korean
Chez es Saada – Moroccan
Frank – Italian
Stingy Lulu's – American
Yaffa Café – American

Union Square

Chat 'n' Chew – American
Mesa Grill – South-western

Gramercy Park

Globe – American

Flatiron District

Gramercy Tavern – American
Metronome – Mediterranean

Chelsea

O Padeiro – Portuguese

Madison Square

Tabla – American Indian

East River

Water Club – American/seafood

Midtown West

Asia de Cuba – Fusion
Barbetta – Italian
Jean Georges – French
Petrossian – Caviar
Supper Club – American
World Yacht Dining Cruise –
Continental

Theater District

Firebird – Russian
Frankie and Johnnie's – American
Les Pyrénées – French
Official All Star Café – American
René Pujo – French

RESTAURANTS

Midtown

44 – American
China Grill – Chinese
Hard Rock Café – American
Harley Davidson Café – American
Motown Café – American
Planet Hollywood – American
Remi – Italian
Rock Center Café – American
Russian Tea Room – Russian
SeaGrill – seafood

Midtown East

21 Club – American
Asia de Cuba – Fusion
Caviar Russe – Caviar
Chin Chin – Chinese
Docks Oyster Bar – Seafood
Europa Grill – American
Four Seasons – Continental
Istana – Mediterranean
La Caravelle – French
La Grenouille – French
Le Cirque 2000 – French
Lespinasse – French fusion
Oyster Bar – Seafood
Palm – Steak and seafood
Palm Too – Steak and seafood
Tapika – South-western
Vong – Thai–French

Upper West Side

Alouette – French
Café des Artistes – French
Picholine – Mediterranean
Republic – Pan-Asian
Ruby Foo's – Asian
Spazzia – Mediterranean

Central Park

Tavern on the Green – American

Upper East Side

Aureole – American
Bolivar – Latin American
Carlyle – French
Celadon – Fusion
Mark's – French–American
Matthew's – Moroccan
Orienta – Fusion
Rosa Mexicana – Mexican
Serafina Fabulous Grill – Italian

Harlem

Rao's – Italian
Sylvia's – Soul food

Brooklyn

River Café – American/seafood
Grimaldi's – Italian

Nolita

Bond Street – Japanese
Indochine – Vietnamese-French

157

CHAPTER 9

Gay New York

INFORMATION

Lesbian and Gay Community Services Center

208 West 13th Street between 7th and 8th Avenues. Tel 212-620 7310, website at **www.gaycenter.org**

By far the best organisation in New York for getting information from, you'll find millions of leaflets and notices about gay life in the city. There are now around 400 groups that meet here and it also houses the National Museum and Archive of Lesbian and Gay History.

Publications

The main gay weeklies are *HX* (Homo Xtra) and *HX for Her* (**www.hx.com**), which tend to be available in gay bars, clubs, hotels and cafés. They include listings of bars, dance clubs, sex clubs, restaurants and cultural events. Good newspapers are the *LGNY – Lesbian and Gay New York*, though it's a lot more serious and covers political issues – and *The Blade*.

★★★★ **INSIDE TRACK** ★★★★

Check out the HX website just before you go for the latest on exactly what is happening in the city for your visit.

ACCOMMODATION

Chelsea Pines Inn: 317 West 14th Street between 8th and 9th Avenues. Tel 212-929 1023, e-mail at **cpiny@aol.com** Subway A, C, East to 14th Street; L to 8th Avenue. Area: Chelsea.

Doubles and triples **$99–$139** including breakfast.

In an excellent location in Chelsea on the border with The Village, this is just about the cheapest accommodation you could hope to get in New York, but you need to book at least six to eight weeks in advance. The hotel was recently given a face-lift and now looks clean and simple. Some rooms have their own baths, others have shared bathrooms. Open to men and women.

Colonial House Inn: 318 West 22nd Street between 8th and 9th Avenues. Tel 212-243 9669, website at **www.colonialhouseinn.com** Subway C, East to 23rd Street. Area: Chelsea. **$80–$140**

A beautiful place to stay and also spotlessly clean. The economy rooms are tiny, but all have cable TV, air con, phone and daily maid service, and smoking is allowed in rooms. The price includes breakfast, which is eaten in the Life Gallery, with works by gay and lesbian artists. Book as early as you can because this place gets packed with groups coming into town for drag conventions and so on. Has a 24-hour doorman. Mostly for gay men.

The Edison Hotel: 228 West 47th Street between Broadway and 8th Avenue. Tel 212-840 5000. Subway N, R to 49th Street. Area: Theater District. **$130–$260**

One of New York's great hotel bargains, the Edison has been totally refurbished and now has a new coffee shop, the Café Edison, which is considered to be the best place to spot lunching theatre luminaries.

The Hotel Wolcott: 4 West 31st Street between 5th Avenue and Broadway. Tel 212-268 2900, website at **www.sales@wolcott.com** Subway N, R to 28th Street. Area: Midtown. **$90–$180**

Well, darling, it's location, location, location, for this hotel. Just three blocks down from 5th Avenue and the Empire State Building, this is a favourite with the serious tourist and budget-minded business traveller.

Incentra Village House: 32 8th Avenue between West 12th and Jane Streets. Tel 212-206 0007. Subway A, C, East to 14th Street; L to 8th Avenue. Area: West Village. Doubles **$99–$150**

A moderately priced guest house in two red-brick townhouses that date back to the 1840s (old by American standards!). The suites all have kitchens, phones and private

bathrooms and some can even accommodate groups of four to five people. All the rooms are well decorated with different themes – the Bishop Room is a lovely split-level suite and the Garden Room has its own private garden filled with flowers and shrubs. There is a 1939 Steinway piano in the parlour and anyone who can is allowed to play.

The Inn at Irving Place: 56 Irving Place between 17th and 18th Streets. Tel 212-533 4600, website at **www.innatirving.com** Subway L, N, R, 4, 5, 6 to 14th Street/Union Square. Area: Gramercy Park. **$295–$475.**

The building is filled with exquisite furniture and elegant décor. All rooms come with private facilities, some even have study areas, there is a 24-hour concierge, plus laptops and fax on request, laundry and dry-cleaning, video rentals, gym within walking distance and 24-hour massage.

Pride Accommodations: Tel and fax: 212-255 0388. E-mail: **info@prideaccommodations.com**

For bed and breakfast accommodation throughout Manhattan, this is where to come to. Fax or e-mail your preference for hosted or unhosted (ie in the owner's house or in a private studio), your dates, desired location, number of guests and your own details, including your name, address, fax and phone number. They can even sort out accommodation on Fire Island if necessary.

9

The Royalton: 44 West 44th Street between 5th and 6th Avenues. Tel 212-869 4400. Subway 4, 5, 6 to 42nd Street; 7 to 5th Avenue. Area: Midtown. **From $350**

Ian Shraeger's beautiful hotel, designed by Philippe Starck, is now considered to be the address for gays and lesbians into the power thing. A chic tone is set by the lively fashion and publishing crowd who love the lobby bar and restaurant.

FOR HIM

Note that, as in the UK, special events and party nights change very frequently so it is always best to check before setting out.

Clubs

Centro Fly: 45 West 21st Street between 5th and 6th Avenues. Tel 212-627 7770. Subway N, R, F to 23rd Street. Area: Chelsea.

Subliminal Sessions, $15, Thursdays from 10pm. Has a rotating cast of famous DJs from all over the world. Popular with everyone, gay or straight.

El Flamingo: 547 West 21st Street between 10th and 11th Avenues. Tel 212-243 2121. Subway C, East to 23rd Street. Area: Chelsea.

Performances of the Off-Broadway *Donkey Show* Wed to Sat, followed by Midnight Disco on Saturdays from 11pm. $15, $10 before midnight.

La Nueva Escuelita: 301 West 39th Street at 8th Avenue. Tel 212-631 0588. Subway A, C, East to 42nd Street. Area: Midtown West.

Thumpin' Thursdays, $5, $10 after 10pm. DJ Steve 'Chip Chop' Gonzalez plays salsa, merengue and house. Spicy Fridays, $10, from 10pm. Dancing and Latin-style drag show starring Angel Sheridan and the divas of Escuelita. Azucar Saturdays, $15, from 10pm with house and Latin music. Sunbeam Sundays, $3. Harmonica Sunbeam hosts the tea dance from 5pm.

Limelight: 660 6th Avenue at 20th Street. Tel 212-807 7780. Subway F to 23rd Street. Area: Flatiron District.

Gay nights on Fridays and Sundays.

Lips: 2 Bank Street at Greenwich Avenue. Tel 212-675 7710. Subway 1, 2, 3, 9 to 14th Street. Area: West Village.

A supper club with continuous drag shows from 5.30pm to midnight, 2am on Fri and Sat. The Bitchy Bingo Show on Wednesdays, free, open from 8pm. Hosts Sherry Vine and Yvon Lame preside over the bitchiest bingo game in the world.

Pyramid Club: 101 Avenue A between 6th and 7th Streets. Tel 212-462 9077. Subway F to 2nd Avenue. Area: East Village.

1984, $5, on Fridays from 10pm for 1980s dance music. Pyramid Saturdays, $6, from 11pm when Austin Downey brings out the funky house vibes.

Roxy: 515 West 18th Street between 10th and 11th Avenues. Tel 212-645 5156. Subway A, C, East to 14th Street; L to 8th Avenue. Area: Chelsea.

Saturdays, $20, from 11pm for an outrageous evening of gorgeous guys, sexy drag queens and brilliant sounds. This is the big night out. Winner of the 1999 *HX* Award for Best Large Club Night.

Splash: 50 West 17th Street between 5th and 6th Avenues. Tel 212-691 0073. Subway L, N, R, 4, 5, 6 to 14th Street/Union Square. Area: Chelsea.

Musical Mondays, free. Door opens 4pm for Happy Hour until 9pm. Dancing after 11pm as VJ Reed McGowan serves showtunes and campy video clips. 98° Tuesdays, free. David Martinez houses it up after 10pm. Wet Me Wednesdays, free. Music and video clips to 10pm, then DJ Carlos Pertuz spins the dance tunes. Virtual Thursdays, free. Dancing after 10pm with DJ Julian Marsh spinning smooth circuit sounds. Full Frontal Fridays, free before 10pm, $7 after. After 10pm DJ Max Rodriguez spins NRG-etic house. X-Zone Saturdays, free before 10pm, $7 after. Dancing after 10pm with Kevin Frank. Extreme Tea on Sundays, free from 9pm till 4am. Splash also has a happy hour every weekday from 4pm until 9pm and at weekends from 4pm until 8pm.

Studio 84: 3534 Broadway at 145th Street. Tel 212-234 8484. Subway 1, 9 to 145th Street. Area: Harlem.

Tu y Yo on Thursdays, $2 before midnight, $5 after. A house party for Dominicans, Puerto Ricans and Nubians.

The Monster: 80 Grove Street at Sheridan Square. Tel 212-924 3558. Subway 1, 2, 3, 9 Christopher Street/Sheridan Square. Area: The Village.

Sabor Latino on Mondays, free. Opens at 4pm, party starts at 10pm with DJ Aurelio Martin and an amateur strip contest. Flashback Tuesdays, free. Opens at 4pm, dancing after 10pm to disco classics. Monster Tea on Sundays, free before 8pm, $3 after. From 5pm DJ Aurelio Martin spins Latin hits until 4am.

Tunnel: 220 12th Avenue at 27th Street. Tel 212-695 4682. Subway C, E to 23rd Street. Area: Chelsea.

Kurfew on Fridays, $20, from 11pm when DJs Jen Pussy-Lee and Michael T spin the grooves for the college kids.

Twilo: 530 West 27th Street between 10th and 11th Avenues. Tel 212-268 1600. Subway C, E to 23rd Street. Area: Chelsea.

Fridays is a mixed night, $25. From 11pm there is a rotating cast of prominent DJs such as Sasha and Digweed and Paul Van Dyk. Saturdays, $25. From 11pm DJ Vasquez spins the discs for the assorted collection of drag queens and clubheads. You won't get out till Sunday afternoon.

Vinyl: 6 Hubert Street between Greenwich and Hudson Streets. Tel 212-343 1379. Subway A, C, East to Canal Street; 1, 9 to Franklin Street. Area: TriBeCa.

Be Yourself on Fridays, $20, from 11pm with DJ/producer Danny

Tenaglia playing the music. Shelter, Saturdays from 11pm, $11, with DJ Timmy Regisford's spirit of the Paradise Garage. An alcohol-free night. Body and Soul, Sundays, $14, from 4pm. DJs Francois K, Danny Krivit and Joe Claussell spin the house classics for a mixed crowd.

Lounges

B Bar: 40 East 4th Street between Lafayette Street and the Bowery. Tel 212-475 2220. Subway B, D, F, Q to Broadway/Lafayette Street; 6 to Bleecker Street. Area: East Village.

Beige on Tuesdays, free, from 9pm. This is a super-trendy hangout filled with models and gorgeous people.

Barracuda: 275 West 22nd Street between 7th and 8th Avenues. Tel 212-645 8613. Subway C, E, 1, 9 to 23rd Street. Area: Chelsea.

Frequent, free drag shows.

Blu: 161 West 23rd Street at 7th Avenue. Tel 212-633 6113. Subway 1, 9 to 23rd Street. Area: Chelsea.

Faggot Feud hosted by Mona Foot on Wednesdays, free. Gay game show at 11pm. Gong Show on Thursdays, free. Show at midnight. Hedda Lettuce presides over the cruel 1970s game show with hilarious results.

The Cock: 188 Avenue A at East 12th Street. Tel 212-777 6254. Subway F to 2nd Avenue, 6 to Bleecker Street. Area: East Village.

Cock-A-Two on Wednesdays, free, from 10.30pm with drag divas at midnight. Cruise on Thursdays, $5, from 11pm with host Mario Diaz and DJs Scott Ewalt and Jo Jo Americo.

Foxy on Saturdays, $5, when the audience competes for the title of 'foxiest'. Opens 10.30pm. Great drag show acts.

g: 225 West 19th Street between 7th and 8th Avenues. Tel 212- 929 1085. Subway 1, 9 to 18th Street. Area: Chelsea.

A super-popular nightly spot for hunks open from 4pm to 4am. It gets incredibly busy later on when the queues build up outside.

Hell: 59 Gansevoort Street at Washington Street. Tel 212-727 1666. Subway A, C, East to 14th Street. Area: West Village.

Tuesday nights hosts Afterlife, free, from 10pm. DJ Barton spins a British blend of sounds. House in Hell on Thursdays is also free. From 9.30pm. DJ Bert Villanueva spins the discs for a cool, chic crowd.

Lucky Cheng's: 24 1st Avenue between 1st and 2nd Streets. Tel 212-473 0516. Subway F to 2nd Avenue; 6 to Bleecker Street. Area: East Village.

The drag lounge and bar beneath the restaurant is past its heyday, but the late-night karaoke is still fun.

Pegasus: 119 East 60th Street between Park and Lexington Avenues. Tel 212-888 4702. Subway 4, 5, 6 to 59th Street; N, R to Lexington Avenue. Area: Upper East Side.

Gentlemen's piano bar featuring karaoke and cabaret shows on various rotating nights of the week. Fri and Sat focus on entertainment for Asian gays.

Top: Comfort Inn

Above: Apple Core Hotel

Above right: Soho Grand

Right: Soho Grand

Below: The Bentley

Above left: Quality Hotel
Above centre: Carlton Hotel
Above right: Holiday Inn
Left: Best Western Manhattan
Below left: New York Hilton
Below right: Marriott Marquis

Photo acknowledgements: New York street scene (p
70) Mark Leet Photography. Lower East Side Tenem
Museum (page 105) Carol Highsmith. The Frick Coll
(page 105). The Children's Museum (105). Fifth Ave
(page 106) NYC & Co. Beauty and the Beast (page
Eduarado Patino. The Lion King and Rent 2000 (pa
139) Joan Marcus.American. Park at the Battery, Pa
View at the Boathouse and Europa Grill (page 140)
Philippe Dollo.Matthews (page 141). The Bentley (p
141). Quality Hotel, Best Western Manhattan, Com
Inn, Apple Core Hotels and The Bentley and Soho (
(page 176) Nancy Friedman PR. Carlton Hotel (page
All other photographs provided by NYCBV.

Wonder Bar: 505 East 6th Street between Avenues A and B. Tel 212-777 9105. Subway F to 2nd Avenue. Area: East Village.

A nightly lounge with a packed, mixed crowd enjoying the soul and classic hits.

Xth Avenue Lounge: 642 10th Avenue at 45th Street. Tel 212-245 9088. Subway A, C, East to 42nd Street. Area: Midtown West.

Open daily with a Happy Hour between 4pm and 8pm. There is a light menu in the back room. A neighbourhood bar not exclusively for gays.

FOR HER

Clubs and lounges

Bar 85: 504 West 16th Street between 10th and 11th Avenues. Tel 212-631 1000. Subway A, C, East to 14th Street. Area: Chelsea.

Hosts Lipstick and Candy on Thursday night – a lovely lounge party with DJ Pride (from 9pm, $15) – and LoverGirl on Saturdays with DJs Kris Spirit, MK, Storm and Mary Mac and go-go girls galore (from 9.30pm, $8 before midnight, $10 after).

Crazy Nanny's: 21 7th Avenue South at Leroy Street. Tel 212-366 6312. Subway 1, 9 to Christopher Street/Sheridan Square. Area: West Village.

This bar is popular with locals, out-of-towners and their friends. A mix of pool, drag shows and karaoke. Fri and Sat are DJ nights. The bar is

open until 4am daily with a Happy Hour from 4pm to 7pm every day.

Flamingo: 219 2nd Avenue at 13th Street. Tel 212-533 2860.

An off-beat, trendy club. From September 2000, this will be the venue of the Clit Club party, an uninhibited bash which ran for nine years at the now-closed Mother club.

Henrietta Hudson's: 438 Hudson Street at Morton Street. Tel 212-243 9079. Subway 1, 9 to Christopher Street/Sheridan Square. Area: West Village.

A neighbourhood girl bar with great jukebox music and a friendly crowd. Tuesday the party is Out Loud (from 10pm, free), then it's Decadence on Wednesdays with DJ Alex 'Tech' Aviance (9pm, free), Mi Tierra on Thursdays with DJ Lisa G (10pm, free), Bliss on Friday with DJ Pride (10pm, free), Beautiful Girl on Saturdays with guest DJs (10pm, $5) and Girl Parts on Sundays (8pm, $4). The bar is open from 4pm to 4am Monday to Friday, 1pm to 4am weekends, with a happy hour from 5pm to 7pm during the week.

Julie's: 204 East 53rd Street between 2nd and 3rd Avenues. Tel 212-688 1294. Subway E, F to Lexington Avenue; 6 to 51st Street. Area: Midtown East.

A cosy bar for stylish and often professional women, it gets packed at the weekends. Monday is R 'n' B night, Tuesday karaoke with Poppi Kramer, Wednesday is salsa and merengue, Thursday is singles' night, Friday is house and reggae, Saturday is Latin night and Sunday is the Tea Dance. Open from 5pm nightly until as late as 4am. Happy hour is from 5pm to 7pm daily.

La Nueva Escuelita: 301 West 39th Street at 8th Avenue. Tel 212-631 0588. Subway A, C, East to 42nd Street. Area: Midtown West.

Her/She Bar on Friday night is a truly upbeat Latin night with a hot crowd. Opens at 10pm, $8 before midnight, $10 after.

Meow Mix: 269 Houston Street at Suffolk Street. Tel 212-254 0688. Subway B, D, F, Q to Broadway/ Lafayette Street; 6 to Bleecker Street. Area: Lower East Side.

A hip neighbourhood bar that welcomes both women and their men friends. Xena fans unite on the second Tuesday of every month for a full three episodes of the sword-wielding heroine ($3). Every Thursday it's Gloss from 10pm ($5), then it's Frisky Friday (from 11pm, free before 9.30pm, $5 after) and Sassy Saturday (from 9.30pm, $5). Happy Hour lasts from 5pm to 8pm from Tuesday to Friday and from 3pm to 8pm at the weekends.

Starlight: 167 Avenue A and 11th Street. Tel 212-475 2172. Subway L to 1st Avenue. Area: East Village.

A fabulous bar and lounge that is open from Wednesday to Sunday until 3am. Sundays are Starlette night with Wanda and DJ Sharee.

Wonder Bar: 505 East 6th Avenue between Avenues A and B. Tel 212-777 9105. Subway F to 2nd Avenue. Area: East Village.

This is a stylish hangout for both men and women, which tends to be fairly mellow during the week, but gets packed out at the weekends. Open every day from 6pm to 4am, the daily happy hour is between 6pm and 8pm.

RESTAURANTS

Chelsea

Big Cup: 228 8th Avenue at 22nd Street. Tel 212-206 0059.

A truly gay local coffee house.

Eighteenth and 8th: 159 8th Avenue at 18th Street. Tel 212-242 5000.

The gay restaurant of the gay district of New York, it serves healthy American food. But be prepared for a long wait outside as it's tiny inside.

Empire Diner: 210 10th Avenue at 22nd Street. Tel 212-243 2736.

A great pit-stop after a night out at a club.

Lola: 30 West 22nd Street between 5th and 6th Avenues. Tel 212-675 6700.

Famous for its American cuisine with Caribbean and Asian influences, it gets packed on Sunday for the gospel brunches.

Pad Thai: 114 8th Avenue at 16th Street. Tel 212-691 6226.

Elegant noodle lounge.

Restivo: 209 7th Avenue at 22nd Street. Tel 212-366 4133.

Great Italian cuisine at good prices.

East Side

Comfort Diner: 214 East 45th Street between 2nd and 3rd Avenues. Tel 212-867 4555.

Authentic and delicious American cuisine served in a 1950s-style diner setting.

Regents: 317 East 53rd Street between 1st and 2nd Avenues. Tel 212-593 3091.

Attracts a fairly posh gay crowd for its eclectic cuisine. Also has an upstairs back terrace and live cabaret nightly.

Townhouse Restaurant: 206 East 58th Street between 2nd and 3rd Avenues. Tel 212-826 6241.

This is a real gay haunt – especially among the more mature crowd. It serves delicious food at reasonable prices.

East Village

Astor Restaurant and Lounge: 316 Bowery at Bleecker Street. Tel 212-253 8644.

The Moroccan-style lounge plays host to a gay party on Wednesdays, while the restaurant serves French–Mediterranean food in an intimate setting.

B Bar: 40 East 4th Street between Lafayette Street and Bowery. Tel 212-475 2220.

Home to Beige on a Tuesday night, this gorgeous bistro serves delicious food to the beautiful people.

Lucien: 14 1st Avenue at 1st Street. Tel 212-260 6481.

Always packed, this tiny French bistro serves delicious food and is particularly known for its Sunday brunch.

Pangea: 178 2nd Avenue between 11th and 12th Streets. Tel 212-995 0900.

Known for its wonderful home-made pastas and Mediterranean cuisine.

Stingy Lulu's: 129 St Mark's Place between Avenue A and 1st Avenue. Tel 212-674 3545.

A gorgeous old-fashioned diner with the East Village twist.

SoHo/Nolita/TriBeCa

Amici Miei: 475 West Broadway at Houston Street. Tel 212-533 1933.

A chic Italian restaurant open for lunch and dinner with outdoor seating that makes it perfect for people-watching.

Basset Café: 123 West Broadway at Duane Street. Tel 212-349 1662.

Tuck into a delicious salad or sandwich.

El Teddy's: 219 West Broadway between Franklin and White Streets. Tel 212-941 7070.

A hip hangout with a great bar scene and excellent food.

La Cigale: 231 Mott Street between Prince and Spring Streets. Tel 212-334 4331.

Simple but imaginative continental food and a magical back garden.

West Side

Coffee Pot: 350 West 49th Street at 9th Avenue. Tel 212-265 3566.

Nice little coffee bar with live music and Tarot card readings.

Mangia East Bevi: 800 9th Avenue at 53rd Street. Tel 212-956 3976.

A popular Italian serving up excellent food in the middle of Midtown's gay district.

Revolution: 611 9th Avenue between 43rd and 44th Streets. Tel 212-489 8451.

A club-like restaurant with great food and music videos. It has a DJ every night, a youngish crowd and American menus.

Vintage: 753 9th Avenue at 51st Street. Tel 212-581 4655.

A hip bar/restaurant that serves dinner till midnight and cocktails till 4am.

West Village

Benny's Burritos: 113 Greenwich Avenue at Jane Street. Tel 212-727 3560.

The incredibly cheap and huge burritos attract a huge student crowd who don't mind the poor service.

Caffe Dell'Artista: 46 Greenwich Avenue between 6th and 7th Avenues. Tel 212-645 4431.

A European-style café serving simple, light meals and desserts.

Cowgirl Hall of Fame: 519 Hudson Street at Charles Street. Tel 212-633 1133.

Great for women who feel at home surrounded by cowgirl memorabilia and enjoy the margaritas. The food's good too as is the people-watching outside in the summer.

Florent: 69 Gansevoort Street between Greenwich and Washington Streets. Tel 212-989 5779.

Good French food served 24 hours a day at weekends and until 5am during the week, making it an excellent pit-stop after clubbing.

Garage Restaurant and Café: 99 7th Avenue South between Barrow and Grove Streets. Tel 212-645 0600.

Serves global cuisine including steaks and a raw bar, with live jazz nightly.

Lips: 2 Bank Street at Greenwich Avenue. Tel 212-675 7710.

A continental–Italian menu with dishes named after popular queens, drag memorabilia and waitresses in drag.

Nadine's: 99 Bank Street at Greenwich Street. Tel 212-924 3165.

Eclectic and good value food in a funky but glamorous setting.

Rubyfruit Bar and Grill: 531 Hudson Street at Charles Street. Tel 212-929 3343.

Not just for lesbians any more, but still for the open-minded. Serves good eclectic food both downstairs and in the fun bar upstairs. Live music nightly.

Sacred Cow: 522 Hudson Street at West 10th Street. Tel 212-337 0863.

Healthy vegan food shop and café.

CHAPTER 10

Sports

sk any New Yorker and they'll tell you that they read their newspapers from back to front – that's just how important sports are to them. And they have plenty to choose between, from two football teams, to baseball, basketball, hockey, tennis and racing. That's the good news. The bad news is that it can be really tough to get into some of the games, especially to see the New York Giants and the Mets, but it's worth making the effort just to see another side to New York life! If you can't get tickets directly through the box offices listed, then try **TicketMaster** on 212-307 7171 – they've got most games covered. An incredibly expensive alternative is to try one of the companies that specialise in selling tickets at exorbitant prices – anything from $100 for a football game to $1,000 for a baseball game. They include **Prestige Entertainment** on 1-800-2-GET-TIX and **Ticket Window** on 1-800-SOLD-OUT. A third alternative is to try a ticket tout – they're known as 'scalpers' in New York – outside Madison Square Garden. Your final and probably best bet of all three is to ask the concierge at your hotel – they have an amazing ability to come up with the goods.

★★★★ **INSIDE TRACK** ★★★★

For a schedule of forthcoming games in all the sports listed, check out the website: *www.sportserver.com*

SPECTATOR SPORTS

Madison Square Garden on 7th Avenue at 32nd Street (subway A, C, E, 1, 2, 3, 9 to 34th Street/Penn Street) is home to the following:

NBA's **New York Knicks** basketball team – season is from November to June. Box office: 212-465 JUMP.

NHL's **New York Rangers** ice hockey team – season is from October to April. Box office: 212-308 NYRS.

WNBA **New York Liberty** women's pro basketball team – season is from May to August. Call TicketMaster on 212-307 7171.

Women's Tennis Association Tour Championships in November. Call TicketMaster.

Football

The two teams are the **New York Giants** and the **New York Jets,** who both play at the Giants Stadium at Meadowlands, New Jersey (get there on a bus from the Port Authority bus terminal at 42nd Street and

8th Avenue). The box office is 201-935 3900 and you'll have more luck getting tickets for the Jets than the Giants. The season runs from September to January.

Baseball

Try the **Yankee Stadium** (see page 106) in The Bronx at 161st Street (take subways C, D or 4 to 161st Street/ Yankee Stadium). The box office number is 718-293 6000.

The **New York Mets** play at Shea Stadium in Flushing Meadows, Queens (take the 7 line from 42nd Street/Times Square to Willetts Point/Shea Stadium). The box office is 718-507 8499. The season for both is from April to October.

Tennis

The **US Open** is held every year at the US Tennis Center in Flushing Meadows, Queens (take subway 7 to Willetts Point/Shea Stadium), from late August to early September. Tele-Charge on 212-239 6250. Tickets for the finals are impossible to get, so go for the earlier rounds.

Horse racing

This takes place at Aqueduct Stadium in Queens (take subway A to Aqueduct Racetrack) from mid-October to May, every Wednesday to Saturday. Call 718-641 4700 for information. Also at the Belmont Racetrack (take the Long Island Rail Road's 'Belmont Special' from Pennsylvania Station at 7th Avenue and 34th Street) from May to July.

GET STUCK IN

If you want to take part in some kind of sporting activity while in New York, your best bet is Central Park. Probably the most popular sports here are boating, biking, in-line skating and running.

Boating

From Loeb Boathouse, Central Park near 5th Avenue and East 74th Street. Tel 212-517 4723). Here you can rent a rowing boat or even a chauffered gondola. $10 per half hour, $30 deposit.

Biking

You can also rent bikes from the Loeb Boathouse. Try tackling the seven-mile road loop that is closed to traffic at the weekend. $20–$30 per hour, $100 deposit.

In-line skating

The Wollman Memorial Rink at the southern end of Central Park is a good place to start, though the more experienced prefer to tackle the seven-mile road loop. You can hire skates from Blades at 160 East 86th Street between Lexington and 3rd Avenues (tel 212-996 1644) or 120 West 72nd Street between Broadway and Columbus Avenues (tel 212-787 3911) for $20 per day plus $200 deposit without a credit card payment.

Running

Joggers go running in Central Park or Riverside Park on the west side of Manhattan.

CHAPTER 11

Hotels

I have deliberately left the matter of choosing your hotel to be your last decision so that you will have the chance first to work out what you want to do while you're in the Big Apple. That way you'll know where you'll be spending most of your time, so you can decide where best to locate yourself. It may be that if you intend to stay for a week it would work out best to stay at two hotels – one in Lower Manhattan and one in Midtown – so you can save on travelling time and expensive cab fares.

It is worth noting a few of the basic facts about New York hotels, too, so you can make a considered opinion about where to stay. For instance, the most expensive hotels tend to be clustered on the East Side from Midtown up to 96th Street. The best deals tend to be around Herald Square and on the Upper West Side, but if you go for these options check you won't be spending too much extra on transportation costs. The average room rate for a room that can accommodate two people is $200 a night – so if you get something for less (and there are plenty of ways to do this) you are doing well.

Here are some more tips:

• Over the last few years more and more hotels have been opening up and existing ones have been expanding to meet the growing demand for beds in the city. It is estimated that there are now around 70,000 hotel rooms in New York, yet demand at certain times of the year is such that you will still have a hard time finding a room. Your best bet for both ensuring a bed and getting the best prices is to go in the off-peak times of January to March and also July and August.

• Most hotels reduce their rates at weekends – including some of the poshest. If you're staying for more than a weekend, negotiate the best rate you can for the rest of your time or switch to a cheaper hotel.

• If noise is a particular problem for you, bear in mind that hotels Downtown and Uptown tend to be quieter than those in Midtown. Also, addresses on streets tend to be quieter than those on avenues except those nearer the river.

• For longer stays, try to choose a hotel room with a kitchenette, then you won't have to eat out all the time.

• Smaller hotels tend not to book large groups, so they often have rooms available even during peak periods.

• If you're having real problems

finding a hotel, stay in nearby Westchester County, which is just north of The Bronx, where there is a good choice of luxury hotels, inns and B and B accommodation that are all much cheaper than in Manhattan and easily accessible to the island via excellent rail links.

• When booking your room, check there isn't going to be a major convention staying at the hotel at the same time as you – if there is, ask to be put on a different floor as some of the people who attend conventions can be very noisy.

• Also ask for a corner room – they are usually bigger, less noisy and have more windows and, therefore, more light than other rooms and don't always cost more than a standard room.

• There is always a lot of renovation work going on in New York hotels, so when reserving a room, ask if any is being done at that particular hotel and, if so, ask for a room as far away as possible from the renovation work.

BOOKING IT YOURSELF

Of course, you can use a travel agent to make room reservations, but you can also do it yourself through companies that specialise in offering excellent rates at off-peak and low-peak times or even just guarantee finding you a room during busy periods. They include:

Hotel Conxions: Tel 212-840 8686, fax 212-221 8686, or check out their website where you can also find out about availability and price, and book a room: **www.hotelconxions.com**

Hotel America Ltd: Tel 01444 410555. A British company providing hotel discounts anywhere in the world. Either phone or use the website at **www.hotelanywhere.co.uk**

Quickbook: Tel 212-779 ROOM, fax 212-779 6120. Website at **www.quikbook.com** A service providing discounts on hotels from coast to coast in America. They

Diamond discounts

There are two ways to cut your room rates through NYTAB. You can take advantage of their tie-up with Express Reservations. Take a look at their website at www.hotelsinmanhattan.com or call 001 303-28 7808. They offer major discounts on over 25 hotels across most price categories.

NYTAB has also made arrangements at a few carefully chosen hotels for discounts of up to 45 per cent. Full details can be found on pages 193–4.

★★★★ **INSIDE TRACK** ★★★★

If you are planning to take in the sights of Downtown Manhattan, Chinatown, Lower East Side, SoHo and the Village, choose a hotel in the area. It'll save you loads of time on travel and money on cab fares.

promise there are no hidden cancellation or change penalties, and pre-payment is not required.

Another great way to find cheaper rates is through the hotel discount service on:

http://usacitylink.com/citylink/ny/new-york

When discussing room rates with any of these organisations, always check that the prices you are quoted include the **New York City hotel tax** of 13.25 per cent and the $2 per night **occupancy tax.**

Below I've given a listing of various hotels in New York, which I have chosen for their location, service, price or the excellent value-for-money they offer. I have divided them up firstly by price, showing also their location, and then listed them by area with a price cross reference. This way if price is more important you know where to look first, or if location is a serious consideration, you will be able to see how much you will have to pay. Happy bed-hunting!

$	Less than $100
$$	$100–$200
$$$	$200–$300
$$$$	$300–$400
$$$$$	$400 and over

SHEER LUXURY

Hotel Carlyle: 35 East 76th Street between Madison and Park Avenues. Tel 212-744 1600, fax: 212-717 4682. Subway 6 to 77th Street. **Area: Upper East Side.**

Famous for its impeccable and discreet service, this is the place where the stars come. The apartment-style rooms are elegant and very plush – some even have grand pianos and all have whirlpools in the bathrooms. By the way, Woody Allen plays jazz here every week. **$$$$–$$$$$**

The Four Seasons: 57 East 57th Street between Madison and Park Avenues. Tel 212-758 5700, fax 212-758 5711. Subway 4, 5, 6 to 59th Street. **Area: Midtown East.**

Put on your best power suits to rub shoulders with New York's movers and shakers. The art deco-style rooms come with electronically controlled drapes and marble-clad bathrooms. **$$$$–$$$$$**

★★★★ **INSIDE TRACK** ★★★★
★ When making a booking directly ★
★ with a hotel, always make sure ★
★ they send you confirmation of ★
★ your reservation (fax is simplest). ★
★ That way, if there is any ★
★ problem when you arrive, you ★
★ have proof of your reservation ★
★ and the hotel is duty-bound to ★
★ find you a room. ★
★★★★★★★★★★★★★★★★★★★★

Hotel Plaza-Athene: 37 East 64th Street between Madison and Park Avenues. Tel 212-734 9100, fax 212 722 0958. Subway 6 to 68th Street. **Area: Upper East Side.**

What its rooms lack in size they make up for with elegant classic French antique furnishings. **$$$$-$$$$$**

The Mark: 25 East 77th Street between 5th and Madison Avenues. Tel 212-744 4300, fax 212-744 2749. Subway 6 to 77th Street. **Area: Upper East Side.**

In terms of luxury, it vies with the Carlyle – only The Mark has Italian neoclassicism compared with the Carlyle's English gentility. There's a complimentary car service to Wall Street and the Theater District, a small health club and a top-notch restaurant. Take advantage of the excellent value-for-money weekend and summer rates. **$$$$-$$$$$**

★★★★ **INSIDE TRACK** ★★★★
★ ★
★ **The posh Mark hotel on the** ★
★ **Upper East Side does such good** ★
★ **weekend rates that you could** ★
★ **afford to stay there and enjoy all** ★
★ **that fabulous luxury.** ★
★★★★★★★★★★★★★★★★★★★★★★★

The Sherry-Netherland: 781 5th Avenue at East 59th Street. Tel 212-355 2800, fax 212-319 4306. Subway 4, 5, 6 to 59th Street. **Area: Midtown East.**

A true New York secret, this is one of the grand hotels with plenty of charm and is also the permanent home of many a celebrity. Discount with a NYCard. **$$$$-$$$$$**

The Stanhope: 995 5th Avenue at 81st Street. Tel 212-288 5800, fax 212-517 0088. Subway 6 to 77th Street. **Area: Upper East Side.**

Well located on Museum Mile, this security-conscious hotel is a real hideaway for Hollywood stars and also caters to top businesspeople. **$$$$-$$$$$**

The Waldorf-Astoria: 301 Park Avenue at 50th Street. Tel 212-355 3000, fax 212-872 7272. Subway 6 to 51st Street. **Area: Midtown East.**

In 1998 a $60-million upgrade was completed which saw the Park Avenue lobby, its surrounding Cocktail Terrace and Sir Harry's Bar restored to full glory of their art deco heyday. The refurbishment of Oscar's restaurant by Adam Tihany, the hottest restaurant designer in town, and the renewal of the fabled Empire Room put the finishing touches on this grand hotel. **$$$$-$$$$$**

★★★★ **INSIDE TRACK** ★★★★
★ ★
★ **I have not included car parking** ★
★ **fees, on the basis that most of** ★
★ **you won't be hiring a car while in** ★
★ **New York (see page 21), but if** ★
★ **you do, bear in mind that most** ★
★ **hotels charge a parking fee of** ★
★ **around $25 a night.** ★
★★★★★★★★★★★★★★★★★★★★★★★

PRETTY DARN LOVELY

Box Tree: 250 East 49th Street between 2nd and 3rd Avenues. Tel 212-758 8320, fax 212-308 3899. Subway 6 to 51st Street. **Area: Midtown East.**

Despite the skyscrapers New York still has a few traditional townhouses now turned into 'boutique' – ie small – hotels. The Box Tree with its romantic décor is one of the best. **$$$–$$$$**

Elysee: 60 East 54th Street between Park and Madison Avenues. Tel 212-753 1066, fax 212-980 9278. Subway 6 to 51st Street. **Area: Midtown East.**

Another boutique offering, this time dating from the 1930s. Its décor includes antique furnishings and Italian marble bathrooms. **$$$$–$$$$$**

Inn at Irving Place: 56 Irving Place between East 17th and East 18th Streets. Tel 212-533 4600, fax 212-533 4611. Subway L, N, R, 4, 5, 6 to 14th Street/Union Square. **Area: Gramercy.**

Delightful, tiny Victorian boutique hotel. Each room comes with a romantic fireplace and four-poster bed. **$$$$–$$$$$**

Inn New York City: 266 West 71st Street between Broadway and West End Avenue. Tel 212-580 1900, fax 212-580 4437. Subway 1, 2, 3, 9 to 72nd Street. **Area: Upper West Side.**

Taking the boutique notion to its limits, this hotel has just four suites, each with a kitchen. **$$$$–$$$$$**

Kitano Hotel: 66 Park Avenue at East 38th Street. Tel 212-885 7000, fax 212-885 7100. Subway S, 4, 5, 6, 7 to Grand Central/42nd Street. **Area: Midtown East.**

A first-class, Japanese-run hotel with top-notch service and a deliciously decadent deep-soaking tub in each room. **$$$$–$$$$$**

Marriott World Trade Center Hotel: 3 World Trade Center between Liberty and Vesey Streets. Tel 212-938 9100, fax 212-444 4094. Subway C, E to World Trade Center; N, R, 1, 9 to Cortlandt Street. **Area: Financial District.**

Geared up to the businessperson thanks to its location, it offers a complimentary breakfast and use of the rooftop health club, swimming pool, indoor track and saunas. **$$$$**

The New York Hilton and Towers: 1335 6th Avenue at 53rd Street. Tel 212-586 7000, fax 212-315 1374. Subway B, D, F, Q to 47th–50th Streets/Rockefeller Center. **Area: Midtown West.**

After a recent $100-million renovation, the city's largest hotel now has a beautiful new façade and entrance lobby, plus two new restaurants and lounges. **$$$$$**

Peninsula New York: 700 5th Avenue at 55th Street. Tel 212-247 2200, fax 212-903 3943. Subway F to 53rd Street; 6 to 51st Street. **Area: Midtown.**

A beautiful hotel which has recently undergone a $45-million renovation in the public areas, restaurants and all 241 guest rooms. **$$$$$**

Royalton: 44 West 44th Street between 5th and 6th Avenues. Tel 212-869 4400, fax 212-869 8965. Subway B, D, F, Q to 42nd Street. **Area: Midtown.**

An 'in' place with the magazine and showbiz crowd, this hotel was designed by Philippe Starck. Each of the rooms has futon beds, slate fireplaces and round bathtubs. **$$$$–$$$$$**

SoHo Grand: 310 West Broadway between Grand and Canal Streets. Tel 212-965 3000, fax 212-965 3244. Subway C, East to Canal Street. **Area: SoHo.**

Famous for its style, this was the first proper hotel to open in the SoHo area. Cocktails and light meals are served in the Grand Bar, an intimate, wood-panelled club room, as well as the fashionable Salon, a lively lounge that is excellent for people-watching. **$$$$**

TriBeCa Grand: 2 Avenue of the Americas at Church Street. Tel 212-519 6600, fax 212-519 6700, UK freephone 0800-028 9874, or look them up on their website at **www.tribecagrand.com** Subway 1, 9 to Franklin Street. **Area: TriBeCa.**

A new sister property to the extremely stylish SoHo Grand, this is the first major hotel to open in the TriBeCa area. In-room amenities include voice mail, data port, complimentary local phone calls and faxes, built-in TV and telephone, personal safes, high-speed internet access and complimentary web access. **$$$$–$$$$$**

MEDIUM-PRICED PLUMS

Casablanca: 147 West 43rd Street off Times Square. Tel 212-869 1212, fax 212-391 7585. Subway 1, 2, 3, 7, 9, N, R, S Times Square/42nd Street. **Area: Midtown.**

Elegant Moroccan theme includes ceiling fans, palm trees and mosaic tiles. Service is good too! **$$$–$$$$**

★★★★ **INSIDE TRACK** ★★★★

If you're a smoker, make sure you book a smoking room as most hotels now predominantly provide non-smoking rooms.

Doral Park Avenue: 70 Park Avenue at 38th Street. Tel 212-687 7050, fax 212-973 2497). Subway 4, 5, 6 to 42nd Street. **Area: Midtown East.**

A beautiful, five-star hotel with a bar, restaurant and excellent room facilities. **$$$–$$$$**

The Dylan: 52 East 41st Street between Madison and Park Avenues. Tel 212-338 0500, fax 212-338 0569, website at **www.dylanhotel.com** Subway S, 4, 5, 6, 7 to Grand Central/42nd Street. **Area: Midtown East.**

Located in the former Chemist's Club building, this new boutique hotel was developed to preserve the 1903 *beaux arts* structure. Facilities include a mezzanine lounge and bar overlooking the dramatic, high-ceilinged restaurant, RX. In-room amenities include a state-of-the-art digital entertainment system with large cable TV, DVD and CD players that can access a library of thousands of video and CD titles, two-line telephones with voice mail and data port, large personal safes and complimentary newspaper. **$$$–$$$$**

Fitzpatrick: 687 Lexington Avenue between East 56th and East 57th Streets. Tel 212-355 0100, fax 212-355 1371. Subway 4, 5, 6 to 59th Street. **Area: Midtown East.**

A cosy Irish venture. The rooms are equipped with everything from trouser presses to towelling robes, useful after indulging in the whirlpool bath included in many rooms. **$$$–$$$$**

Fitzpatrick Grand Central: 141 East 44th Street between Lexington and 3rd Avenues. Tel 212-351 6800, fax 212-355 1371. Subway S, 4, 5, 6, 7 to Grand Central/42nd Street. **Area: Midtown East.**

The Fitzpatrick Family Group of hotels continues its Irish theme at this new hotel just across from Grand Central Station. The hotel includes an Irish pub and you can order a traditional Irish breakfast. **$$$**

Franklin: 164 East 87th Street between 3rd and Lexington Avenues. Tel 212-369 1000, fax 212-369 8000). Subway 4, 5, 6 to 86th Street. **Area: Upper East Side.**

Known for its good service, this pleasant hotel has lovely touches in its rooms that include canopies over the beds, fresh flowers and cedar closets. **$$$**

Mansfield: 12 West 44th Street between 5th and 6th Avenues. Tel 212-944 6050, fax 212-764 4477. Subway B, D, F, Q to 47th–50th Street/Rockefeller Center. **Area: Midtown.**

A beautiful lobby with vaulted ceiling and white marble marks the Mansfield out as an elegant hotel for those also wanting the charm of a boutique hotel. **$$$–$$$$$**

Millennium Hilton: 5 Church Street between Fulton and Dey Streets. Tel 212-693 2001, fax 212-571 2316. Subway 1, 9, N, R to Cortlandt Street. **Area: Financial District.**

A black skyscraper geared to business, with fitness centre and a pool. If you want a stunning view of the harbour, ask for a high floor. **$$–$$$$$**

Moderne: 243 West 55th Street between Broadway and 8th Avenue. Tel 212-397 6767, fax 212-397 8787. Subway C, E, 1, 9 to 50th Street. **Area: Midtown West.**

Opened in 1998, this bijou hotel was converted from a five-storey dance studio. **$$$–$$$$**

New York Marriott Marquis: 1535 Broadway at 45th Street. Tel 212-398 1900, fax 212-704 8926. Subway N, R, S, 1, 2, 3, 7, 9 to Times Square/42nd Street. **Area: Theater District.**

In 1998 the hotel completed a $25-million upgrade of all its room so each one now includes console desks, ergonomic chairs, two phone lines and voice mail. A new sushi bar, Katen, is in the atrium lobby. **$$–$$$$**

Paramount: 235 West 46th Street between Broadway and 8th Avenue. Tel 212-764 5500, fax 212-575 4892. Subway C, E, 1, 9 to 50th Street. **Area: Theater District.**

A hip hotel with a glorious, sweeping staircase in the lobby. **$$-$$$$$**

The Premier: 45 West 44th Street between 6th Avenue and Broadway. Tel 212-768 4400, fax 212-768 0847. Subway N, R, S, 1, 2, 3, 7, 9 to Times Square/42nd Street. **Area: Theater District.**

The Millennium Broadway in Times Square built this 22-storey tower in 1999 to increase its total room count to 752. The Premier has its own private entrance on 44th Street and elegant, modern guest rooms with large bathrooms, two phone lines, voice mail and a separate modem and fax machine. **$$$-$$$$**

★★★★ INSIDE TRACK ★★★★
★ ★
★ If you're on a budget, it's worth ★
★ noting that hotels in the Herald ★
★ Square area tend to be very well ★
★ priced, yet are a good ★
★ compromise in terms of ★
★ location for both Downtown and ★
★ Midtown sights; the subway ★
★ connections to the Upper East ★
★ Side are also good. ★
★★★★★★★★★★★★★★★★★★★★★★★

The Roosevelt Hotel: 45 East 45th Street at Madison Avenue. Tel 212-661 9600, fax 212-885 6161, website at **www.theroosevelthotel.com** Subway S, 4, 5, 6, 7 to Grand Central/42nd Street. **Area: Midtown East.**

Built in 1924, this classy hotel completed a $70-million renovation in 1998 in which the lobby was restored to its original grandeur with crystal chandeliers, columns and lots of marble. **$$-$$$$**

Shoreham: 33 West 55th Street at 5th Avenue. Tel 212-247 6700, fax 212-765 9741. Subway F to 5th Avenue. **Area: Midtown.**

This hotel has recently undergone a renovation and now has a new bar, restaurant, fitness centre and more rooms. **$$$-$$$$$**

Time Hotel: 224 West 49th Street between 8th Avenue and Broadway. Tel 212-320 2900, fax 212-245 2305. Subway C, E, 1, 9 to 50th Street. **Area: Theater District.**

This boutique hotel opened in the heart of Times Square in 1999 and features colour-saturated rooms in red, yellow or blue designed by Adam Tihany and a restaurant run by celebrity chef Jean-Louis Palladin. **$$$**

Wall Street Inn: 9 South William Street opposite 85 Broad Street. Tel 212-747 1500. Subway 2, 3 to Wall Street; J, M, Z to Broad Street. **Area: Financial District.**

A boutique hotel in an old office building in the heart of the historic district. Original features include mahogany panels on the walls, and granite floors. **$$$**

West New York: 541 Lexington Avenue between 49th and 50th Streets. Tel 212-755 1200, fax 212-644 0951. Subway 6 to 51st Street; E, F to Lexington/3rd Avenue. **Area: Midtown East.**

In 1998 Starwood Lodging joined forces with designer David Rockwell, celebrity restaurateur Drew Nieporent and nightlife impresario Rande Gerber to transform the former Doral Inn into an urban oasis for travellers looking for comfortable, sophisticated accommodations. **$$$–$$$$$**

EXCELLENT VALUE FOR MONEY

Algonquin Hotel: 59 West 44th Street between 5th and 6th Avenues. Tel 212-840 6800, fax 212-944 1618. Subway B, D, F, Q to 47th–50th Streets/Rockefeller Center. **Area: Midtown.**

Famous for the literary meetings held here by Dorothy Parker and her cohorts, the Algonquin has recently undergone a $45-million refurbishment. **$$–$$$** (includes discount with a NYCard)

The Ameritania: 1701 Broadway at 54th Street. Tel 212-247 5000, fax 212-247 3316. Subway 1, 9 to 50th Street; B, D, East to 7th Avenue. **Area: Midtown West.**

Located just outside the Theater District and near Restaurant Row, this well-priced hotel is well appointed with reasonable rooms. **$$**

Bentley: 500 East 62nd Street at York Avenue. Tel 212-644 6000, fax 212-207 4800. Subway 4, 5, 6, N, R to Lexington Avenue/59th Street. **Area: Upper East Side.**

A recently-renovated gem of a hotel near Bloomingdales. It also offers a complimentary breakfast. **$$–$$$**

Carlton: 22 East 29th Street between 5th and Madison Avenues. Tel 212-532 4100, fax 212-889 8683. Subway 4, 5, 6 to 28th Street. **Area: Madison Square Garden.**

A tourist-class hotel overlooking the Empire State Building and in an excellent location for 5th Avenue and Garment District shopping. Restaurant, lounge and business services. **$$–$$$**

Clarion Hotel 5th Avenue: 3 East 40th Street just off 5th Avenue. Tel 212-447 1500, fax 212-213 0972. Subway 7 to 5th Avenue; S, 4, 5, 6, 7 to Grand Central/42nd Street. **Area: Midtown East.**

In an excellent location near Grand Central Station. Rooms are geared to businesspeople and have all the latest equipment. **$$–$$$**

★★★★ **INSIDE TRACK** ★★★★
Hotels in the Financial District can be especially good value for money at weekends when many businesspeople leave the city.

Courtyard by Marriott Times Square South: 114 West 40th Street between 6th Avenue and Broadway. Tel 212-391 0088, fax 212-391 6023. Subway B, D, F, Q to 42nd Street. **Area: Theater District.**

This new hotel, which opened in 1998, is part of the massive redevelopment of Times Square. The spacious rooms all have a sitting area, large work desk, two phones with data ports and in-room coffee. **$$–$$$**

The Empire Hotel: 44 West 63rd Street between Broadway and Columbus Avenues. Tel 212-265 7400, fax 212-315 0349, website at **www.empirehotel.com**

Subway A, B, C, D, 1, 9 to Columbus Circle/59th Street. **Area: Upper West Side.**

In an excellent location just next door to the Lincoln Center, this is one of hotel-wizard Ian Schrager's most recent acquisitions. Professional and great value for money. **$$–$$$**

Holiday Inn Martinique on Broadway: 49 West 32nd Street at Broadway. Tel 212-736 3800, fax 212-277 2681. Subway B, D, F, N, Q, R to 34th Street. **Area: Herald Square.**

Opened in 1998 on the site of the former Hotel Martinique, this hotel is decorated in a French Renaissance style. **$$–$$$$$**

Holiday Inn Downtown: 138 Lafayette Street at Canal Street. Tel 212-966 8898, fax 212-966 3933. Subway N, R to Canal Street. **Area: border of Chinatown and SoHo.**

Well-equipped, spotless rooms at excellent prices. **$$**

Holiday Inn Wall Street: 15 Gold Street at Platt Street. Tel 212-232 7700, fax 212-425 0330. Subway J, M, Z, 2, 3, 4, 5 to Fulton Street. **Area: Financial District.**

Opened in 1999, billing itself as the most high-tech hotel in New York, complete with T-1 speed internet connectivity. **$$–$$$$**

Hotel Beacon: 2130 Broadway at 75th Street. Tel 212-787 1100, fax 212-724 0839. Subway 1, 2, 3, 9 to 72nd Street. **Area: Upper West Side.**

Good-sized rooms with kitchenettes, plus the hotel is well located for the American Museum of Natural History, the Lincoln Center and Central Park. **$$**

Mayflower Hotel on the Park: 15 Central Park West between 61st and 62nd Streets. Tel 212-265 0060, fax 212-265 0227. Subway A, B, C, D, 1, 9 to Columbus Circle/59th Street. **Area: Upper West Side.**

You'll get great views of Central Park without paying through the nose for them. **$$**

Metro: 45 West 35th Street between 5th and 6th Avenues. Tel 212-947 2500, fax 212-279 1310. Subway B, D, F, N, Q, R to 34th Street. **Area: Midtown.**

Well-located near the Empire State Building, which can be seen from its roof terrace, this hotel offers good service. **$$–$$$**

New York Marriott Brooklyn: 333 Adams Street at Tillary Street. Tel 718-246 7000, fax 718-246 0563. Subway A, C, F to Jay Street/Borough Hall; N, R to Court Street; 2, 3, 4, 5 to Borough Hall just five minutes' walk away. **Area: Brooklyn.**

Opened in 1998, this is Brooklyn's first hotel in 68 years. Over the water from Manhattan, but you get excellent business and fitness facilities at very good prices. **$$–$$$**

Quality Hotel and Suites Rockefeller Center: 59 West 46th Street between 5th and 6th Avenues. Tel 212-719 2300, fax 212-790 2760. Subway B, D, F, Q to 47th–50th Streets/Rockefeller Center. **Area: Midtown.**

A well-priced hotel with excellent amenities that include a fitness centre, coffee makers and irons in the rooms, free local phone calls and a complimentary continental breakfast. **$$**

Washington Square Hotel: 103 Waverly Place between 5th and 6th Avenues. Tel 212-777 9515, fax 212-979 8373. Subway A, B, C, D, E, F, Q to West 4th Street/Washington Square. **Area: Greenwich Village.**

A family-run hotel overlooking Washington Square. The rooms are small but the rates very reasonable and include a complimentary breakfast. **$$**

Wyndham: 42 West 58th Street between 5th and 6th Avenues. Tel 212-753 3500, fax 212-754 5638. Subway B, Q to 57th Street; F to 5th Avenue. **Area: Midtown West.**

Large, basic rooms with walk-in closets. Great location. **$$–$$$**

BARGAIN GEMS

Gershwin Hotel: 7 East 27th Street between 5th and Madison Avenues. Tel 212-545 8000, fax 212-684 5546. Subway 6 to 28th Street. **Area: Madison Square.**

A character-crammed budget boutique with some of the best rates in the city. Discount with the NYCard. **$–$$**

The perfect apple

A major hotel chain called **Apple Core** has recently opened five renovated hotels in excellent Midtown locations with extremely reasonable rates – from $89 to $199 a night. They are: Red Roof Inn Manhattan on 32nd Street, west of 5th Avenue; the Comfort Inn Midtown on 46th Street west of 6th Avenue; Quality Hotel and Suites Rockefeller Center on 46th Street off 6th Avenue; the Best Western Manhattan on 32nd Street west of 5th Avenue and Quality Hotel East Side at 30th Street and Lexington Avenue.

All the hotels offer complimentary continental breakfast, well-equipped fitness centres and business centres. In-room facilities include cable television and pay-per-view movies, telephones with data port and voice mail, coffee makers, irons and ironing boards. The modern bathrooms all come with marble vanities and hair dryers.

Be warned, though, these hotels are already so popular that average occupancy rates are above 90 per cent – so book early if you want to get a room! You can book rooms at any of the hotels through Apple Core's central reservations on tel 212-790 2710, fax 212-790 2760, **www.applecorehotels.com**

11

Herald Square Hotel: 19 West 31st Street between 5th Avenue and Broadway. Tel 212-279 4017, fax 212-643 9208. Subway N, R to 28th Street. **Area: Herald Square.**

Once the headquarters of *Life* magazine, this is now a small, extremely well-priced hotel near the Empire State Building and Macy's. **$**

Hotel 17: 225 East 17th Street between 2nd and 3rd Avenues. Tel 212-475 2845, fax 212-677 8178. Subway L, N, R, 4, 5, 6 to Union Square/14th Street. **Area: Gramercy Park.**

A very basic hotel with shared bathrooms. **$–$$**

Larchmont: 27 West 11th Street between 5th and 6th Avenues. Tel 212-989 9333, fax 212-989 9496. Subway F to 14th Street. **Area: Greenwich Village.**

This is a clean, well-sought-after Village boutique hotel. No private baths in any of the rooms, however. **$–$$**

Off SoHo Suites: 11 Rivington Street between Chrystie Street and the Bowery. Tel 212-353 0860, fax 212-979 9801. Subway F to Delancey Street. **Area: Lower East Side.**

Good-sized, clean suites with fully equipped kitchens. **$–$$**

Pickwick Arms Hotel: 230 East 51st Street between 2nd and 3rd Avenues. Tel 212-355 0300, fax 212-755 5029. Subway 6 to 51st Street. **Area: Midtown East.**

A cheap place to stay in a pricy neighbourhood. The rooms are tiny but the hotel does have a roof garden and cocktail lounge. **$**

Portland Square Hotel: 132 West 47th Street between 6th and 7th Avenues. Tel 212-382 0600, fax 212-382 0684. Subway B, D, F, Q to 47th–50th Streets/Rockefeller Center. **Area: Midtown West.**

A family-run hotel (they also run the Herald Square Hotel). The rooms are small but the hotel is very near the Theater District **$**

ThirtyThirty New York City: 30 East 30th Street between Park and Madison Avenues. Tel 212-689 1900, fax 212-689 0023, website at **www.3030nyc.com** Subway 6 to 29th Street. **Area: Herald Square.**

Formerly the Martha Washington Hotel, this was turned into a modern, sophisticated hotel in 1999. **$–$$**

HOTEL LISTINGS BY AREA

Upper West Side

The Empire Hotel	$$–$$$
Hotel Beacon	$$
Inn New York City	$$$$–$$$$$

Upper East Side

Bentley	$$–$$$
Franklin	$$$
Hotel Carlyle	$$$$–$$$$$
Hotel Plaza-Athene	$$$$–$$$$$
The Mark	$$$$–$$$$$
The Stanhope	$$$$–$$$$$

Midtown West

The Ameritania	$$

Moderne	$$-$$$	The Sherry-	
The New York Hilton		Netherland	$$$$-$$$$$
and Towers	$$$$$	The Waldorf-Astoria	$$$$-$$$$$
Portland Square Hotel	$	West New York	$$$-$$$$$
Wyndham	$$-$$$		

Herald Square

Herald Square Hotel	$
Holiday Inn Broadway	$$-$$$$$
ThirtyThirty New York City	$-$$

Theater District

Courtyard by Marriott	
New York Marriott	
Marquis	$$-$$$$
Paramount	$$-$$$$$
The Premier	$$$-$$$$
Time Hotel	$$$

Gramercy Park

Hotel 17	$-$$
Inn at Irving Place	$$$$-$$$$$

Madison Square

Carlton	$$-$$$
Gershwin Hotel	$-$$

Midtown

Algonquin	$$-$$$
Casablanca	$$$-$$$$
Mansfield	$$$-$$$$$
Metro	$$-$$$
Peninsula New York	$$$$$
Quality Hotel and Suites	
Rockefeller Center	$$
Royalton	$$$$-$$$$$
Shoreham	$$$-$$$$$

Greenwich Village

Larchmont	$-$$
Washington Square Hotel	$$

SoHo

Holiday Inn Downtown	$$
SoHo Grand	$$$$

Lower East Side

Off SoHo Suites	$-$$

TriBeCa

TriBeCa Grand	$$$$-$$$$$

Midtown East

Box Tree	$$$-$$$$
Clarion Hotel 5th Avenue	$$-$$$
Doral Park Avenue	$$$-$$$$
The Dylan	$$$-$$$$
Elysee	$$$$-$$$$$
Fitzpatrick	$$$-$$$$
Fitzpatrick Grand Central	$$$
The Four Seasons	$$$$-$$$$$
Kitano Hotel	$$$$-$$$$$
Pickwick Arms Hotel	$
The Roosevelt Hotel	$$-$$$$

Financial District

Holiday Inn Wall Street	$$-$$$$
Marriott World Trade	
Center Hotel	$$$$
Millennium Hilton	$$-$$$$$
Wall Street Inn	$$$

Brooklyn

New York Marriott	
Brooklyn	$$-$$$

OTHER OPTIONS

Abode Ltd: PO Box 20022, New York, NY 10021. Tel 212-472 2000, fax 212-472 8274, website at **www.abodenyc.com**

Unhosted, good-quality studios or apartments all over the city, but youhave to book a minimum of four days. **$–$$$**

Bed and Breakfast (and Books): 35 West 92nd Street, Apt. 2C, New York, NY 10025. Fax 212-865 8740.

Hosted and unhosted apartments – and you may end up the guest of a writer. **$–$$**

Bed and Breakfast in Manhattan: PO Box 533, New York, NY 10150. Tel 212-472 2528, fax 212-988 9818.

From comfortable to smart and both hosted and unhosted. **$–$$$**

Jazz on the Park: 36 West 106th Street at Central Park West. Tel 212-932 1600, visit their website at **www.jazzhotel.com**

Clean, safe and comfortable rooms for the budget traveller. Double and 'dormitory' rooms, laundry room, roof-top terrace and garden. Price includes breakfast. **$**

Westchester

Not only is Westchester a good alternative to Manhattan when you're having trouble getting a room, it can also be far cheaper – usually half the going rate of Manhattan, with many seasonal promotional rates under $100 a night.
Westchester County borders the New York City borough of The Bronx and is just 20 minutes away from Manhattan via the Metro-North Railroad system, which runs three lines – the Hudson, the Harlem and the New Haven. There are also 43 Metro-North stations throughout Westchester County, with Grand Central Station in midtown Manhattan as the terminal station. Some hotel options include:

The Castle at Tarrytown: 400 Benedict Avenue, Tarrytown. Tel 914-631 1980. **$285–$625**

Courtyard by Marriott: 631 Midland Avenue, Rye. Tel 914-921 1110. **$130–$225**

Crowne Plaza: 66 Hale Avenue, White Plains. Tel 914-682 0050. **From $150**

Peekskill Inn: 634 Main Street, Peekskill. Tel 914-739 1500. Very close to station. **$100**

Ramada Plaza Hotel: One Ramada Plaza, New Rochelle. Tel 914-576 3700. Close to station. **$125–$160**

Royal Regency Hotel: 165 Tuckahoe Road, Yonkers. Tel 914-476 6200.A long walk from the station. **$99**

Doral Arrowwood: Anderson Hill Road, Rye Brook. Tel 914-939 5500. Also a little remote from the station. **$150–$210**

CHAPTER 12

Safety First

GENERAL HINTS AND TIPS

Don't allow your dream trip to New York to get spoilt by not taking the right kind of precautions – be they for personal safety or of a medical nature.

In the sun

Although the biggest season for New York is winter, many Brits still travel to America at the hottest time of the year – the summer – and most are unprepared for the sheer intensity of the sun. Before you even think about going out for the day, apply a high-factor sun block as it is very easy to get sunburnt when you are walking around sightseeing or shopping. It is also a good idea to wear a hat or scarf to protect your head from the sun, especially at the hottest times of the day from 11am to 3pm, so you do not get sunstroke. If it is windy you may be lulled into thinking that it's not so hot, but this is an illusion.

At your hotel

In America, your hotel room number is your main source of security. It is often your passport to eating and collecting messages so keep the number safe and secure. When checking in, make sure none of the hotel staff mentions your room number out loud. If they do, give

them back the key and ask them to give you a new room and to write down the new room number instead of announcing it (most hotels follow this practice in any case). When you need to give someone your room number – for instance when charging a dinner or any other bill to your room – write it down or show them your room card rather than calling it out. When in your hotel room, always put on the deadlocks and security chains and use the door peephole before opening the door to strangers. If someone knocks on the door and you don't know who it is, or they don't have any identification, phone down to the hotel reception desk. When you go out, make sure you lock the windows and door properly and even if you just leave your room to go to the ice machine, still lock the door.

★★★★ **INSIDE TRACK** ★★★★

Always carry plenty of water around with you – even if you're in New York in the depths of winter. The air con and heating used in buildings are incredibly dehydrating and you'll find yourself wanting to keel over very quickly without a good lubricant. It is also best to avoid alcohol during the day.

Cash and documents

Most hotels have safe deposit boxes so use these to store important documents such as airline tickets and passports. Keep a separate record of your travellers' cheque numbers. When you go out, do not take all your cash and credit cards with you – always leave at least one credit card in the safe as an emergency back-up and only take enough cash with you for the day. Using a money belt is also a good idea and if your room does not come with its own safe, leave your valuables in the main hotel safe. Also, be warned: American banknotes are all exactly the same green colour and size so familiarise yourself with the different bills in the safety of your hotel room before you go out. Keep larger denominations separate from smaller bills.

Emergencies

For the police, fire department or ambulance, dial **911** (9-911 from a

hotel room). If it's a medical emergency, call the front desk of your hotel as many have arrangements with doctors for house calls. The alternative is to contact **Dial-a-Doctor on 212-971 9692.** There are several 24-hour pharmacies, most run by the Duane Reade chain (to New York what Boots is to Britain). The most centrally located are at Broadway and 57th Street (tel 212 541 9208) and Lexington and 47th (tel 212 682 5338).

Cars

Unless you have a driver, a car in New York is not a good idea. If you do hire a car, however, be sensible. Never leave your car unlocked and never leave any valuable items on the car seats or anywhere else where they can be seen. And put away maps and brochures in the glove compartment as these will be obvious signs that your car belongs to a tourist.

New York street savvy

The city is nowhere near as dangerous as it used to be, but it is still a large city and there are always people on the lookout for an easy opportunity. To reduce your chances of becoming a victim, there are some simple things you can do and important advice to follow:

• Always **be aware** of what is going on around you and **keep one arm free** – criminals tend to target people who are preoccupied or have both arms laden down with packages or briefcases.

- Stick to **well-populated, well-lit areas** and, if possible, stay in the company of others.

- Don't engage any suspicious people, such as street beggars, though you can tip **buskers** if you wish.

- Visible **jewellery** can attract the wrong kind of attention. If you are a woman wearing rings, turn them round so that the stone or setting side is palm-in.

★★★★ INSIDE TRACK ★★★★
★ It cannot be stressed enough that ★
★ you should only every walk about ★
★ with as little cash as possible ★
★ and never, ever count your ★
★ money in public. ★
★★★★★★★★★★★★★★★★★★★★★★★

- If you're wearing a coat, put it on **over** the strap of your shoulder bag.

- Men should keep **billfolds** in their front trouser or coat pockets or in a shoulder strap.

- Another trick you can use is to **have two wallets** – one a cheap one carried in your hip pocket or bag containing about $20 in cash and some out-of-date credit cards and another hidden somewhere on your body, or in a money belt containing the bulk of your cash and credit cards.

- If you are approached by someone who demands money from you, your best bet is to **get away** as quickly as possible. Do this by throwing your fake wallet or purse in one direction, while you run, shouting for help, in another direction. The chances are that the mugger will just collect the wallet rather than chasing after you. If you hand over your wallet and just stand still, the mugger is more likely to demand your watch and jewellery too. This advice is even more important for women who are more vulnerable to personal attack or rape if they hang around.

- Watch out for **pickpockets and scam artists** especially in busy areas, as you would in any big city.

- **Pickpockets work in teams,** often involving children who create a diversion.

- **Do not carry your wallet or valuables in a bumbag.** Thieves can easily cut the belt and disappear into the crowds before you've worked out what has happened.

★★★★ INSIDE TRACK ★★★★
★ Don't be tempted to chance your ★
★ hand at any version of the old ★
★ three-card trick – you'll lose! ★
★★★★★★★★★★★★★★★★★★★★★★★

TRAVEL INSURANCE

The one thing you should not forget when travelling anywhere around America is insurance – medical cover is very expensive and if you are involved in any kind of an accident you could be sued, which is very costly indeed in America. If you do want to make savings in this area, don't avoid getting insurance cover, but do avoid buying it from tour operators as they are notoriously expensive. I took a random selection of premiums offered by tour operators specialising in North America and found that two weeks' worth of cover for one person varied in cost from £39 to a staggering £82.25. If you're travelling for up to four weeks, the premiums go up to nearly £100 per person.

The alternative, particularly if you plan to make any more than one trip in any given year, is to go for an **annual world-wide policy** direct from the insurers. These can start at around £55 and go up to £112, and will normally cover all trips taken throughout the year up to a maximum of 31 days per trip. These world-wide annual policies make even more sense if you're travelling as a family. For instance, cover for four people bought from your tour operator could easily cost you £160 for a two-week trip; compare that to an annual world-wide family policy premium of between £90 and £140.

Check your cover

Policies vary not only in price, but in the cover they provide. In all cases, you need to ensure that the one you choose gives you the following:

• Medical cover of at least £2 million in America.

• Personal liability cover of at least £2 million in America.

• Cancellation and curtailment cover of around £3,000 in case you are forced to call off your holiday.

• Cover for lost baggage and belongings of around £1,500. Most premiums only offer cover for individual items up to around £250,

so you will need additional cover for expensive cameras or camcorders.

• Cover for cash (usually around £200) and documents, including your air tickets, passport and currency.

• 24-hour helpline to make it easy for you to get advice and instructions on what to do.

Things to watch out for

Sharp practices: In some cases your tour operator may imply that you need to buy their travel insurance policy. This is **never** the case: you can **always** arrange your own. Alternatively, they may send you an invoice for your tickets that includes travel insurance **unless** you tick a certain box – so watch out.

Read the policy: Always ask for a copy of the policy document before you go and if you are not happy with the cover offered, cancel and demand your premium back – in some cases you will only have seven days in which to do this, so look sharp!

Don't double up on cover: If you have an 'all risks' policy on your home contents, this will cover your belongings outside the home and may even cover lost money and credit cards. Check if this covers you abroad – and covers your belongings when in transit – before buying personal possessions cover.

More things to check

Gold card cover: Some bank gold cards provide you with insurance cover if you buy your air ticket with the gold card, though only the Nat

West Gold MasterCard provides sufficient cover for travel in America.

Dangerous sports cover: In almost all cases, mountaineering, racing and hazardous pursuits such as bungee jumping, skydiving, horseriding, windsurfing, trekking and even cycling are not included in normal policies. There are so many opportunities to do all of these activities and more – and they are so popular as holiday extras – that you really should ensure you are covered before you go.

Make sure you qualify for full cover: For instance, if you have been treated in hospital in the six months prior to travelling or are waiting for hospital treatment, you may need medical evidence that you are fit to travel. If your doctor gives you the all-clear (the report may cost £25) and the insurance company still says your condition is not covered, shop around to find the right cover.

Annual policies: Companies offering annual world-wide insurance policies include AA (0191-235 6513), Barclays (0345 573114), Bradford & Bingley (0800 435642), Columbus (020 7375 0011), Direct Travel (01903 812345), General Accident Direct (0800 121007), Our Way (020 8313 3900), Premier Direct (0990 133218) and Travel Insurance Direct (0990 168113). Many of these companies also offer straightforward holiday cover for a given period, such as two weeks or three weeks, which again will be cheaper than insurance offered by tour operators.

If you are a UK or EU resident, your NYCard gives you access to an excellent 12-month multi-trip travel insurance policy for £49.95 plus insurance premium tax. Many policies cost more for a single visit. This one is valid for a whole year regardless of the number of trips and a single payment covers you anywhere inthe world. There are also good prices for families. To get full details contact ExtraSure, one of the longest-established Lloyd's underwritten specialists in the UK. Tel 202 7480 6871. Quote the code SS00027 on your NYCard to get the unique NYTAB rates. As with all policies, you should check it to make sure it covers what you want.

Index

Location references in italics indicate maps; those in bold type indicate major references.

INDEX

INDEX

HOW TO USE YOUR NYCARD

Your NYCard is attached to the back flap of your *Brit's Guide to New York*. It is a discount card that will enable you to save from 10 per cent to 50 per cent on a range of things from travel insurance and airport transfers to accommodation and museum entry. Simply ask for the NYCard rates when calling, booking or buying tickets. Show your NYCard when checking in. You automatically receive the discount. Some of the deals are listed below, but new deals are constantly being added, so keep in touch by visiting NYTAB's web site at **http://www.nytab.com**

If your card is missing, you can obtain another card, together with a copy of NYTAB's pocket guide to New York, *NYPages*, which includes full details of all the NYCard offers, by sending £1.95 per visitor pack to: NYTAB, 11 Berkeley Street, London, W1J 8DS.

Alternatively, within the UK you can call 09060 40 50 60. Calls cost £1.50 per minute, and you'll spend about £4.50. But *Brit's Guide* readers can get up to three visitor packs for no further charge by saying the magic words 'I'm a *Brit's Guide* reader'. Allow 28 days for delivery.

Hotels and Reservations
The NYCard offers the best rates available – up to 45% off – at the following three hotels. Each is the best in its class. Visitors should simply contact the hotels directly, ask for the NYTAB rate and present their NYCard at check in. Rates vary by season.

The Sherry–Netherland: Old-world luxury. Tel (001) 212-355 2800, Fax (001) 212-319 4306.

The Algonquin: Historic mid-range. Tel (001) 212-840 6800, Fax: (001) 212-944 1449.

The Gershwin: Art scene economical. Tel (001) 212-545 8000, Fax: (001) 212-684 5546.

NYTAB's partner, **Express Reservations**, can also help visitors save on quality accommodation. Express block-books discounted rooms in over 25 hotels and has agreed to give its best rates to NYCard holders. Express will make the reservation and confirm it. You pay the hotel as usual, at check out. There are no fees and no pre-payment requirements. Call in the US (001) 303-218-7808 or visit their website at: **http://www.hotelsinmanhattan.com**

SuperShuttle
With the NYCard, door-to-door service to and from any airport and any hotel in Manhattan is just $14. Between any airport and a private residence in Manhattan it's $18, with other passengers in the same small group or family travelling for only $9. All prices include tolls, and credit cards are accepted. Rates are subject to change.

When you land, call SuperShuttle from the courtesy phones at the Ground Transportation Desk near baggage claim (all airports, all terminals) to arrange for a pick up. SuperShuttle has become very popular and there can sometimes be a bit of a wait. Be sure to reserve a seat for your return to the airport at least 24 hours before your departure. Tel (001) 212-209-7011.

Sightseeing and Museums
Look out for the following NYCard discounts:

Top of the World Observatories at the World Trade Center: Tel 212-323 2340, $2 off.

Circle Line Cruises: Tel 212-563 3200, $3 off all cruises. Full Island, Semi-circle, Harbor Lights and Seaport Liberty Cruises; Seaport Music Cruises Tel: 212-630 8888; The *Beast* Speedboat Ride; *World Yacht* Dinner Cruise.

NY Waterway Cruises: Tel 800-533 3779, 15% off all cruises. Full Manhattan, Lower Harbor and Twilight Cruises; The Yankee Clipper and the Mets Express Baseball Cruises; Historic Hudson Valley Cruises.

New York Visions and Harlem Spirituals Tours: Tel 212-391 0900, $5 off all tickets purchased at West 43rd Street office.

Guggenheim Museum: Tel 212-535 7710, $2 off.

Intrepid **Sea-Air-Space Museum:** Tel 212-245 0072, $2 off.

Lower East Side Tenement Museum: Tel 212-431 0233, 25% off.

Morgan Library: Tel 212-685 0610, free admission + 10% gift shop discount.

Morris-Jumel Mansion: Tel 212-923 8008, 2 for 1 admission.

Museum of the City of NY: Tel 212-534 1672, 2 for 1 admission.

Bloomingdales
Take the receipt from any Bloomingdale's purchase with your NYCard to the visitor centre and receive a fabulous free gift.

Cohen's Fashion Optical
Receive 20% off contact lenses (not disposable or opaque) or 30% off designer frames and lenses for prescription or sunglasses. Participating branches are at 40 West 57th Street (between 5th and 6th Avenues), 389 5th Avenue (at 36th Street), 767 Lexington (at East 60th Street), 50 East 42nd Street (at Madison Avenue), 2561-2575 Broadway (at West 96th Street), 1900 Broadway (between West 63rd and West 64th Streets).

Telephone
You can use your NYCard as a phone card and receive toll-free access numbers for 40 countries. NYTAB's partner in this service is Swiftcall, and the per-minute rates are hugely discounted when compared with other calling cards.

To activate your NYCard's telephone function, call the number on the back of the card and press ##100 to obtain your personal PIN number and charge your card with any amount over $16. If you charge or re-charge your card with $40 you get an extra $8 worth of calls free. Swiftcall will also send you a comprehensive information kit with full details of all your savings. The service works from any regular, mobile or pay touch-tone phone, anywhere in the world.

Travel Insurance
UK residents can obtain a 12-month, multi-trip insurance for less than some policies charge for a single visit, plus there's equally good rates for families, longer trips and EC residents – even car insurance. For details, call Extrasure in the UK on 020 7480 6871 and quote the special code SS00027 for NYTAB rates.